Desktop Database Marketing

Jack Schmid - Alan Weber

NTC Business Books
NTC/Contemporary Publishing Company

Library of Congress Cataloging-in-Publication Data

Schmid, Jack.
    Desktop database marketing / Jack Schmid, Alan Weber.
       p.   cm.
    Includes index.
    ISBN 0-8442-3235-1
    1. Database marketing.   2. Direct Marketing—Data processing.
  I. Weber, Alan.   II. Title.
  HF5415.126.S25   1997
  658.8′00285—dc21   97-21275
                                         CIP

Interior design by Hespenheide Design

Published by NTC Business Books
An imprint of NTC/Contemporary Publishing Company
4255 West Touhy Avenue, Lincolnwood (Chicago), Illinois 60646-1975 U.S.A.
Manufactured in the United States of America
International Standard Book Number: 0-8442-3235-1

18   17   16   15   14   13   12   11   10   9   8   7   6   5   4   3   2   1

To my wife, Trish, and to our three children: thank you for giving me the chance to complete a dream. A special thank you to Errett Schmid for her help in revising and tweaking and for pretending not to understand until I made each point clear.

Alan Weber

I dedicate this book to my loving wife of 36 years and to a great staff of coworkers at J. Schmid & Assoc. Inc. Without their wise counsel, guidance, and support this book would not have been possible.

Jack Schmid

Contents

Introduction   vii

Section I   The World of Database Marketing

1 Database Basics   3
2 Database Marketing and Improved Customer Communication   10
3 The Economics of Database Marketing   19

Section II   Setting Up Your Day-to-Day Database Operations

4 Key Elements of a Decision Support System   33
5 Building a Marketing Database   41
6 Designing for Flexibility   54
7 Using Data Storage Tools   73
8 Using Statistical Tools   82
9 Examining and Reporting Data   95

Section III   Developing Your Database Strategy

10 Customer Loyalty and Relationship Marketing   107
11 RFM (Recency-Frequency-Monetary Value)   119
12 Lifetime Value   132
13 Selecting Internal Data   142
14 Selecting and Using External and Research Data   154
15 Choosing a Database That Fits   164

Section IV   Managing Your Database

16 The Art of Testing   177
17 Customer Cloning   190
18 Customer and Prospect Communication   206
19 Turning a Communication Plan into a Financial Plan   225
20 Managing a Marketing Database: Day-to-Day Issues   245

Section V   Case Studies

21 Case Studies   257

Index   271

Introduction

You can learn from a number of books, speakers, and seminars what database marketing is. Odds are you not only know what database marketing is, you are also at least partially sold on the idea that it works. (If you weren't, you never would have opened this book.) Perhaps you've already read books and articles about database marketing, but you didn't have the expertise to set up and manage a marketing database yourself (or the budget needed to hire a service bureau).

Perhaps you've said to yourself, "If only someone would just tell me how to do it myself!"

The reason we've written this book is to tell how you can do it. Of course, we can't promise you this is an easy topic, but it really is not difficult. You will learn new concepts that make marketing databases work, as well as how-to techniques to put these concepts into action. But you'll get more than just how-to. You'll get "why-to." And perhaps, most important of all, you'll learn that you can do it.

There are no rules in this book about how big you must be, or how much money you have to spend. You can use these ideas if you are a one-person business, have 100 employees, or are in the Fortune 500. You can use these rules if you sell to consumers, to businesses, by catalog, or even in person. The rules are the same, whether you are big or small. What is more, we promise never to say, "Then get a programmer. . . ." If we can't or don't actually use something or do something ourselves, we won't tell you to use it or to do it.

A lot of people have the idea that the computer should be operated only by technical experts. As a result, we have computer experts doing all sorts of marketing analyses. While they probably use the computer's resources competently, wouldn't it make more sense to have marketing experts doing marketing analyses? Who could know more about your business, about what you do, than you? So the challenge becomes putting you in charge, letting you look, test, retest, and uncover the kind of information only you know to look for.

The chapters in this book are laid out in a logical sequence that reflects the order in which you will work to design, build, and use a marketing database. This is for two reasons. The first is so the steps will be clearly presented so you can follow them. The second is so the idea of how the whole process works will more easily gel in your mind. The concept would be much more difficult to grasp if the sequence of chapter topics was different than the sequence in which you will approach each task as you complete your database project.

If you are a little fuzzy about what the differences between an MIS (Management Information System) and a DSS (Decision Support System) are, that's OK. You don't have to be a programmer or a technical expert, and frankly it's better if you're not. There are important concepts you will need to grasp, but once you do, the "technical" things won't seem so technical at all.

Computers have finally found their way to people's desks, and these PCs are powerful enough to analyze millions of customers. Database software, and even statistical software, is becoming faster and far more user-friendly. Simply put, the resources are finally available and the timing is right for people like you to be in control of your marketing database. The computer has become easier to use and maintain, just as the automobile has.

In the early part of the 20th century, the only people who drove automobiles were quite wealthy and either were "tinkerers" or they hired a chauffeur who maintained their automobile. Over the years, as technology progressed, automobiles became far more user-friendly. It is no longer necessary to be able to repair an automobile in order to drive one regularly, and almost no one has a chauffeur. Most people have no idea how a car works, and yet they drive quite well by themselves.

In much the same way, computers have also become more user-friendly. There are still those who will tell you that it takes a professional service bureau with a mainframe computer and a budget of at least $100,000 to create a marketing database. However, more and more people are creating and operating marketing databases on inexpensive PCs. As PCs become more powerful and database software easier to use, people whose expertise is in marketing are beginning to use computerized databases as tools . . . by themselves.

Just as with the automobile, there are certain new skills that must be learned by any new operator. Not everyone gets the hang of it easily. But there are simple procedures that, if followed, will consistently lead to good results.

Most of you will need to work with other people to get the information, time, and perhaps the equipment you need. Be aware that information is power, and you will be asking others to put you in control of information. Believe me, those folks in accounting and MIS are fully aware of how important the power of information is. You will have to do more than use hard numbers to convince people your database project will pan out. You will have to carry the project through diplomatically.

There is a very important rule that you need to know before you start. The rule is: You don't need to know how to complete a project to start it. But if you don't start, you can't finish.

Here is an example. A friend of ours wanted two new storm doors put on his house, but he had never installed a storm door before. After finding out how much installation would cost, however, he concluded he could learn. So he bought two good-quality doors, read the instruction book first, then carefully installed each door.

The first one took four hours. The second one took an hour and a half. Now he has his storm doors installed correctly, and his relatives asked him to install storm doors for them!

If you already knew how to create and operate a marketing database you wouldn't need this book. The point is not that by reading this book you will know exactly where you will finish before you start. The point is that you will know exactly where you will start, and you can find where you will finish, one step at a time, using the book as a guide. Once you have gotten through your first project, you'll have a whole new set of skills you can use again and again.

View your time reading and studying this book as an investment in yourself. When you are done, you'll have a lot of difficult tasks ahead of you. You have to justify the cost, set up a database that works, and then implement a database marketing program. But while you are reading, learning, and even practicing, you will be building a set of job skills truly prized in business today. Once this knowledge is in your head, nobody can take it away. So don't hurry off too soon. Your first successful project will be only one of many.

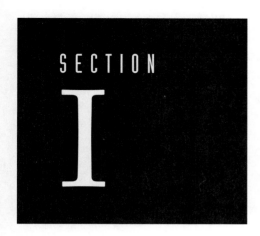

SECTION

I

The World of Database Marketing

CHAPTER

1

Database Basics

It has long been an axiom of mine that the little things are infinitely more important.

Sherlock Holmes in *A Case of Identity* (1892), by Arthur Conan Doyle

This is not just another database book, and it's not just another database marketing book. Lots of companies have databases—or at least the technology for having them. Many executives in these companies believe they are "doing" database marketing because they have multimillion-dollar mainframes and large customer lists.

But they aren't. This book will show them and you how to develop *real* database marketing programs. You may be hooked up to an expensive, sophisticated network, or you might be part of a small company with only two or three PCs. No matter. This book will show you how to get the benefits of database marketing—from your desktop.

What Is Desktop Database Marketing?

If all those companies mentioned above aren't doing database marketing, what are they doing? They are recording customer purchases without getting additional information. *Database marketing* is the process of extracting all relevant information from a customer purchase for use in future marketing programs and customer contacts. Basic information includes what customers purchase, how much (in units, dollars, or both), and how often they purchase. At more sophisticated levels, it can include demographic information (age, income, etc.) as well as psychographic information (e.g., buying preferences, likes and dislikes).

True database marketing allows you to achieve the ultimate goal—one-to-one relationships with your customers. *Desktop* database marketing is simply an extension of that strategy. Using the newer PC technology, it brings database marketing down to the level of individual marketers or marketing managers—right to their desktops. For a large company, that means that each individual marketing manager can know each customer and that customer's needs much more intimately and individually. For the smaller operator, even the company with a staff of one, it means being able to be as effective with a single PC as a company with a megamainframe.

The many benefits of desktop database marketing all come down to the increased marketing efficiency and effectiveness that result from knowing one's customers better and being able to predict more precisely their likelihood to buy. Specifically, this means higher response rates, higher average order value (AOV), greater repeat purchase activity, and more efficient prospecting for new customers.

WHERE DID DATABASE MARKETING COME FROM?

This book contains some new technical information, but the principles of database marketing aren't new. In fact the principles of getting close to your customer are as old as smart marketing itself. Although all sorts of marketing models and paradigms are touted these days, the simplest, most easily understood model for database marketing is reflected in an old-style retail setting, as the following will illustrate.

Jack's Men's Clothing

Bob Staley is a typical retail salesperson. He works long hours and is paid on commission: the more he sells, the more he earns. Over the years, he has built up a clientele of customers who know him and whose likes and dislikes he has come to know.

One day Bob gets an idea. Many of his customers are repeat buyers. He starts to keep track of what some of his best customers buy. He first records just names and phone numbers but quickly expands his list to include some basic purchase information, such as kinds of purchases and other preferences. In short order he realizes that it makes more sense to put the information for each customer on a separate $3'' \times 5''$ card. The following is a sample card for customer Bill Smith:

> 42 long suit or sport coat
> $16^{1}/_{2}'' \times 35''$ shirt size
> $10^{1}/_{2}$ shoe size
> $36'' \times 32''$ pant
> Bright, geometric-pattern ties
> Likes to have his wife confirm his purchases, especially of suits and
>   sport coats

Then Bob begins keeping track of customers' visits to the store, how many times they purchase, and how much they buy and spend.

As the new fall season approaches, he realizes that he has a gold mine on those $3'' \times 5''$ cards. To announce the arrival of the new fall line, he sends each customer on his list a postcard with the following handwritten message:

Our new fall line of suits and sport coats has just arrived. If you call me, I'll be happy to give you a private showing any morning next week between 8:00 and 9:00 A.M., before the store officially opens. Just give me a call at your convenience at 555-2965.

Your friend at Jack's

Bob Staley

As his business doubles almost overnight, Bob becomes the envy of the other salespeople in the store and a "marvel" to his boss.

Bob expands his customer file until he has nearly 300 names. He religiously keeps track of the purchase behavior of each customer—when, how often, how, and under what circumstances they buy—and he continuously updates their personal information (changes in size and taste preferences). The following fall he reaps another harvest.

The Heart of the Matter

Although this elementary example doesn't hint at computers or technology of any sort, it shows the heart of database marketing—and smart marketing in general: successful marketing is based on building relationships with your customers, and your ability to build sustainable relationships is directly related to your knowledge of your customers' buying habits and preferences. This retail example is especially appropriate because it could have happened at almost any time in any century. The principles are near-universal and eternal. And larger businesses have just begun to rediscover them in recent years.

Distinguishing Between Lists and Databases

The logical question that flows from the previous discussion is "What is the difference between a list and a database?" The answer is relatively simple. A *list* is a group of names and addresses put in ZIP code order for mailing. Often it is rented from a list broker and used to find new customers. It also can be one's own "house" list and might have other information, such as past customer purchases, but it is not organized in any particular fashion.

A *database*, on the other hand, is a list of names to which additional information has been added (appended) in a systematic fashion. That additional information is the basis of organization. As mentioned previously, it might be purchase history (quantity, dollar value, frequency), phone number, source of the name, method of purchase, or any combination of these.

Database marketing often relies on lists but is not list driven. It is transaction (sales or contact) driven. The difference is critical. Your customers tell you about themselves at each point of contact—when they buy something and when they don't. And it only stands to reason: the more you know about what people want to buy, the better you can serve them by offering the kinds of products they prefer and presenting those products in ways they prefer. Thus if you know that Ms. Jones is a budget-conscious car buyer who hates telemarketing calls and the color green, you won't call her during dinner time to tell her about a new, top-of-the-line green Mercedes. To extend this to the obvious point: the better you serve people, the more likely it is that they will buy again—and probably buy more.

Lifetime Value and Customer Value

When you have built detailed histories of customers, you can determine the lifetime value (LTV) of their purchases. Two things happen here. First, you begin to get an idea of how much you should spend to get or keep that customer. Second, you discover what study after study has shown: all customers are not created equal. As Exhibit 1-1 shows, the majority of your sales will come from a minority of your customers. The proportions might be 80/20 or 70/30, but this basic principle holds. Having LTV information, you are able to identify your most valuable customers and profit from them over the long term by building relationships with them.

Thus database marketing enables you to know how your customers want to be served and how much you can afford to do to keep them.

Getting Started

Exhibit 1-2 shows the four basic steps in database marketing. (You'll notice they reflect the sequence of steps Bob Staley took in building his homegrown database.)

1. Build: gather information about your customers and prospects.
2. Analyze: evaluate the information you have; determine what it means and how it can best be organized.
3. Strategize: determine what you want to do by answering five questions:

    a. To whom will you communicate?
    b. When will you communicate?
    c. How often will you communicate?
    d. How will you communicate—by phone, fax, personal sales call?
    e. How will you organize or group the customers you attempt to contact?

The critical aspect of step 3 is planning for the measurement (tracking) of communications with customers by assigning a distinguishing code to each group.

Exhibit 1-1

ALL CUSTOMERS ARE NOT CREATED EQUAL

Best Customers
N = 1,200 (10%)

- High profit
- Spent > $1,000
- Multiple purchases
- Purchased in last 6 months
- LTV: High

Total annual sales
= $1,200,000

Next-Best Customers
N = 2,400 (20%)

- Good profit
- Spent approximately $500
- Multiple purchases
- Purchased in last 12 months
- LTV: Good

Total annual sales
= $1,200,000

Average Customers
N = 3,600 (30%)

- Average profit
- Spent $250
- One purchase
- Purchased in last 18 months
- LTV: Average

Total annual sales
= $900,000

Poor Customers
N = 4,800 (40%)

- Low profit
- Spent < $100
- One purchase
- Purchased in last 24 months
- LTV: Low

Total annual sales
= $504,000

LTV = Lifetime values
N = Number of customers in category.
Total annual sales: $3,804,000

Total number of customers: 12,000
Total number of orders per year: 20,000
Average order value: $190.20

4. Communicate: make the contacts and track responses. Some people will respond to your offer; others will not. What is crucial is to capture as much information as possible about response activity, which can be fed back into step 1 for future programs.

Database marketing is a continuous process of collecting information, analyzing information, building communication strategy, and talking to customers and prospects.

WHAT DATABASE MARKETING WON'T DO AND WHEN IT WON'T WORK

Database marketing isn't a miracle drug or a magic formula for success. It is old-fashioned hard work. It is a tool that runs on information and thinking. It won't think for you or develop your marketing strategy for you, but it can be a wonderful source of information for building better strategies. It won't substitute for new product development by magically turning dogs into winners, but it can provide invaluable information for refining the new product development process.

Exhibit 1-2

DATABASE MARKETING: A CONTINUOUS PROCESS

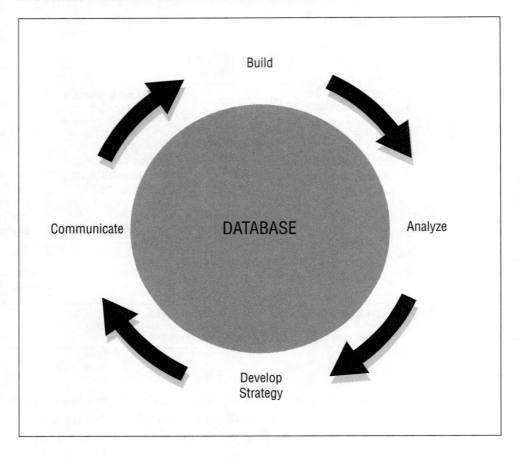

A marketing database can provide information only if it is developed. As a repository of information, it takes attention, management, thought, and investment to work effectively.

Marketing databases are not for all marketers. Three situations can make a database impractical:

1. The business is not based on repeat buyers; for example, a baseball fan buying a hot dog from a vendor at a baseball game. This probably is a one-time sale, and it is unlikely the fan will be buying another hot dog at another time from the same vendor.

2. The unit of sale is extremely low. True, some direct marketers make money selling inexpensive items through the mail. However, the lower the price, the lower the

likelihood for profitability. In the case of the hot-dog buyer and vendor, the unit of sale is, in all probability, too low.

3. The ability to capture information is low or nonexistent. Again, the example of the hot-dog vendor is a good one. Neither the fan nor the vendor has the time or inclination to capture information.

THE FUTURE OF DESKTOP DATABASE MARKETING

The above-listed exceptions aside, all sorts of established marketing concepts apply to database marketing, the way business will be done in the future. As is true for most "new" ideas that will be the "wave of the future," it is based on solid principles that have been tested and proved for generations.

The fundamental principle of database marketing is "The more you know, the more you can tell [in the right way]; and the more you can tell, the more you can sell." That principle—selling one-to-one—is as old as smart business.

The future of desktop database marketing, made possible by advances in PC technology, is equally certain. Although the basics of database marketing can be realized without technology, the ability to use relatively inexpensive technology to manage the collection and analysis of customer-related information has made desktop database marketing practical for businesses of every size. Because individual marketing managers can work a database from their desktops, the large corporation with dozens or even hundreds of marketing managers can recapture the level of customer intimacy it may have lost. Also, the power of the PC enables the smaller business or the individual to develop a level of customer knowledge and account penetration not previously possible on a small budget.

This book contains information on technical operations and on the economics of desktop database marketing. Keep in mind that technical operations are merely tools for making the economics work to your benefit. Specific suggestions can be customized to meet the marketing needs of your particular business.

2 Database Marketing and Improved Customer Communication

Mere parsimony is not economy. . . . Expense, and great expense, may be an essential part in true economy.

Edmund Burke (1729–97), Irish philosopher and statesman, in *A Letter to a Noble Lord* (1796)

"Improved communication" is a phrase one hears all the time—in seminars, in corporate meetings, and in general business conversation—and it is observed more in the breach than in the practice. It also is a key element to successful marketing and successful business profitability and is much more than the "spray and pray" approach of old-time, traditional mass marketing.

Your ability to communicate with your customers when they want to hear from you, with the kind of message they want to hear, in the way they want to hear it is itself a special kind of communication. Communications with these qualities tell potential buyers that you know them and have their best interests at heart. You aren't "just selling something" to any warm body; by demonstrating that you have some knowledge of their needs and preferences, you are sending them a message that is likely to be important to them.

A very simple analogy from farming (also a term used in some industries to describe territory management) applies here. Farmers can throw seed anywhere in a field and get a crop. But if they plant systematically and measure the yield from different parts of the field, they substantially increase their chances for a better yield in future years. The kind of investment implied by this analogy can be considerable. In-depth customer knowledge has a real, tangible price. It takes some combination of money, time, effort, and people; it also takes an investment in technology. But the payoff can be enormous.

This chapter will discuss database marketing from a communications viewpoint. Chapter 3, which is about the economics of database marketing, will discuss the financial implications of successful relationship marketing based on database marketing.

REQUIREMENTS FOR SUCCESSFUL CUSTOMER RELATIONSHIP MARKETING

Envisioning a successful relationship or loyalty marketing program is easy. This is a program where a number of things are happening:

◆ Customer purchase history is being actively tracked through a database.
◆ Suspects, prospects, inquiries, catalog requests—all those nonbuyers who have expressed some interest in your company's products or service are also tracked and maintained by date.
◆ The customers react to communications and loyalty efforts. They have a high response to promotions, surveys, and so on. In effect they are really interactive with you, as in a partnership.
◆ The customer feels good about the relationship, believing it is a win/win situation for them and the company with which they are dealing.
◆ Sales and profits are increasing because your company can be more selective about to whom it mails, can increase the frequency with which it communicates with its better customers, and can get higher response and higher dollar levels to orders.
◆ The company can target its promotions with personalized messages about past items or categories purchased or with special offers. Reliance on general, mass communications is a thing of the past.

Use of the Database

What's making all of these positive, relationship-building things happen? They are all driven by the optimal use of the database:

◆ All orders are expertly tracked and maintained on the company database.
◆ The database is used to drive marketing based on segmentation of the prospect and customer lists.
◆ The company applies research and statistical modeling techniques to understand better who the elite customers are and to find others who match that profile.

Data Requirements

Data requirements for database marketing will be stated in a half-dozen ways throughout this book, but customer data can be generally categorized within two main groupings:

For Customers

- Name, address, and telephone information for individuals
- Company name, address, and telephone and fax information for companies
- Company contact(s) who might be involved in the purchase activity
- Purchase history, specifically

    - Recency—date of last purchase
    - Frequency—number of purchases
    - Monetary—total dollars of all sales activity

- Merchandise purchase information:

    - Product category
    - Specific item or stockkeeping unit (SKU) purchased
    - Return or exchange history
    - Cancellation history (back order where the customer is unwilling to wait)

- Original source code (where the name came from: list, space ad, etc.)
- Method of placing the order (phone, fax, mail, salesperson, store visit, etc.)
- Method of payment (cash, check, credit card, purchase order, "bill me," etc.)
- Promotional history (date and type of communication)*
- Demographic information (census data for individuals and SIC and size data for companies)*

For Prospects

In addition to all the name, address, and phone information, include these:

- Original source code
- Date of lead
- Promotional history*

COMMUNICATIONS STRATEGY: USING THE CUSTOMER HIERARCHY TO BUILD CUSTOMER SHARE

As we have mentioned previously (and will mention again), all customers are not created equal. Different kinds of customers buy in different quantities, in different dollar amounts, at different times, and in response to different kinds of sales messages. The kind of sales message you use depends upon your knowledge of your customers. And that in turn depends on your understanding of the customer hierarchy.

---

*Not maintained by all companies.

Understanding the Customer Hierarchy

Fundamental to gaining customer loyalty is an understanding of the hierarchy of customers (Exhibit 2-1). What does this chart tell us? At the bottom of the ladder are persons or companies labeled *suspects*. They fit every demographic aspect of your best customers. You can identify them on response lists (known mail-order buyers), subscriber lists, or even compiled lists. But they have never bought from your company.

On the next rung on the ladder are the *prospects*. These persons or companies still have not purchased from your company, but they have done something to distinguish themselves from the suspects. They might have visited your booth at a trade show or requested your catalog in response to an ad in a magazine. They may be identified as a newly incorporated business, or your outside sales force passed their new business location and reported their existence. They could have called your 800 number or

Exhibit 2-1

THE CUSTOMER HIERARCHY

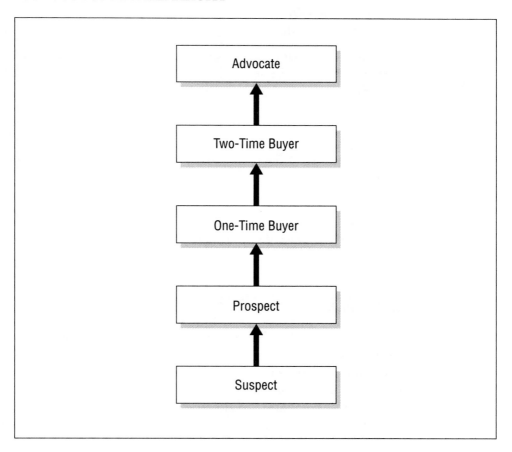

responded to a sweepstakes offer without buying. Perhaps they visited your store or asked for more information about the company. Generally, to be a bona fide prospect, the person or company must have taken some action toward becoming a buyer.

The *one-time buyer* has passed the first of three hurdles present in the customer hierarchy. Caution epitomizes these people or companies. Call them "tryers" because they are literally trying out your store, catalog, or services. You can count on three facts:

- They will have a low percentage response.
- They will have a low average order value (AOV).
- Only about half of them will ever return for another purchase.

This is not a group of customers upon whom you can build a successful business, and you have hardly won their undying loyalty.

Many people consider the next step the most significant hurdle in the hierarchy process. It is getting one-time buyers to purchase a second time, to become *two-time buyers*. These customers are sending you an important message:

- Your products are OK.
- Your service is OK.
- Your pricing is OK.

These buyers will have higher response rates, higher average order values, and more buying confidence because they know your company and what you stand for. In effect they have started on the road to customer loyalty, not the total, undying kind but "puppy" loyalty. They need to be nurtured, loved, and told how much they are appreciated.

The ultimate hurdle on the hierarchy ladder is for customers to become *advocates*. Advocates will recommend your company and its services to others. These persons have

- a higher likelihood of responding to your mailings
- a higher AOV when responding
- a greater likelihood of buying more often during the year

In defining customer loyalty, this is as close as you will get.

Understanding Front-End and Back-End Marketing

Several years ago, Don Beaver, president of the New Pig Corporation and a budding business marketer, gave a classic description of how his company was organized. He said that it had two primary groups. One was in charge of *getting* new customers, and the other was responsible for *keeping* those customers. Don's "get 'em and keep 'em" description (others have called it "shoot 'em and clean 'em") was really a simple way of describing front-end and back-end marketing. Understanding the fact that all marketing can be broken into *front-end* and *back-end* is essential. Exhibit 2-2 highlights the differences.

Front-end marketing goes by a lot of names, such as prospecting or new customer acquisition, but they all mean the same thing. As the table shows, the goal of front-end marketing is to get first-time customers. Generating leads and inquiries and converting those prospects to buyers is what it is all about. Typical measurement of the success of the prospecting function rests on cost per lead or per customer, or the cost of converting inquiries or leads into customers.

Generally, front-end marketing is viewed as an investment in the future. Most businesses are willing to invest in promotion and communication costs to bring in new customers in the hope of keeping them over time to recoup the investment and generate profits. Companies that find they can profitably prospect (acquire first-time buyers and make money) should count their blessings.

Back-end marketing, as Exhibit 2-2 portrays, is where the profits of the business come from: moving buyers up the hierarchy, maximizing the number of communica-

---

Exhibit 2-2

FRONT-END/BACK-END MARKETING

| Prospects = Costs | Customers = Profits |

OBJECTIVE	HOW RESULTS ARE MEASURED
Front-End Marketing	
• Acquire new, first-time customers	• Cost per customer
• Acquire new leads	• Cost per lead
• Acquire new inquiries	• Cost per name
• Convert leads and inquiries to customers	• Cost of conversion
• Minimize cost of building the customer file	
Back-End Marketing	
• Convert one-time buyers into two-time buyers	• Growth of multibuyer file
• Maximize number of mailings to customer list	• Number of customer mailings per year
• Make a profit	• Return on investment
	• Return on sales
	• Value of a customer over three years

tions with these customers, and starting to differentiate best buyers from average buyers from poor buyers, using the customer database. Back-end marketing will be measured by return on sales for each promotional event, return on investment of each communication, and the long-term value of a customer (lifetime value) over a period of at least three years.

Communicating with Each Customer Group

Are the type and level of communication the same for each of the groups in the buyer hierarchy? Absolutely not! Just start with the gross difference between the front end and back end (nonbuyers and buyers). Much customer communication or promotion that occurs in business today fails to differentiate these fundamental differences.

Look at some examples of how businesses change their communication, based on whether the person has purchased from the company before.

Large Catalog Companies

Larger catalog companies such as L.L. Bean regularly produce separate catalogs, one for customers and one for prospects, or nonbuyers. The difference: the buyer catalog has more pages and is filled with *new* products. Repeat-buying customers are looking for what's new in the catalog and probably will not be satisfied with the same styles and items they saw last season. For the prospect, the entire catalog is new; the catalog company can concentrate on products that are proven winners, with the best margins. This catalog has fewer pages and fewer items. The covers need to work harder to grab the readers' attention, getting prospects inside and presenting offers to motivate the people to place that important first order.

Retailers

Retailers looking for repeat purchase activity often use frequency-purchase devices, such as a card that can be punched or initialed with each purchase. A small retailer such as the Wild Bird Center uses a "Frequent Feeder Card" (see Exhibit 2-3) to encourage multiple purchases with the reward of one free 40-pound bag of birdseed after purchasing nine. This technique is very common with restaurants, fast-food shops, pet stores, and so on. The secret is getting the card in the hands of first-time buyers and letting them know about the reward/offer.

Business to Business

Business-to-business selling, whether done directly or through a salesperson, is often a two-step process. The process really highlights the difference between the prospect and the customer. Businesses use a wide variety of front-end, or prospecting, techniques:

Exhibit 2-3

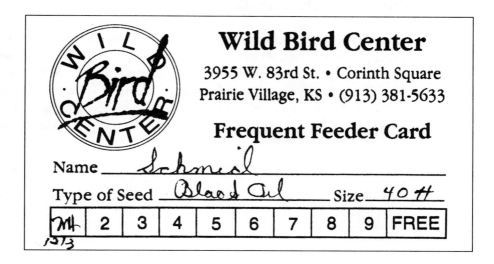

- Display ads in trade journals
- Postcard mailings to a rented list of attendees, for a trade show
- Classified ads in yellow pages
- Outbound telephone calling
- Cold calls by a salesperson
- Solo mailings to rented names of subscribers or compiled lists
- Card deck promotions

Building a Smarter Marketing/Promotional Plan with Key Data

Everything discussed in this chapter is predicated on capturing and using prospect and customer information to enhance future marketing efforts. Moving from mass communication such as network television, newspapers, or general consumer magazines to a highly targeted, personalized communication can't happen overnight. Even for small and medium-size companies, service and professional groups, or retailers, the process is one of gathering and maintaining key customer information to use for future promotional efforts. It requires changing from:

- general communication to specific communication
- average (group) history to individual history
- nonpersonal to personal communication
- nontrackable to precisely tracked orders and response

BENEFITS OF IMPROVED CUSTOMER COMMUNICATION

The ability to target customers and prospective customers more closely is the key to greater profitability and greater competitiveness. And "Time is of the essence" is more true than ever. The more quickly you make decisions based on reliable data, the more effectively you can send your message to the right audience in the right way. The more often you accomplish that, the stronger the relationships you will build with your customers. Chapter 3 will show how that translates to the bottom line.

The Economics of Database Marketing

There is nothing new in the world except the history you do not know.

Harry Truman

Why is being able to target one's repeat buyers and one's best buyers so vitally important? Simple: the bottom line. All sorts of studies—from *Harvard Business Review* to small-circulation, specialized business publications—point to the numbers. Some indicate that most businesses get the majority (60 to 80 percent) of their revenue from current customers; these customers represent a numerical minority of a business's total pool of customers. Other studies show that a 5 percent increase in current-customer business can translate into as much as a 50 percent increase in the bottom line. Still others point out that the ability to tailor messages to different audiences can easily double response rates.

Key to increasing response rates and profitability is the value of a customer—specifically, in direct marketing terms, the lifetime value (LTV) of a customer. A very simple example demonstrates the varied levels of value that can be assigned to customers. Suppose you have three customers: Mr. A, Ms. B, and Ms. C. Here are their purchases over three years.

	Year 1	Year 2	Year 3
Mr. A	$100	$100	$100
Ms. B	$100	$100	None
Ms. C	$100	None	None

Evaluation is simple. The three customers are equally important for the first year. A and B are equal through the second year. For the third year, Mr. A stands apart; he is clearly most valuable.

Customers such as Mr. A are the basis for a long-term, sustainable business. You need to find out what it will take to get each of them to buy more and to buy more often. Ultimately you need to determine which of these customers is most profitable for you.

WHAT YOU NEED

Before developing any marketing program, you need to know how much you can afford to invest in getting a new customer. You need to know the breakeven, and you need to know the lifetime value of your customers. That knowledge comes from tracking (by coding) all response to your marketing messages.

Determining Breakeven

Before starting any database-driven marketing campaign, before deciding how much to spend on advertising, and before deciding who should be contacted, knowing how much investment is needed to gain a new customer is vital. You can accomplish this through a break-even analysis. Exhibit 3-1 shows a simplified analysis, assuming a $50 average sale, a 50 percent cost of goods sold, a $3 per sale "fulfillment" cost (cost of making the sale), and a 55 cents (per prospect) advertising piece.

The break-even analysis is a first step for any database-driven marketing effort that will be held accountable for results. By determining what is required to get customers at breakeven and comparing that to actual results, a baseline is established. As the first step in judging any campaign, this analysis should always be done in the initial planning stages.

In a later chapter, we will revisit the break-even analysis to discuss how to deal with returns, cancellations, fixed and variable costs, and profit objectives. For now, try

---

Exhibit 3-1

BREAK-EVEN ANALYSIS WITH KNOWN AVERAGE ORDER

Average order	$50.00
Cost of goods percentage	50%
Net cost of goods sold	$25.00[1]
Cost to make a sale (fulfillment):	
Average per sale	$3.00
Advertising cost per prospect contacted	$0.55
Break-even response percentage	2.50%[2]
Break-even cost per prospect contacted	$1.25[3]

[1]$50 × 50%

[2]$0.55 ÷ ($50 − $25 − $3)

[3]2.5% × $50

to make a simple breakeven on one or two campaigns, using your own company's figures. If you have never done this before, you may be in for a shock!

Understanding Lifetime Value

Lifetime value (or LTV) is the value today of future profits. Using a transaction-driven marketing database, LTV can be calculated and used to make marketing decisions. Is a loyalty program a profit generator or a money drain? Calculating LTV with and without the loyalty program will reveal the answer. A sample case involving Bob Staley, whom you met in Chapter 1, will illustrate this comparison.

Jack's Men's Clothing: Measuring the Value of Customer Loyalty

Exhibit 3-2 shows the economics that Bob Staley is living with at Jack's.

On average, each new customer spends $500 a year—probably a new suit or sport coat, a pair of shoes, and some accessories. For every 100 new customers that Jack's brings in with general advertising, word of mouth, and so on, there is 50 percent attrition. Attrition declines in second-year customers but still occurs, as follows:

> First year = 50 percent: 50 percent of first-time customers buy in the next year.
> Second year = 40 percent: 60 percent of second-time customers buy again.
> Third year = 30 percent: 70 percent of third-time customers buy again.

Cost of goods is 50 percent, the "keystone margin" typical of most retailers. In this equation, the company buys a men's shirt for $20 and sells it for $40—a 50 percent cost of goods or a 50 percent gross margin. Finally, Jack's spends 10 percent of revenues on advertising, typically through local newspapers, flyers, and an occasional television ad. Bob Staley's small database efforts are entirely self-funded and come out of his commissions.

Column 1 shows the economics for the first year:

◆ 100 customers spending $500 each, on average, generate a total of $50,000 revenue.
◆ With cost of goods at 50 percent ($25,000) and advertising cost at 10 percent ($5,000), the profit contribution before overhead is $20,000.
◆ Since there is no time value of money discount in the present year, the net present value profit is also $20,000.
◆ The first-year annual value of each customer is $200 ($20,000 profit divided by 100 customers).
◆ Lifetime value of each customer after one year is $200.

In column 2, the second year's numbers start to change:

◆ Only 50 customers return to make the annual purchase of $500, yielding $25,000 total revenues.

- Cost of goods and advertising percentages are the same at 50 percent and 10 percent, respectively.
- Profit contribution is reduced to $10,000.
- There is a 20 percent cost of money or time value of money, as though one were going to have to borrow extra dollars to finance this effort.
- Net present profit is therefore reduced to $8,333.
- Annual customer value for year 2 is $166.67.
- Lifetime value (after two years) is up to $366.67 per customer.

The third column is similar to column 2 except the number of original customers is now down to 30.

Jack's New Personalized Communication Initiative

Exhibit 3-2 is the base case Jack's has lived with for years. Following the initiative of Bob Staley with his personalized database-driven efforts, management at Jack's decides to see if it can change the economics of the business. The goal is to communicate directly with customers to improve retention and get them to spend more. This is called building customer lifetime value.

The managers decide to test three personalized communications with new customers who are likely to become regular customers. In other words, they want to identify the customers more likely to repeat and send those customers a series of specialized communications: a birthday card, a holiday greeting card, and a postcard to highlight either special sales or new seasonal merchandise. Advertising will cost an additional 2 percent of revenues, which will cover creative and mailing costs.

Exhibit 3-3 shows the effects of this personalized, database-driven loyalty program on the value of a customer. Column 1 starts to explain the change in economics:

- Customer retention jumps to 55 percent from 50 percent.
- On average, each first-year customer spends an additional $100 with Jack's.
- Advertising goes up 2 percent, but cost of goods remains the same at 50 percent.
- Profit contribution grows by $4,000 to $24,000, a 20 percent gain.
- Annual value of a customer grows by $40 to $240, also a 20 percent gain.

The second year's results (column 2) are even better:

- Attrition is down by 5 percent.
- Sales per customer are up $150 over the base case.
- Profit contribution is up by 19 percent.
- Lifetime value of a customer is up 30 percent.

The trend continues into the third year and beyond. By capturing and tracking key customer information, such as customer purchase history and birth date, and then implementing a personalized loyalty-building communication program to the customer, you can improve short-run and longer-range sales and profitability.

Exhibit 3-2

MEASURING CUSTOMER LTV AT JACK'S: No Loyalty Program

	First Year	Second Year	Third Year
Sales			
Customers	100	50	30
% customers from previous year who buy again		50%	60%
% customers from first year who buy again		50%	30%
Sales per customer	$500	$500	$500
Total sales	$50,000	$25,000	$15,000
Costs			
Cost of goods %	50%	50%	50%
Cost of goods sold (COGS)	$25,000	$12,500	$7,500
Advertising cost % of sales	10%	10%	10%
Advertising costs	$5,000	$2,500	$1,500
Profits			
Profit contribution (before overhead)	$20,000	$10,000	$6,000
Time value of money discount factor	100%	120%	144%
New present value profit	$20,000	$8,333	$4,167
Annual lifetime value per customer	$200.00	$166.67	$138.89
LTV (cumulative)	$200.00	$366.67	$505.56

Lifetime value can be used in the same way to compare customers by original source. For example, Jack's could compare the LTV of customers who first bought with a coupon in a newspaper supplement against customers who first heard about them on the radio or who simply were walking through the mall and decided it was time for a new suit. If radio-generated new buyers bought more over time than coupon-generated new buyers, Jack's would know that it was worth spending more (per customer) to gather new buyers through radio.

Often the best place to gain new customers is from the sources that have the highest initial average purchase. For example, if coupon buyers have an average first purchase of $50, they are likely to make small purchases in the future, as well. If radio-generated buyers spend an average of $500 on their first purchase, they are likely to make large purchases in the future. Calculating lifetime value by source will uncover the potentially huge difference in future profits.

Exhibit 3-3

MEASURING CUSTOMER LTV AT JACK'S:

Database-Driven Loyalty Program

	FIRST YEAR	SECOND YEAR	THIRD YEAR
Sales			
Number of customers	100	55	36
% customers who buy again		55%	65%
Sales per customer	$600	$650	$700
Total sales	$60,000	$35,750	$25,025
Costs			
Cost of goods %	50%	50%	50%
Cost of goods sold (COGS)	$30,000	$17,875	$12,513
Advertising cost % of sales	12%	12%	12%
Advertising costs	$7,200	$4,290	$3,003
Profits			
Profit contribution (before overhead)	$22,800	$13,585	$9,510
Time value of money discount factor	100%	120%	144%
New present value profit	$22,800	$11,321	$6,604
Annual lifetime value per customer	$228.00	$205.83	$184.72
LTV (cumulative)	$228.00	$433.83	$618.56
Profit gain with database marketing	$2,800	$1,321	$604
% profit gain with database marketing	14%	13%	10%
$ gain in LTV (cumulative)	$28.00	$67.17	$113.00
% gain in LTV (cumulative)	14%	18%	22%

USING THE DATABASE TO MANAGE CUSTOMER AND PROSPECT COMMUNICATION

Database marketing is more than just remarketing to past customers (although remarketing is a very important part). Database marketing can be used to grow business, use advertising media more effectively, and manage the entire process of communicating with customers and prospects.

In the case study that follows, two similar instant oil change shops both operate out of a single location, and both compete for customers and market share. Traditional Oil advertises through the local newspaper, its local "shopper" publication, radio spots, postcards to people near its shop, and postcards to customers. It never tracks the results of its ads, but it does find that business increases with advertising.

Smart Oil Change, up until last year, advertised in exactly the same way as Traditional Oil. However, last year management began tracking the results from each ad, radio spot, and postcard promotion. They store these results in Smart Oil's marketing database. As a result, they now advertise differently!

Look first at how these two companies were advertising before Smart Oil Change began tracking and adjusting its customer and prospect communication. Both companies began with

◆ annual sales of $400,000, with a profit margin of 50 percent
◆ four advertising "pushes" per year, one each for spring, summer, fall, and winter
◆ 10,000 customers buying each year
◆ 20,000 sales, with an average sale of $20
◆ repeat customers accounting for about two-thirds of their business

The two companies advertised exactly the same way. Each quarter, they would

◆ send postcards to each of their 10,000 recent customers, at a cost of $3,500 per quarter, or $14,000 per year
◆ place $4,000 in radio spots, for a total of $16,000 per year
◆ place $4,000 in newspaper ads, for a total of $16,000 per year
◆ place $500 in shopper ads, for a total of $2,000 per year
◆ send 10,000 postcards to people near their shops, at $4,000 per quarter or $16,000 per year

In total, each company spent $64,000 per year on advertising, or about 16 percent of sales. Smart Oil Change wants to expand the business by using its advertising dollars more wisely. The near-term goal is to continue to spend an average of 16 percent of sales on advertising while growing sales by 20 percent, to $480,000 per year. This will increase annual profits by around $27,000 per year. This increase in profits will allow Smart Oil Change to expand and build a second shop. How can the company do this?

To start, Smart Oil Change puts a unique code on each promotion it runs. Then it asks each and every customer how he or she heard about Smart Oil Change, or which offer had been received, every time a sale is made. This is entered into the computer, along with the customer's name, address, vehicle information, and which parts and services bought. To begin, the company uses a simple source coding plan (see Exhibit 3-4).

Right away, Smart Oil Change managers realize they have missed a few things. First, every customer received a postcard at the same time; therefore, every repeat customer was coded with Q1A. Management couldn't tell if the postcard actually caused them to come in, or if they would have come in anyway. Instead of sending all the postcards at once, management will send them six weeks apart. Then the differ-

Exhibit 3-4

SMART OIL CHANGE: INITIAL SOURCE CODES

ADVERTISING METHOD	SOURCE CODE
Repeat-customer postcards	Q1A
Radio spots (either of two stations)	Q1B
Newspaper ads	Q1C
Shopper ads	Q1D
Prospect postcards	Q1E

ence in the two customer groups can be tracked for that six-week period, to permit judging of the effectiveness of this particular method of communication.

Second, all radio-derived customers were not from the same station. Some were from KTRY, the local country station, and some were from KOOL, the easy-listening station. Smart Oil Change wants to know which station was more effective.

Newspaper and shopper ads are simple enough to track, but the prospects who were sent postcards should be divided into three groups: businesses, consumers under $50,000 per year income, and consumers over $50,000 per year income. Exhibit 3-5 shows the source codes in the second quarter.

Now Smart Oil Change can really see some differences in the list segments, such as the difference between customers who received a postcard and those who did not. Management finds that, on average, each dollar spent on postcards accounts for around $7 in business. It also finds that customers who received a postcard closer to the time they will need an oil change, either three months or 3,000 miles, were more likely to respond.

Exhibit 3-5

SMART OIL CHANGE: SECOND-QUARTER SOURCE CODES

ADVERTISING METHOD	TARGET AUDIENCE	SOURCE CODE
Repeat-customer postcards: first mailing	Recent customers	Q2A
Repeat-customer postcards: second mailing	Recent customers	Q2B
Radio spots: KTRY	All categories	Q2C
Radio spots: KOOL	All categories	Q2D
Newspaper ads	All categories	Q2E
Shopper ads	All categories	Q2F
Prospect postcards	Businesses	Q2G
Prospect postcards	Consumers < $50K	Q2H
Prospect postcards	Consumers > $50K	Q2I

As a result of the findings with the customer postcards, Smart Oil Change will contact its customers more frequently. Instead of reaching all of them every three months, Smart Oil Change will contact some 2½ months after their last change. High-mileage customers, those who drive more than 1,000 miles per month, will be contacted more frequently. So, instead of sending an average of four postcards per year per customer, Smart Oil Change will now contact its customers an average of six times per year.

By tracking responders from both radio stations, Smart Oil Change finds that the country station KTRY gets about 50 percent better response than KOOL. Every dollar spent on KTRY brings in about $3 in sales; every dollar spent on KOOL about $1.50. In the next quarter, Smart Oil Change will advertise less on KOOL and will test advertising on KWBY, the other country station.

Sending the postcards to three different groups also teaches Smart Oil Change a lesson. Overall it gets $2 in sales for every $1 spent on advertising. Business performs well, but seemingly only certain kinds of businesses respond. By a wide margin, the higher-income consumer lists perform better than the lower-income list. In the next quarter, only businesses likely to have one or more company vehicles will be targeted. Smart Oil Change will increase its mailing radius (the distance from the store it is willing to mail) for consumers with over $50,000 annual income and will reduce the mailing radius for under-$50,000 consumers.

The third-quarter codes are modified again. They are listed in Exhibit 3-6. By targeting customers at the appropriate times, Smart Oil Change is still able to increase sales by $7 for every dollar spent on postcards—an excellent return. Also, the spots on KWBY are just as effective as the KTRY spots, so KOOL will be dropped, and radio advertising will be split between KTRY and KWBY. Newspaper ads are returning

---

Exhibit 3-6

SMART OIL CHANGE: THIRD-QUARTER SOURCE CODES

ADVERTISING METHOD	TARGET AUDIENCE	SOURCE CODE
Repeat-customer postcards	High-mileage customers	Q3A
Repeat-customer postcards	2½-month customers	Q3B
Radio spots: KTRY	All categories	Q3C
Radio spots: KOOL	All categories	Q3D
Radio spots: KWBY	All categories	Q3E
Newspaper ads	All categories	Q3F
Shopper ads	All categories	Q3G
Business postcards	SIC select	Q3H
Prospect postcards	Consumers < $50K	Q3I
Prospect postcards	Consumers > $50K	Q3J

$2 for every $1 spent, or about 50 percent of sales. Although newspaper advertising won't be dropped, it will be reduced. The shopper, on the other hand, is producing $3 for every $1 spent, on par with radio. As a result, advertising in the shopper will be increased.

Dropping businesses in categories that do not respond is a smart move. Instead of a $2 return for each dollar spent on postcards, the return is now $3 for every $1 spent. Smart Oil Change will continue to target all the likely businesses in its area.

Higher-income consumers perform well, at $2 in sales per $1 spent, but lower-income consumers return substantially less. In the future, Smart Oil Change will send prospecting postcards only to businesses and to consumers with incomes above $50,000 a year.

In the fourth quarter, both Traditional Oil and Smart Oil Change will spend $16,000 in advertising. However, Smart Oil Change will spend its dollars differently. To show the changes in sales, Exhibit 3-7 presents a comparison of what both companies *were* getting by using the same methods and what Smart Oil Change will get with its new advertising mix.

By making what amounts to minor adjustments based on actual data, Smart Oil Change can increase business $15,000 per quarter, or $60,000 per year, while spending the same amount on advertising. Increased sales will allow the company to spend more to find new customers, since for every dollar in sales it can spend 16 cents on advertising. To meet the goal of an $80,000-a-year sales increase while still spending 16 percent of sales on advertising, Smart Oil will need to make further tweaks. Exhibit 3-8 (page 30) outlines a plan for increasing sales an additional $10,000 per quarter while spending less than $3,000 per quarter more than the previous year, well within the initial goal.

In fact, the benefits of database marketing go beyond those this case illustrates. By managing its customer base, Smart Oil Change increases the lifetime value of each new customer it gathers. This allows the company to spend more per customer to get new business, knowing repeat sales will more than make up for it. Smart Oil Change could grow much faster, if it chose to!

Using the Economies of Database Marketing

In this chapter we've touched on these basic areas of database marketing:

◆ Measuring marketing cost versus incremental revenue
◆ Lifetime value
◆ Marketing to repeat customers
◆ Communication planning

Each of these areas will be explored in greater depth later in the book. Later chapters geared toward technical, computer-related issues are presented only as a

Exhibit 3-7

SALES COMPARISONS UNDER DIFFERENT ADVERTISING PLANS

Initial Communication Plan Results

TARGET AUDIENCE	COST	SALES FROM ADVERTISING
Repeat-customer postcards	$3,500	$24,500
Radio spots (either of two stations)	$4,000	$9,000
Newspaper ads	$4,000	$8,000
Shopper ads	$500	$1,125
Prospect postcards	$4,000	$8,000
Total	**$16,000**	**$50,625**

Fourth-Quarter Results

TARGET AUDIENCE	SOURCE CODE	COST	RETURN PER DOLLAR SPENT	SALES FROM ADVERTISING
High-mileage customer	Q4A	$2,500	$7.00	$17,500
Three-month customer	Q4B	$2,750	$7.00	$19,250
KTRY radio spots	Q4C	$2,500	$3.00	$7,500
KWBY radio spots	Q4D	$2,500	$3.00	$7,500
Newspaper ads	Q4E	$2,000	$2.00	$4,000
Shopper ads	Q4F	$1,250	$3.00	$3,750
Business postcards	Q4G	$1,000	$3.00	$3,000
Postcards to consumers > $50K per year	Q4H	$1,500	$2.00	$3,000
Total		**$16,000**		**$65,000**

means to an end. What makes marketing databases valuable tools is not their ability to store data but rather how they can be used to change the economics of marketing communication. With this focus clearly in mind, we approach how database marketing should be conducted.

Exhibit 3-8

SMART OIL CHANGE: PLAN FOR SECOND-YEAR FIRST QUARTER

TARGET AUDIENCE	SOURCE CODE	COST	RETURN PER DOLLAR SPENT	SALES FROM ADVERTISING
High-mileage customer	Q5A	$3,000	$7.00	$21,000
Three-month customer	Q5B	$3,250	$7.00	$22,750
KTRY radio spots	Q5C	$3,000	$3.00	$9,000
KWBY radio spots	Q5D	$3,000	$3.00	$9,000
Newspaper ads	Q5E	$2,000	$2.00	$4,000
Shopper ads	Q5F	$2,000	$3.00	$6,000
Business postcards	Q5G	$1,000	$3.00	$3,000
Postcards to consumers > $50K per year	Q5H	$1,500	$2.00	$3,000
Total		**$18,750**		**$77,750**

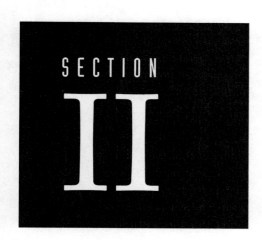

SECTION

II

Setting Up Your Day-to-Day Database Operations

Key Elements of a Decision Support System

You can't teach a pig to sing. It won't work, and what is more, it annoys the pig.

Mark Twain

The Goal for a Marketing Database

The drive to create marketing databases has as much to do with the popularity of the spreadsheet as it does with database technology. Managers have become used to being able to play "what if" games with their spreadsheets: change a number and immediately see what impact the change might have.

Traditionally days, weeks, or months were needed to create reports showing differences in sales by region, item, or salesperson from data stored in different computer systems. When programmers had to write a program, load a tape, and run it overnight to answer any question that could not be resolved with a standard report, managers tended not to ask too many questions. In contrast, with a database with the flexibility of a spreadsheet, the analyst could make the same kind of charts, graphs, and so on and could respond to a what-if question not in hours, days, or weeks but in seconds.

For example, a what-if database question might be "What if we had sent the last offer only to the top 40 percent of our customers instead of the top 50 percent?" This could easily lead to comparing the top 30 percent to the top 40 percent to the top 50 percent—in just a few seconds. If response in one area seemed different, perhaps in California, the California customers could be analyzed separately. If that analysis showed that Sacramento seemed to be different, then just Sacramento could be analyzed. Analyses can extend all the way down to the individual customer and transaction level.

Now imagine this fast, flexible database being analyzed not by programmers interpreting a management request and then having to write a new program but by the managers themselves. The tool would have to be capable of allowing people who are experts at what they do (when what they do is something other than programming computers for a living) to explore the data, ask their own what-if questions, and get fast answers. When decision-makers can go from one question to the next in seconds rather than days or weeks, they can ask not only more questions but better and, hopefully, the right questions. Rather than create "data overload," this approach allows managers to get what they want when they want it.

Ultimately, the goal of a marketing database is to give spreadsheet-like what-if flexibility to managers who need to analyze their own company's data. Achieving the first part of this goal, spreadsheet capabilities, makes the benefits of marketing databases available to people in the company, who then bring their own insights together with the information in the marketing database to make better decisions. That is the true benefit of a marketing database.

Data Warehousing

Over time, businesses gather information about customers, their transactions, and about how they operate their business. Naturally, they want to be able to use that data to make better decisions. The challenge for most businesses is not to gather more information; it is simply to get at the information they've already amassed, to make some sense of it, and then to put it to use making decisions that can be long term and strategic, or day to day. Whether deciding which new products to develop, which services to offer, or which customers and prospects to call or mail this month or even today or right this minute, managers desire to use the data they already have to make a better decision.

Data warehousing is best described as an *action term*. It is the process of moving data, not just storing it but moving it from where it is gathered to where it can be analyzed and acted upon. Data is gathered at many points: during the process of making a sale, through contact management programs used by salespeople, in the accounting process, from prospecting, and through many other possible means. Data warehousing brings together data from different sources to be analyzed and used to support business decisions.

Data is analyzed most effectively in a single database. A marketing database tends to house information that originated in several other databases: transactions from one system, advertising costs from somewhere else, and so on. This collection of data from several "source" databases into one database to facilitate analyzing and making better marketing decisions is what we will refer to as a data warehouse.

A marketing database that is also a data warehouse does not have to be big or small. It can be a collection of a few hundred customer names from a contact management program, transactions taken from accounting reports or actual invoices, and some product information, all stored in a simple database on a small PC. It also can be a collection of tens of thousands of customers from different corporate divisions, years of diverse sales histories, and information on thousands of products, promotions, and salespeople.

So, the amount of data does not define a data warehouse. If the database is a collection of data from more than one database, if it is normalized and available for analysis,[1] and if it is intended for use as a tool to make better decisions, then it is a data warehouse—and warehousing is the method used to create and store the marketing database.

Three Types of Computer Systems

Computer systems are designed to accomplish certain tasks, and different systems are used to perform different functions. A system may be designed to take orders from multiple operators at once, tie all the cash registers together, or transfer information from place to place. A well-designed system will effectively accomplish the tasks for which it was intended. It may not, however, be good for other tasks.

Three basic types of computer systems are commonly used in business, each designed to perform a particular task very well. They are transaction processing systems, management information systems, and decision support systems.

Transaction Processing Systems

A transaction processing system handles the business of running the business. It can be a cash register system, an order entry system, or a credit card approval system. Transaction processing systems tend to have several things in common:

♦ They can handle a lot of small lookups, changes, insertions, and deletions in a database, often by several operators at once.
♦ They are very fast at handling a single transaction or lookup, usually while a customer is either standing at the register or waiting on the phone.
♦ If the system is not working, the business is not doing business. (For example, a store can't sell without cash registers; a catalog company can't take orders without an order processing system.)

Management Information Systems

Most managers use management information systems to produce the reports they use on a day-to-day, week-to-week, month-to-month basis. These systems are used for

---

[1] Normalization is the process of deciding into which database file to put each piece of data.

tasks such as accounting, producing financial reports, storing personnel records, managing inventory, and summarizing data from transaction processing systems. Management information systems tend to have several things in common:

- They produce reports based on summarized data, usually based on sets of facts rather than on individual pieces of data.
- They integrate data between such departments as production, accounting, marketing, and human resources.
- They have a structured information and report flow that is planned and stable (e.g., weekly/monthly sales reports produced in a certain way at a certain time).

Decision Support Systems

The third type of system, decision support systems, provides a tool for top management and decision-makers to explore data and make unplanned analyses. These systems contain summarized data, as well as data describing individual buyers, individual transactions, and individual products. Decision support systems tend to have several things in common:

- They allow nontechnical users to explore data and ask unplanned questions.
- They can add large amounts of new information to the database very quickly and can complete large-scale updates of data very rapidly.
- They are optimized to produce fast answers to broad questions, such as "What was the average sale price of hammers sold in California last month, and is that more or less than it was in Colorado?"

A data warehouse is usually built to house a decision support system. Data is taken from transaction processing systems, management information systems, and even outside data sources and placed into the data warehouse for accessing through a decision support system.

Using the data warehousing approach allows the other systems in a company to do the jobs they were designed to do and still provides the decision support flexibility managers need. Requesting data from a data warehouse does not affect the other systems and prevents situations where information requests can crash a transaction processing system or slow it to a crawl. Making unplanned data inquiries does not upset the management information system's structure or information flow when the inquiries are made in the data warehouse.

DIFFERENT DATABASES FOR DIFFERENT SYSTEMS

Each of the three different types of systems—transaction processing, management information, and decision support—uses its own database. The three usually are on different computer systems and do not compete for the same piece of data at the same time. Why are these systems different and often separate? Why can't one big system do it all?

One reason is that different users often compete for the same data at the same time. All three systems may need to change or update data, but when data is being changed, only one user in one system can have access to the records being changed. This is called *record locking*. It prevents two people from changing something, such as an address, at the same time. Record locking is necessary to ensure data integrity.

Record locking is usually not an issue with a transaction processing system, because only the person talking with the customer is likely to be modifying the information. For example, someone placing an order may report a new address, but rarely does the company modify names and addresses in large batches or all at once. However, when data is summarized, addresses cleaned, and other changes made in batches by the management information or decision support system, many records can be locked in the process. This makes getting at customer's information difficult or impossible, effectively taking the transaction processing system down.

Another issue that arises when systems compete for the same data is speed. Entering large numbers of inquiries, summarizing data, and updating files can drastically slow a system's abilities to process transactions. Speed becomes a critical issue when nightly batch runs become so large that they cannot be completed by the next start of business.

Finally, data security and integrity are major reasons the three systems are often separate. An inexperienced user can easily erase data, recode important information, lose information, and create a situation where the transaction system could be down for anywhere from hours to days. Imagine someone accidentally erasing customer ID numbers and wiping out a good part of the database! It simply isn't worth the risk of having every manager in the company a mouse click away from destroying working data and forcing a system backup at any moment.

A well-planned decision support system using a well-planned data warehouse makes managers and decision makers more effective at their jobs without hindering other people and other systems.

Finding relevant Marketing Data——and Ignoring the Rest!

Not all information used or created in other systems belongs in a marketing database. Bin locations of items in the warehouse, for example, probably won't be of any use for decision support. The sale amount on invoices will be very useful and must be stored. The number sold, quantity on hand, and current cost are also important and should be kept.

Certain questions need to be answered when you decide which pieces of data to use and which pieces are not relevant. Some questions seem quite basic, such as, "How much is a sale?" However, the answer to that question is not necessarily the number of units sold multiplied by the price of each item. What if the invoice had a discount? What about shipping, taxes, or some miscellaneous charge? How much of the total amount is the sale amount should be determined before deciding which fields from a transaction table should be stored or discarded.

Another example of a simple question: "When does a sale become a sale?" Is it when the product is ordered, when the credit card is charged, or when the item is shipped? All these potentially different dates are likely to be entered and stored in a transaction processing system. The date that describes when each sale occurred (according to the definition established) is the date that should be kept in the marketing database.

The first consideration in selecting which data to retain and use is making sure all relevant data will be available for any inquiry. The second consideration is to take in each data point only once. For example, a transaction date could redundantly be stored in several places in the transaction processing system. To avoid problems with inconsistent data and to streamline the process, the transaction date should be taken from only one place (a single data point) when the data warehouse is updated.

All the information in the marketing database example in the next chapter will be useful in a data warehouse. In addition, other information about customers, products, and salespeople may be useful, along with information not related to sales and marketing: product specifications, engineering data, and component assembly information.

Summarizing Data for Fast Answers

When data is first put into a marketing database, it is stored in many separate files referred to as *tables*. The process of deciding where to store each piece of data is called *normalization*. Summaries of important pieces of information are then created and stored, to speed up finding answers to common questions. This is called *denormalization*.

A data warehouse may contain as much as seven times as much information in summary tables and indexes as it has in original data. All this denormalized data is used as a quick way to find answers to likely questions. Examples of common summaries are sales by month, by region, or by product. The planned storage of summarized data makes a wide variety of unplanned inquiries go extremely fast. Knowing how to summarize and what should be summarized is important when putting a data warehouse together.

Pictures from catalog pages, product manuals, and even employees' photos can be stored in a data warehouse. For example, an insurance company could scan photos of an accident and store them with data about a claim. Sound, either for instructions or as the data itself, can be part of the warehouse. There is really no limit, except for what is defined by needs, availability, and common sense.

Permanent Storage and Constant Update

Product costs change, customers move, and employees change positions. Once database managers decide that a particular piece of data needs to be in the marketing database, the next step is to decide how, when, and how often it should be updated or replaced. Having an update strategy that takes into account the changes that occur in the database is important.

Some facts never change, and others are constantly changing. That Bill Clinton is the 42nd president of the United States will never change. As the 43rd, 44th, and 45th presidents are elected and added to the list of presidents, who was president before does not change. The address of someone serving as U.S. president is the White House on Pennsylvania Avenue in Washington, DC. When a president leaves office, his personal address is no longer the White House and must be changed.

Based on this kind of simple logic, decisions can be made about what kinds of information are added to and what kinds of information will need to be updated. For example, last month's invoices are exactly that, last month's. If an invoice from last month is found to be incorrect today, the past invoice is not changed. The correction is made through another invoice. For this reason, new invoices can simply be added to the invoice table, and old invoices do not require updating.

On the other hand, if a customer's phone number has changed, the old phone number is replaced by the new phone number. This changes the customer's record in the customer table. In addition to new customers being added to the customer table, the records of old customers that have any changes must be updated in the data warehouse.

Data Access and Security

Decision-makers having access to the data on which they will base their decisions is a primary goal in data warehousing. In larger companies a data warehouse resides on a server, which is either a PC or a midrange computer. Managers access the data through a PC network, using database and statistical tools.

Data warehouses can be very complete, with a tremendous amount of information about the company and its clients, products, people, costs, and sales. They should not be stored where competitors or hackers can get access to them. Every reasonable precaution should be taken to ensure that only people who have a "need to know" can use the data warehouse.

Control Issues

Marketing is not the only area of a company that can benefit from having a data warehouse. Production, planning, engineering, and other departments can all use this information. The Management Information Systems (MIS) department is often in charge of the day-to-day running of the data warehouse.

MIS control can sometimes become a point of conflict, however. When MIS tries too hard to make a "structured environment," that can ultimately stymie the "free-form" ability managers need to ask unstructured questions. That Management Information Systems does not want some other department in charge of the data warehouse is almost certain, even if MIS management doesn't understand why it is needed or why it should be built a certain way. Crucially, however, user managers' know-how and business understanding must be used to both build and use the data warehouse. MIS cannot make or manage a successful data warehouse without the involvement of the managers who will use it.

What makes a decision support system successful is not who initiates it or who is ultimately in charge. What makes a decision support system successful is planning, bringing in the right data so managers can have confidence in their findings, and having a fast, flexible way of finding the answers to questions based on the data being stored.

Making a system that works involves far more than technical knowledge. Marketing knowledge must be a part of what goes into making a marketing data warehouse. Some database software is better for transaction processing, and some is specifically designed for decision support. However, what software a big computer has does not matter if the data is wrong or incomplete.

For a marketing data warehouse to succeed as a marketing decision support system, it must be able to produce fast answers to a wide variety of unplanned questions about large and small groups of customers. It must have complete information about customers and transactions, and that data must be accurate. Speed, flexibility, ease of use, and accurate, credible data—that is what decision support is all about.

Building a Marketing Database

Knowledge is of two kinds. We know a subject ourselves, or we know where we can find information upon it.

Samuel Johnson (1709–84), English author and lexicographer

How Will the Marketing Database be Used?

Thinking about the kinds of information a marketing database will provide is important, before the database is assembled. Once information needs have been decided, appropriate data can be gathered to support the decisions the business must make. These are the kinds of questions that need to be answered:

- Who should be targeted for certain offers?
- Who are the best customers?
- Who are the best prospects?
- Which offer(s) should they receive?
- How should they be contacted?
- Who can be contacted more often?
- Who can be cross-sold?

The specific kinds of information required by different businesses varies greatly, but certain kinds of data are common to nearly all marketing databases. In this chapter, we review those common data elements.

Building Blocks of a Marketing Database

Before we describe each marketing database "building block," you need to understand how the data is stored and understand the terminology.

Each building block, or set of information, is referred to as a *file*—for example, customer file or product file. A file is a unique set of information about a specific grouping of items, people, or events. If you are at all familiar with computers, you have heard and probably used the term *file.*

A database file must follow certain rules. Unlike a file that contains a letter, a picture, or a program, a database file must be arranged in rows and columns. When you look at a database file, it looks very much like a spreadsheet. There are column headings at the top and data going across each row.

	Column/Field #1	Column/Field #2	Column/Field #3
Row/Record #1	Data = "Bob Jones"	Data = "101 Main St"	Data = "66208"
Row/Record #2	Data = "Sue Evans"	Data = "105 E 10th"	Data = "61820"

In a database file, the columns are referred to as *fields.* For example, if the first column in a customer file contains only customer names, the first column is referred to as the "name field," not the name column. If the second column contains only addresses, it is called the "address field." If one contains only the postal code, it's the "postal code field," and so on. Fields (columns) in a database file do not vary. Names are always in the name field, addresses are always in the address field, and so on.

This arrangement makes it easy to find information (e.g., a customer by name). Simply look down the name column to locate the customer you want, and the row you find the name in will contain fields with other information about that customer.

Fields in a database file are usually of a certain type and width. For example, a name field could be 20 characters long. That means up to 20 letters or numbers can be stored there, but a 21-character name (a name 21 letters and spaces long) would have to be truncated (shortened) to fit. Sometimes to help avoid typos or so that math functions can be done a field is restricted to only character data (names, addresses, etc.) or only numeric data, such as dollar amounts. A letter (*A, B, C*) will not be allowed in a numeric field; only numbers will. Fields are displayed with a set width so they will line up in straight columns when you look at the data.

Each row of a database is referred to as a *record.* For example, if customer John Doe is listed in the first row of the database, his information can be found in record number one. If Jane Smith is listed in the fourth row, her information can be found in record number four.

Exhibit 5-1 shows what a database file looks like. Looking down each column (field), you find only information that is related. The name field has only names, not addresses or cities. Also, the state field needs to be only two characters wide, as it never contains more than two letters. The name field must be large enough to hold customers' names without truncating them and so is much wider than the state field.

Looking across each row (record), you find information about only one person. Record number one has only John Doe's name, address, city, state (or province), and ZIP (postal) code. Jane Smith's information is only in record number four.

Exhibit 5-1

RECORD #	NAME	ADDRESS	CITY	STATE	ZIP
1	John Doe	101 Waverly Dr	Champaign	IL	61821
2	Jack Schmid	4550 W 90th Ter #200	Shawnee Mission	KS	66207
3	Alan Weber	4638 W 70th St	Prairie Village	KS	66208
4	Jane Smith	PO Box 101	Minneapolis	MN	55450

When referring to information about one person, you could say, "Based on Jane Smith's record, she lives in Minnesota." On the other hand, if you referred to the information in one field, this would be based on information from all the records. For example, you could say, "Based on the state field, two customers live in Kansas, one in Illinois, and one in Minnesota."

Database files are often referred to as *tables*, meaning that the file is part of a database that contains other files and that those files are related to one another. Files are related by *key fields*, which contain unique ID numbers: customer numbers, part numbers, invoice numbers, and so on. Exhibit 5-1 is simply a file because it does not have a unique identifier that would make it part of a larger database.

Exhibit 5-2 shows a pair of related files that can be correctly referred to as tables.

Exhibit 5-2

CUSTOMER TABLE

NAME	ADDRESS	CITY	STATE	ZIP	CUST ID
John Doe	101 Waverly Dr	Champaign	IL	61821	0001
Jack Schmid	4550 W 90th Ter #200	Shawnee Mission	KS	66207	0002
Alan Weber	4638 W 70th St	Prairie Village	KS	66208	0003
Jane Smith	PO Box 101	Minneapolis	MN	55450	0004

INVOICE HEADER TABLE

INVOICE ID	DATE	AMOUNT	PAID BY	CUST ID
10001	2/10/98	50.00	Check	0002
10002	2/11/98	20.00	Visa	0001
10003	2/11/98	35.00	Cash	0003
10004	2/12/98	30.00	Cash	0004
10005	2/12/98	40.00	Visa	0001

By looking at the pair of tables, you can relate customers to their purchases by the "CUST ID" field. For example, you can see that Jane Smith made a purchase of $30 on February 12, and she paid cash. You can also see that John Doe made two purchases and used his Visa credit card both times.

Together, the two files in Exhibit 5-2 can be referred to as a database. A database is a set of tables (more than one) that are files related by key fields. We would not refer to files or tables by themselves as a database, as they are correctly called either files or tables. To qualify as a database, there must be more than one file, or at least two tables.

Starting from the smallest pieces and working up, a database is made up of

1. rows and columns of data making up individual files
2. files with key fields that relate to other files, which are now called tables
3. two or more related tables

Now that we have described the basic parts of a database, let's look at the parts of a marketing database. Most marketing databases have pieces of information that are common to all. We will discuss the most common pieces in detail.

CUSTOMER INFORMATION

Customers are the most important part of database marketing. However, they are only one element. What they do, what they buy, and what you offer them are other elements. A customer is not a transaction, a customer is not a product, and a customer is not the special offer you made last fall.

Neither is a customer a row of several columns of information, but that is how a customer is represented in the database: by name, address, phone number, and so on. Finding a customer in the database means you have found a description of that customer. From this description, you can mail, call, or locate the actual customer.

Whether a person is a customer or a prospect or has requested information, assume that each person will be given a single record in the customer table. It may be easier for you to think of the customer table as the "people" table, because that is exactly what it is in the example in Exhibit 5-3.

Exhibit 5-3 shows the column categories and their parameters in a sample customer table. The descriptions on the left side are the column, or field, descriptions. The customer ID number listed first in the customer table is the unique ID code that can also be found in other tables that describe what a customer has done. As in Exhibit 5-2, a customer's ID number also can be spotted in the invoice records, where that customer's purchase information is found.

The name, address, and phone number portion tells who the customers are and where they can be reached. The fields are summaries based on the customer's transactions with the company. These fields are useful for quick lookups and analysis. We discuss how to create them later in the book.

Exhibit 5-3

SAMPLE CUSTOMER DATABASE

CUSTOMER	
Customer ID	↔**Key Field**
Mr/Ms	4 characters
First Name	14 characters
Middle Initial	1 character
Last Name	19 characters
Title	30 characters
Company	30 characters
Address One	30 characters
Address Two	30 characters
City	19 characters
State or Province	2 characters
ZIP or Postal Code	10 characters
Phone #	12 characters

Initial Source Code

Date Entered in the System
Do Not Rent
Change of Address

Cash
Charge
Phone
Mail

First Purchase Date
Last Purchase Date **R**
Total # of Purchases **F**
Total $$ of Purchases **M**

Last Return Date
Total # of Returns
Total # of Exchanges
Total $$ of Returns
Last Cancellation Date
Total # of Cancellations

Last Mailing Date
Total # of Mailings

Gift Giver

Product Classification One
Product Classification Two
Product Classification Three
Product Classification Four

INVOICE HEADER	
Customer ID	↔**Key Field**
Invoice Number	↔**Key Field**
Salesperson ID	↔**Key Field**
Source ID	↔**Key Field**
Order Date	
Method of Payment	
Gross Sales	
Discounts	
Other Charges	
Net Sale Amount	

INVOICE DETAIL	
Invoice Number	↔**Key Field**
SKU (Item Number)	↔**Key Field**
Invoice Line Number	
Ship Date	
Quantity	
Total Price	

PRODUCT	
SKU (Item Number)	↔**Key Field**
Product Classification (Category)	
Cost per Unit	
Retail Price	
Number in Stock	
Description	
Weight	

SALESPERSON	
Salesperson ID	↔**Key Field**
Salesperson Name	
Department or Division	

OFFER	
Source ID	↔**Key Field**
Description	
Number of Offers Made	
Cost per Reach	

The name and address areas in Exhibit 5-3 have a recommended number of characters as a minimum width for each field so that truncating important information can be avoided. A last-name field only 12 characters wide would not be wide enough for many long, hyphenated last names, such as Schwing-Hammer or Smith-Ellington.

Having first and last names in separate fields is important. Otherwise, it is difficult to send a letter to John Doe. Rather than start with "Dear John," the letter may start with "Dear John Doe." This will be a problem every time the customer is to be contacted. Keeping first and last names separate makes far more sense.

Title and company are important to have, whether the target customer group is businesses or consumers. One problem that occurs when needed fields are either too short or unavailable is that data will be entered in the wrong field to make it "fit." Exhibit 5-4 shows just such a situation.

In the case of Audrey Kennedy-Jones, letters will be addressed Dear Ms. Kennedy-, and her address label will place her last name on two lines. The resulting incorrect address label, and the corresponding correct label look like:

Incorrect:	*Correct:*
Audrey Kennedy-	Audrey Kennedy-Jones
Jones	101 Main
101 Main	Big City, US 01000
Big City, US 01000	

In the case of John Doe at Doe & Co., since the company name is on an address line, he cannot be easily distinguished as a business customer. He also has only one address line left, and many business addresses require two lines. His incorrect address label and the corresponding correct label look like:

Incorrect:	*Correct:*
John Doe	John Doe
Doe & Company	Sales Manager
101 Main St	Doe & Company
Anytown, IL 61821	Suite 1415
	101 Main St
	Anytown, IL 61821

Exhibit 5-4

First Name	Last Name	Address #1	Address #2	City	State	Zip
Audrey	Kennedy-	Jones	101 Main	Big City	US	01000
John	Doe	Doe & Co.	101 Main	Anytown	IL	61821

Not having all the fields needed, such as company and title, or having fields that are too narrow for the data creates problems in the future. In the case of Audrey Kennedy-Jones, it is both embarrassing to the company and insulting to the customer to have her name broken apart every time she is contacted. In the case of John Doe, his mail may not reach him at all.

The *initial source code* is in bold in Exhibit 5-3. This is the ID code of the offer through which the customer initially came into contact with the company. It might be the source code of the first catalog a person ordered from or the source code of a magazine ad call-in to request more information. The original source code is a very important piece of data that will stay with the customer record forever.

Date entered is the date the customer was initially included in the database. In the case of someone who goes into the database as a prospect and buys later, this date will be prior to the first purchase date. *Do not rent* can indicate whether or not customers want their name rented to other companies; it should be a part of all customer tables. Change of address indicates when the address was last updated or corrected. This is either listed as a specific date or is left blank.

Cash, charge, phone, or mail simply indicates that this person has or has not used one of these methods to pay or order products. Similar fields, such as store charge, purchase order, or OK to bill, could also be needed for some retailers or business-to-business sellers. The information in these fields makes it easy to target offers to either credit or noncredit buyers.

First purchase date, when a customer made the first purchase, is useful in lifetime value calculations. Recency-frequency-monetary (RFM) is a summary of purchase data that helps target customers more efficiently. Chapter 11 is devoted entirely to a discussion of RFM.

Returns and *cancellations* are an important enough part of purchasing behavior that they are broken out separately. The impact of returns and cancellations is greater in some businesses (e.g., fashion retailers) than in others but is well worth tracking and analyzing.

Tracking the last contact or mailing date and total number of contacts helps prevent contacting a single customer too many times. This can be important when a large number of different or overlapping offers are being made and when contacts are expensive, such as large catalogs or personal sales calls.

The *product classification* fields can represent either categories or departments and are used to note whether or not the customer has bought certain kinds of products. For a clothing store, classifications could be coats, men's trousers, suits, ladies' sportswear, lingerie, evening wear, and shoes. For a hardware store, it could be power tools, hand tools, gardening, household, and lumber. This type of classification is very useful either when groups of customers are found to be very different based on the categories of merchandise they buy or when buyers in one category are good cross-selling prospects for another category of merchandise.

By now the question "What about the prospect file?" may have occurred to you. Or, maybe you're wondering about the customers from different stores or divisions. Again, the customer table is the people table. Try to put all the people into this table. Only if having one and only one table with all the people in it is impossible should more than one people table be considered. Note the word *impossible*. It may be difficult, but unless it is impossible there should be one and only one table—the customer table—for all people the company either sells to or keeps on file as prospects.

TRANSACTION INFORMATION

Transactions are fully represented by two tables, the invoice header and the invoice detail (see Exhibit 5-3, page 46). This is because a transaction is a single event made up of the purchase of one or more items.

As an example, consider buying a hammer, two boxes of nails, and a tube of glue at the same time. The total transaction (see Exhibit 5-5) is represented by one record in the invoice header file, and each of the three types of items purchased is represented by a record in the invoice detail file. In this respect, transactions are different from customers: customers are not a grouping; they are whole, unique beings.

A transaction can be compared to a family. A family is one unique thing but is also made up of its members, each of whom is in turn unique. In the same way that a family can be made up of a father, a mother, a daughter, and a son, a transaction is made up of the purchase of one or more items. In Exhibit 5-5 the nails part number, Nails-264, is listed only once in the invoice detail, with a quantity of two; for each

Exhibit 5-5

INVOICE HEADER

Invoice Number	Paid By	Source ID	Salesperson ID	Date	Total Amount
001001	Cash	HO98A	AW	2/12/98	20.00

INVOICE DETAIL

Invoice Number	Line Number	Quantity	Part Number	Amount
001001	1	1	Hamr-100	5.00
001001	2	2	Nails-264	10.00
001001	3	1	Glue-789	5.00

unique type of item (part number) in the invoice detail, there is only one record corresponding to each invoice header. If one box or one million boxes of nails is purchased, the transaction is still one record.

However, if one box had been roofing nails, part number Nails-150, and the other nails were for hanging pictures, part number Nails-300, each would have a separate record in the invoice detail file.

In the invoice detail file is stored the information of exactly which items were sold, in exactly what quantities. If the question "Who bought roofing nails, part number Nails-150, and paid cash?" is asked, the invoice detail must be used, along with the invoice header file, to ultimately relate to the customer table. The part number information is in the invoice detail, but the method of payment is in the invoice header.

Often businesses try to have only one invoice file, usually the invoice header. The invoice detail is often the largest file to store on computer in a marketing database, and eliminating it allows computer people to have a much easier job. However, next to the customer table, the invoice detail is the most important file. Without it there is no way to know who bought what.

A marketing database with both an invoice header and an invoice detail can gather all the information about who bought what, when they bought, how they paid, who sold it to them, and to which offers they have responded. The longer that information is gathered into these two files, be it months or years, the more a company will know about the buying habits of its customers.

PRODUCT INFORMATION

Information about the products and services a company sells is stored in the product table (Exhibit 5-3, page 46). This table describes each product (or service), shows the classification (suits, shoes, etc.), of each, and contains product cost, list price, and other information about what is being sold.

In Exhibit 5-6 the invoice detail does not have a product description, only the part number. If you wanted to know whether hammer Hamr-100 had a graphite or wooden handle or what it cost, you would look it up in the product table.

The product table may contain list prices, which are not always the same as the customer's price. The price in the product table is more of a suggested retail price; the actual price, what a customer paid, is found in the invoice detail table.

SALESPERSON INFORMATION

The salesperson table provides additional information about transactions, similar to the product table. The salesperson table contains information about who made the sale. Looking up the salesperson ID from a transaction (found in the invoice header) tells who made the sale and whether he or she is an outside salesperson, a telemarketer, or an inside salesperson (see Exhibit 5-7).

From the salesperson ID and information in the sales table, sales can quickly be analyzed by person and by department.

Exhibit 5-6

INVOICE DETAIL

Invoice Number	Line Number	Quantity	Part Number	Amount
001001	1	1	Hamr-100	5.00
001001	2	2	Nails-264	10.00
001001	3	1	Glue-789	5.00

PRODUCT

Part Number	Description	Cost	List Price
Hamr-100	Standard Wood Hammer	2.50	5.00
Nails-264	Roofing Nails	2.00	5.00
Glue-789	Sealing Glue	2.75	5.00

Exhibit 5-7

INVOICE HEADER

Invoice Number	Paid By	Source ID	Salesperson ID	Date	Total Amount
001001	Cash	HO98A	AW	2/12/98	20.00
001002	Visa	HO98B	JS	2/12/98	15.00

SALESPERSON

Salesperson ID	Name	Department
AW	Alan Weber	Hardware
JS	Jack Schmid	Gardening

OFFER INFORMATION

Offer information is information about what was offered and to which group it was offered. For example, assume two groups of customers, buyers from the last 6 months and buyers from 7 to 12 months ago, are sent the same offer. If the two groups are going to be tracked separately, each needs a unique record with a unique source ID in the offer table. In Exhibit 5-8, invoice number 001001 is a sale with a source ID of HO98A. Looking up HO98A in the offer table, you see that it was a flyer sent to the last six months' buyers, that 5,567 were mailed to this group, and that each flyer cost 50 cents.

With the source ID, offers that individuals responded to can be quickly identified. More commonly, the sales with each source ID in the invoice header are summed to find total sales for a particular offer or promotion. For example, sales can be totaled for each source ID, such as HO98A, and for each promotion. This could be either all sources starting with HO98, or all the 98 Winter Flyer source IDs.

ADDITIONAL INFORMATION

All the preceding tables—customer, invoice header, invoice detail, product, salesperson, and offer—represent information gathered in the course of doing business. To ship products, you must have the customers' names and addresses. You know what

---

Exhibit 5-8

INVOICE HEADER

INVOICE NUMBER	PAID BY	SOURCE ID	SALESPERSON ID	DATE	TOTAL AMOUNT
001001	Cash	HO98A	AW	2/12/98	$20
001002	Visa	HO98B	JS	2/12/98	$15

OFFER

SOURCE ID	TARGET GROUP	DESCRIPTION	QUANTITY	COST EACH
HO98A	0–6 mo Buyer	98 Winter Flyer	5,567	$0.50
HO98B	7–12 mo Buyer	98 Winter Flyer	4,312	$0.50

you shipped them, when you shipped it, how much they paid, who sold it, and whether or not they got a discount.

Often it is useful to know more about customers than simply who they are and what they bought. You may want to know how they use your product, if they are happy with it, and if they buy your competitor's products. These are questions you can try to answer through surveys.

When a company has a marketing database, it often makes sense to have survey responses listed in a survey table in the database. To make a survey table possible, the customer ID must be attached to the survey. This is usually done by printing it on the survey and entering it along with the survey responses when the survey is returned.

An example of a survey table appears in Exhibit 5-9. By putting survey information into a table in the database, it is possible to compare opinions with behaviors. For example, are buyers of power tools as satisfied as those of hand tools? Which

Exhibit 5-9

SURVEY

CUSTOMER ID ↔KEY FIELD
Satisfaction Rating
Competitors Considered
Type of Use
Would Recommend to a Friend

CONSUMER DEMOGRAPHICS

CUSTOMER ID ↔KEY FIELD
Age
Household Income
Family Size

BUSINESS INFORMATION

CUSTOMER ID ↔KEY FIELD
SIC Code
Years in Business
Annual Sales
Number of Employees
Years in Business

competitors are most often considered for each category of purchase? These questions can be answered through survey data that is part of the marketing database.

Demographic information—age, estimated income, family size, and so on—can be added to a database for pennies a name. It may or may not be useful and may or may not be appropriate, but it is available. Similar information about businesses, such as the Standard Industrial Classification (SIC) code, years in business, annual sales, and number of employees, is also available and relatively inexpensive. Demographic information changes over time and must be updated to remain useful.

Demographic information is helpful in painting a picture of who the customers are, what they are like, and how many other people there are like them. Although targeting people only by demographics rarely is effective, there are cases where demographics combined with other data are very helpful in eliminating unlikely prospects.

Exhibit 5-9 also shows the consumer demographics table and the business information table. With the exception of SIC code, the information is quite comparable: age versus years in business, income versus annual sales, and family size versus number of employees.

Far more information can be included than is shown in the examples in Exhibit 5-9. Generally speaking, the more fields of information desired, the greater the cost. Very complete sources, those that have information on a higher percentage of consumers or businesses, generally charge more for their data than do sources that cannot add data to as many records.

All the Building Blocks

The Exhibit 5-9 tables are basic building blocks that should be represented in every marketing database. More information than these samples show may be needed for some businesses. If more tables or fields are required, by all means include them.

By far the most important job of a marketing database is to track customers, prospects, and their interactions with the company. Additional data can always be added later or left out entirely. The basic information about who customers are and what they buy should always be available. If it is, the marketing database will be a good place to go to find answers when you have marketing questions.

6

Designing for Flexibility

In general, commanding a large number is like commanding a few. It is a question of dividing up the numbers. Fighting with a large number is like fighting with a few. It is a question of configuration and design.

Sun-tzu (ca. 500 B.C.), Chinese general, from *The Art of War*

All the marketing data in the world is of no use if you cannot get access to it. Storing important information is one thing, but storing it in such a way that it can be retrieved is another. Marketing databases are usually designed to be *relational* databases, so that any information stored can be used in the future. A relational database that allows flexible access to all the stored data is designed in a certain way. This method of design, called *normalization*, requires the use of well-defined principles.

However, before we can describe how normalization is done, we must fully describe what a relational database is. To do that, we start with some explanation of what computer databases are and how different types of databases differ in the way the information is accessed and stored.

A Little Database History

When the only choice in computers was the mainframe, files were usually maintained on tapes, normally large, reel-to-reel tapes. Many mainframe systems today still use files stored on these reel-to-reel tapes. Files were not related to other files by key fields and were typically updated on some periodic basis (nightly, weekly, monthly, etc.). Today files that are not related are called *flat files*.

When customer data is stored on tape as a flat file, all the fields of information readily available about a customer are kept in one file. A particular customer's transaction information, similar to that stored in the invoice detail table described in Chapter 5, is not readily available. A transaction flat file stores all the information about transactions but none of the information about customers. For example, it is relatively easy to find out how many of a particular hammer were sold, but it is not

Exhibit 6-1

FLAT CUSTOMER FILE LAYOUT

DATASET LAYOUT

Record ___ **Consumer** ___ Application ___ Date ___

Record Layout ___ Prepared By ___ Page ___ of ___

Data Name ___ **Record Layout**

(INSTRUCTIONS: P • Pucked B • Binary C • Character)

TITLE

First Name | Last Name | Address

City | St. | ZIP + 4 | Date of Last Activity | Total # Purchased | Total $ | Original Source Code | Do Not Rent | COA | # Canc. | Cancellation Recency Date

Cash | Charge | Phone | M a i l

Product Classification: 1 2 3 4 5 6 7 8 9 10

Returns: Date | # of Ret. | # of Each

Column markers: 5, 10, 15, 20, 25, 30, 35, 40, 45, 50, 55, 60, 65, 70, 75, 80, 85, 90, 95, 100, 105, 110, 115, 120, 125, 130, 135, 140, 145, 150, 155, 160, 165, 170, 175, 180, 185, 190, 195, 200, 205, 210, 215, 220, 225, 230, 235, 240, 245, 250, 255, 260, 265, 270, 275, 280, 285, 290, 295, 300 easy to find out who bought hammers or who bought which hammer. This is because the customer flat file and the transaction flat file are not related.

Blank spaces are often kept in each record of a flat file, in case any new fields of information need to be added. If no blank spaces are available, adding a field requires converting the file to a new layout. For an example of a customer flat file layout, look at Exhibit 6-1 (on previous page). The customer flat file in this chapter is very similar to the customer table shown in Chapter 5. The key difference is that the customer table in Chapter 5 is related to other tables but the customer flat file is not.

How does this make a difference operationally? The flat file example has more product categories than the relational table. It is often necessary to have many categories of information in a flat file, because the transaction files cannot be quickly compared for additional information.

For example, using the customer flat file, you can find customers who bought an item in a particular category. However, you cannot easily find out who bought exactly which item and when. Compare this to storing the customer data in a table. By comparing the customer, invoice header, and invoice detail tables, it is possible to find buyers of a particular item from a particular day. Whether the item was sold by phone, mail, fax, or at the store or how the item was paid for (by cash, credit, or check) can also be determined. You can even find who sold a particular item to a customer through the salesperson table.

Exhibit 6-2 shows data for a company selling ski equipment. All the company's customer and transaction information is kept in separate flat files. The customer file in Exhibit 6-2A has three summarized product categories: skis, clothing, and related gear. Assume that buyers of the beginner's ski set, which is item number Ski-101 and in the product category skis, are very likely to buy a better pair of skis the year after they buy the beginner's set. If you look through the customer file, you find you can only select from the product category of skis. You cannot tell who are the buyers of item number Ski-101, the beginner's ski set.

You are faced with two choices: forget about targeting an offer for a more advanced pair of skis to these customers or change the customer file. Many marketing people opt out here and go the easy way; they contact all previous buyers of skis. To avoid this waste, you have to, at a minimum, add a field called beginner to account for purchasing item number Ski-101 (see Exhibit 6-2B). The program that periodically updates the customer file must be modified so you can put the information into the beginner field during future updates. Finally, a special program will be needed to add the information from past purchases of item number Ski-101 to the customer flat file. This means all the old transaction flat files must be rerun one at a time to update the new beginner field in the customer flat file.

Again, by using only the information stored in the customer flat file, it is not possible to tell if buyers of one type of skis are different from buyers of another type of skis. Therefore, these kinds of questions must be answered with something other

Exhibit 6-2

SKI COMPANY'S CUSTOMER FILE

A. Flat Customer File

NAME	ADDRESS	TOTAL PURCHASE	SKIS	CLOTHING	RELATED GEAR
Bill Smith	100 Main	$120	$80	$40	$0
Frank Edward	PO Box 9	$75	$50	$0	$25
Susan Fowler	305 6th St	$250	$150	$75	$25

B. Flat Customer File with Beginner Ski Set

NAME	ADDRESS	TOTAL PURCHASE	SKIS	BEGINNER	CLOTHING	RELATED GEAR
Bill Smith	100 Main	$120	$0	$80	$40	$0
Frank Edward	PO Box 9	$75	$50	$0	$0	$25
Susan Fowler	305 6th St	$250	$150	$0	$75	$25

than the information stored in the customer flat file. For this reason, many good marketing questions go unanswered or unasked; the desired information is simply too difficult to retrieve.

Relational databases are far more flexible than flat file systems for on-the-fly retrieval of all sorts of different data. Flat file systems are designed primarily to store data, but relational databases are designed to explore and use data as well as store it. Although both relational and flat file systems can store data and create periodic reports, a relational database makes it much easier to look at data in different and often unplanned ways. With a relational database, it is fairly simple to explore and track the buying behavior of the customers who bought the beginner's ski set, or any other items, without requiring program changes or updates.

Relational database theory was first explained by E. F. Codd in 1970. The first commercially successful relational database was created by Jake Ruf, founder of the Ruf Corporation, in 1976. Relational databases didn't come into wide use, however, until the PC became commonplace.

In Chapter 5 a table is defined as a file that is part of a database containing other files, and those files are related to one another. Tables are normally stored on hard drives (random-access disk drives), and the user can gather information simultaneously from a combination of tables. Since PCs have hard drives that tend to work well with relational databases, the rising popularity of relational databases has mirrored the rising popularity of the PC.

Describing the things a relational database can do is a bit like saying you can drive your car anywhere you choose. A car won't go where there is no road, and a database needs data to be useful. If a car is poorly designed or poorly maintained, it won't get far. Neither will a database.

FIVE RULES OF RELATIONAL DATABASE DESIGN

Thankfully, normalization is based on only five basic principles, or *normal forms*. If a database satisfies the first principle, it is in first normal form. If a database satisfies the second principle, it is in second normal form, and so on. The five principles, or normal forms, are

1. no repeating groups of data
2. no redundant data
3. no data fields that are not dependent on the key field(s)
4. no fields with multiple values
5. tables cannot reflect logically related many-to-many relationships

Normalization is intended to eliminate one or more of the following four problems:

◆ Data duplication
◆ Inconsistent data
◆ Deletion of data
◆ Insertion or addition of data

To illustrate the five normal forms, we will use an example based on an automobile repair shop. Look at the repair order in Exhibit 6-3. Notice how a repair order has all the information about the customer, the parts that were used, who made the sale, and so on.

The repair order shown represents typical information created when a sale is made. It records a transaction with a customer, has one or more lines of invoice detail, includes the products being sold, shows who made the sale, and even mentions special offers or coupons used by the customer. In this example, all the major tables from Chapter 5 are represented on one sheet of paper.

Assume you have a stack of repair orders from this shop and want to create a relational database to hold marketing information, so you can communicate appropriately with your customers. You'll need to create, at a minimum, a customer table, invoice header, invoice detail, product, salesperson, and an offer table where the information from the repair orders can be stored. You'll do this by taking the information on the repair orders and putting it into tables based on the principles of normalization.

Exhibit 6-3

SAMPLE REPAIR ORDER

Jack's Classic Car Repair

"In business since 1967"

Date: 02/14/98

Salesperson: Darryl

Invoice Number:	10101
Customer ID:	123123
Customer Name:	Alan Weber
Address:	4638 West 70th Street
City, State, ZIP:	Prairie Village, MN 11111

Home Phone: 555-7759   **Work Phone:** 555-0220

Vehicle Year: 1970   **Make:** Plymouth   **Model:** Road Runner

Serial Number: RM23VOA6H001500

Mileage: 56,712   **Offer:** 10% off Winter Special

Purchases:	Cost/Item	Line Total
Two rear tires	$69.50 each	$149.00
4 headlights	$ 5.00 each	$ 20.00
1 quart motor oil	$ 1.00 each	$ 1.00
1/2 hr labor in shop	$40.00 hour	$ 20.00
	Transaction Summary:	$190.00
	Less Discounts:	$ 19.00
	Total Before Taxes:	$171.00

Paid by: Check_____ **Cash** X **Visa**_____ **M/C**_____

First Normal Form

For a table to be in first normal form, *there can be no repeating groups of data.* Each group of information requires a separate table, and each table requires a key field. (See Exhibits 6-4 and 6-5.)

The example in Exhibit 6-4 is not in first normal form, because the customer's name and ID are repeated for every transaction. This would make contacting customers difficult, as their names and addresses could be repeated differently. This would likely result in duplication, and some customers would get duplicate mailings or phone calls. To satisfy first normal form, the information must be split into two tables.

Exhibit 6-4

EXAMPLE NOT IN FIRST NORMAL FORM

KEY FIELD	KEY FIELD	DATA FIELD	DATA FIELD	DATA FIELD
INVOICE NUMBER	CUSTOMER ID	CUSTOMER NAME	DATE	TOTAL AMOUNT
10101	123123	Alan Weber	02/14/98	$171.00
10102	123124	John Doe	02/14/98	$ 76.50
10103	123125	Jane Smith	02/14/98	$211.00
10104	123123	Alan Weber	02/15/98	$ 32.50

Exhibit 6-5

EXAMPLE IN FIRST NORMAL FORM

Customer Table

KEY FIELD	DATA FIELD
CUSTOMER ID	CUSTOMER NAME
123123	Alan Weber
123124	John Doe
123125	Jane Smith

Transaction Table

KEY FIELD	KEY FIELD	DATA FIELD	DATA FIELD
INVOICE NUMBER	CUSTOMER ID	DATE	TOTAL AMOUNT
10101	123123	02/14/98	$171.00
10102	123124	02/14/98	$ 76.50
10103	123125	02/14/98	$211.00
10104	123123	02/15/98	$ 32.50

With a database design such as in Exhibit 6-4, the customer's name is repeated in the database for every transaction. Splitting transactions and customers apart, as in Exhibit 6-5, allows any customer to have an unlimited number of transactions while still having only one listing in the customer table. With only the key field of customer ID repeated in the transaction table, data duplication is eliminated. Since most databases are compiled to track *repeat* purchase activity, this is a critical factor.

Key fields, such as customer ID, can and likely will be repeated in the transaction table. If customers make more than one purchase, their customer ID numbers are expected to be listed in more than one transaction. This does not violate first normal form, *because a key field is not a data field.*

The date, 2/14/98, is repeated through several of the transactions in the example. This is because the date describes the transaction, not vice versa. Different customers or the same customer could have more than one transaction on the same date or for the same purchase amount. Therefore, having two or more invoices with the same date is not duplication; neither is selling two different customers a similar product for the same price.

Second Normal Form

A table in second normal form will have *no redundant data.* By redundant, we mean listing the same data twice or listing data along with a key field that means the same thing. For example, listing both the customer ID and the customer name in a transaction table (or any table other than the customer table) is redundant; both describe who the customer is. There is no advantage to storing both pieces of information in more than one place, but there are many disadvantages.

Second normal form is needed in tables that have more than one key field. When a table (e.g., the transaction table) has several keys, the keys can be referred to as a multivalued key. If data in one field depends on only part of a multivalued key (i.e., depends on only one of two or more key fields), it should be stored in a separate table. This separate table would include the key field the data is dependent upon. (See Exhibits 6-6 and 6-7.)

Exhibit 6-6 is not in second normal form, because it contains data that is dependent on only part of the key fields. There are three key fields—customer ID, invoice number, and part number. Together they are a multivalued key. Now look at the cus-

---

Exhibit 6-6

EXAMPLE NOT IN SECOND NORMAL FORM

Key Field	Data Field	Key Field	Data Field	Key Field	Data Field
Customer ID	**Customer Name**	**Invoice Number**	**Date**	**Part Number**	**Description**
123124	John Doe	10102	2/14/98	Tir-100	15" Tire
123125	Jane Smith	10103	2/14/98	Rad-153	Van Radiator

Exhibit 6-7

EXAMPLE IN SECOND NORMAL FORM

Customer Table

KEY FIELD   DATA FIELD

CUSTOMER ID	CUSTOMER NAME
123124	John Doe
123125	Jane Smith

Transaction Table

KEY FIELD   KEY FIELD   KEY FIELD   DATA FIELD

INVOICE NUMBER	CUSTOMER ID	PART NUMBER	DATE
10102	123124	Tir-100	2/14/98
10103	123125	Rad-153	2/14/98

Product Table

KEY FIELD   DATA FIELD

PART NUMBER	DESCRIPTION
Tir-100	15″ Tire
Rad-153	Van Radiator

tomer name field. The customer name is dependent on only one key field, customer ID. Customer ID 123124 is John Doe; customer ID 124125 is Jane Smith. Name is not dependent on invoice number or part number. Therefore, customer name is dependent on only part of a multivalued key. The same is true for part number and description. Part number Tir-100 is always the 15″ tire; Rad-153 is always the van radiator. Description has nothing to do with invoice number or customer number. It does not matter who buys part number Tir-100 or which invoice reflects the purchase. Tir-100 is always a 15″ tire.

If product information is stored this way, and you want to change the description of a certain item, you have to change the description in every record where the item was purchased. If you do not change all of them, there will be two descriptions for the same item number in the database, an example of inconsistent data.

Another problem can occur if a customer is the only one to buy a certain product. Assume Jane Smith's van is a 1965 Ford Econoline and she is the only customer to buy a van radiator, part number Rad-153, of the three you had in stock. Now assume Jane gets a great job offer in another city and moves away. If you remove her from the database, you also remove part number Rad-153, of which you still have two left.

Second normal form handles several problems. The table in Exhibit 6-6 contains both redundant data, inconsistent data, and potential problems with deleting data. Exhibit 6-7 shows how to handle these problems. As with the tables in second normal form, data based on a key field is not repeated. John Doe's name can be found only in the customer table, not spread over all the transactions he has made. If he gets his Ph.D. and wants to be known as Dr. John Doe, you can change his name once, and it will be used as corrected every time in the future. If his name were in several places and you missed one, there would be a loss of integrity because his name would be inconsistent throughout the database.

If Jane Smith moves away and you want to delete her as a customer, you will not automatically remove the van radiator from the database in the process. This is especially good since you still have two in stock. Without affecting any customer's information, you can even add a comment to the record where information on the radiator is stored, such as "obsolete item, sell at any price."

Third Normal Form

For a table to be in third normal form, *it can contain no data fields that are not dependent on the key field(s)*. Another way to say this is that each table is made up of information about the key field, the whole key field, and nothing but the key field. For example, if a transaction table is keyed on invoice number, it should contain only information about transactions. (See Exhibits 6-8 and 6-9.)

It seems simple enough to just put the salespeople's names along with their titles in the transaction table, particularly when only a few people are making sales.

Exhibit 6-8

EXAMPLE NOT IN THIRD NORMAL FORM

Transaction Table

KEY FIELD	DATA FIELD	DATA FIELD	DATA FIELD
INVOICE NUMBER	TOTAL AMOUNT	SALESPERSON	TITLE
10101	$171.00	Jack Schmid	Owner
10102	$ 76.50	Darryl Erickson	Service Manager
10103	$211.00	Darryl Erickson	Service Manager
10104	$ 32.50	Jack Schmid	Owner

Exhibit 6-9

EXAMPLE IN THIRD NORMAL FORM

Transaction Table

KEY FIELD	KEY FIELD	DATA FIELD
INVOICE NUMBER	**SALESPERSON ID**	**TOTAL AMOUNT**
10101	JS	$171.00
10102	DE	$ 76.50
10103	DE	$211.00
10104	JS	$ 32.50

Salesperson Table

KEY FIELD	DATA FIELD	DATA FIELD
SALESPERSON ID	**SALESPERSON**	**TITLE**
JS	Jack Schmid	Owner
DE	Darryl Erickson	Service Manager

However, the transaction table should be about transactions, not salespeople. To be in third normal form, there should be two tables: one for transactions and one for salespeople.

Notice that we added salesperson ID to the transaction table and removed the salesperson's name and title from the transaction table. Now the information in the transaction table is only about transactions, and the salesperson table is only about salespeople.

In the table in Exhibit 6-8, it is not possible to have a salesperson without a transaction. When new salespeople are hired, they are not in the database until after they make a sale—an example of a problem with inserting new data. If the transactions of former salespeople are removed from the system, there is no record of them ever having made a sale—an example of a problem with deleting data. You will want to put new employees into your database as soon as they are hired, and you may need to keep records of past employees longer than you need to keep transaction-level data.

Fourth Normal Form

For a table to be in fourth normal form, *there can be no fields with multiple values.* This situation can occur in a "one-to-many" relationship. For example, a salesperson has many sales, but each sale has one salesperson. A customer has many transactions, but each transaction has one customer. The problem can also occur with a many-to-many relationship. For example, a car uses many parts, and a part can be used by many cars.

Because this concept is more difficult than the first three normal forms and because mistakes are commonly made designing databases with one-to-many and many-to-many relationships, here are two wrong examples. The first places multiple pieces of data into the same field; the second places the same kind of data into different fields.

In the first bad example (Exhibit 6-10A), having a multivalued field, such as items sold, makes it very difficult to quickly find who bought antifreeze. This is a bit like trying to find everyone in the phone book who's first name is Bob; it also forces the database to have a very large field to store the largest possible number of items sold or to create two or more records to describe items sold if the maximum number of items that will fit into the items sold field is exceeded.

Exhibit 6-10

EXAMPLES NOT IN FOURTH NORMAL FORM

A. Transaction Table with Multiple Pieces of Data in One Field

KEY FIELD	DATA FIELD	DATA FIELD	KEY FIELD
INVOICE NUMBER	TOTAL AMOUNT	DATE	ITEMS SOLD
10101	$171.00	02/14/98	Tir-101, Hed-050, Oil-W30
10102	$ 76.50	02/14/98	Tir-100, Val-100
10103	$211.00	02/14/98	Rad-153, Ant-200
10104	$ 32.50	02/15/98	Val-100, Tal-100

B. Transaction Table with Multiple Fields for the Same Kind of Data

KEY FIELD	DATA FIELD	DATA FIELD	KEY FIELD	KEY FIELD	KEY FIELD
INVOICE NUMBER	TOTAL AMOUNT	DATE	ITEMS 1	ITEMS 2	ITEMS 3
10101	$171.00	02/14/98	Tir-101	Hed-050	Oil-W30
10102	$ 76.50	02/14/98	Tir-100	Val-100	
10103	$211.00	02/14/98	Rad-153	Ant-200	
10104	$ 32.50	02/15/98	Val-100	Tal-100	

In the second bad example (Exhibit 6-10B), data of the same kind, an item sold, is spread among three fields. An item such as a valve stem can be found in the items 1 field and in the items 2 field and could someday appear in the items 3 field. That's like trying to find Bob Jones in any one of three phone books. The database will have to either store a lot of blank items fields or occasionally create two or more transaction records to store all the items sold, the same problem as with multivalued fields.

Exhibit 6-11 shows how to correct both problems. Splitting the transaction table into its two parts, the invoice header and the invoice detail, solves the problem of multivalued fields and places all like data into the same field. Remember from Chapter 5 that a transaction is like a family. One family has many family members. In the same way, there is one invoice header for each transaction, and each transaction is made up of the simultaneous purchase of many items.

Exhibit 6-11

EXAMPLE IN FOURTH NORMAL FORM

Invoice Header

KEY FIELD	DATA FIELD	DATA FIELD
INVOICE NUMBER	**TOTAL AMOUNT**	**DATE**
10101	$171.00	02/14/98
10102	$ 76.50	02/14/98
10103	$211.00	02/14/98
10104	$ 32.50	02/15/98

Invoice Detail

KEY FIELD	KEY FIELD	KEY FIELD
INVOICE NUMBER	**LINE NUMBER**	**PART NUMBER**
10101	1	Tir-101
10101	2	Hed-050
10101	3	Oil-W30
10102	1	Tir-100
10102	2	Val-100
10103	1	Rad-153
10103	2	Ant-200
10104	1	Val-100
10104	2	Tal-100

Fifth Normal Form

For a table to be in fifth normal form, *it cannot reflect logically related many-to-many relationships*. This rule is not likely to have practical value for working with marketing databases. In theory, fifth normal form can reduce the number of updates required to maintain information in tables with many-to-many relationships. In actual use, however, database performance is likely to be better if fifth normal form is ignored. It is mentioned for your interest. And should you choose to study database design in depth, you may encounter fifth normal form.

Marketing Design Considerations

Normalizing a marketing database perfectly—that is, following all the rules of normalization—does not mean the database is perfectly designed. Marketing databases often have missing data, incomplete data, and other problems that need to be planned for in the design phase.

In the customer table example in Chapter 5 (Exhibit 5-3, page 46), most of the fields represent summaries of data from other tables. These summary fields in the customer table are an example of denormalization. Denormalization is the planned violation of normalization principles, done to make certain reports or pieces of information faster to retrieve. Sometimes it is better to store summarized information in a separate field calculated from fields in other tables than it is to recalculate the information on a frequent basis.

The recency-frequency-monetary value (RFM) fields are good examples of information that summarizes data from other tables. These fields represent the last date a customer made a purchase, the number of purchases the customer has made, and the amount the customer has spent on all purchases. Retrieving counts and mailing lists based on RFM can be time consuming and difficult if it is not precalculated. Since RFM is a very common way to select groups of customers for targeted offers, storing the information with each customer's record makes sense. Calculating RFM can be done periodically while other people are not using the database. When a contact list of recent customers or a list of customers who have made more than one purchase is needed, it can be pulled quickly based on information stored in the precalculated summary fields.

A number of common problems or design considerations must be faced when you set up a marketing database. Here are some of the most typical.

Companies Are Customers

Business-to-business marketers may think that each person who buys from them is their customer. If this is true, the database design in Chapter 5 may work well. In business-to-business selling, however, different people often have different buying roles; each plays a part in the purchases the company makes. Here *the company is the customer*, and each person involved with purchasing decisions is a decision-maker related to that company. The customer table in Exhibit 5-3 will not work. Why?

Commonly, in business-to-business selling, one person influences the decision, another makes the buying decision, another approves the purchase, and a purchasing agent might place the order. All have a role in the buying process. Exhibit 6-12 shows what can happen when people and companies are stuck into one customer table in a business-to-business database. In this case, each person involved in purchasing is represented in the database. What also happened is that a check was received that had no person's name on it; it was just a check from The XYZ Inc. This created a new record in the customer table. The alternatives were assigning the company's purchases to one person in the database or spreading the purchases across several people, even though it is in fact one company buying.

Exhibit 6-13 offers one solution to this problem. In addition to correctly assigning purchases to the company, this design also prevents redundant company data (e.g., company name) that may be inconsistent from being repeated in the customer table. Sometimes these relationships can be even more complex. Buyers can be at plants that have headquarters locations, headquarters locations can have parent companies, and so on.

If some buyers are individuals and some are companies, this will usually force a design compromise. The key questions to ask when planning are these:

◆ Who makes the buying decision?
◆ Who influences the buying decision?
◆ Who approves the buying decision?
◆ Is he or she responsible for all or part of the buying process?
◆ Who will be contacted how often, why, and by what method?
◆ Which is more practical, to make the design more complex or to work around the limits of a less complex design?

Exhibit 6-12

CUSTOMER TABLE WITH COMPANY BUYERS

Customer ID	Name	Company	Title	Rec	Freq	Mon
001099	Bill Smith	XYZ Inc	Purchasing		0	0
001100	Frank Edward	XYZ Inc	Comptroller		0	0
001102	Joe Peterson	XYZ Inc	Foreman		0	0
001101	Susan Fowler	XYZ Inc	President		0	0
001158		XYZ Inc		2/10/98	6	$5,200

Exhibit 6-13

BUSINESS-TO-BUSINESS DATABASE DESIGN

Customer Table

CUSTOMER ID	COMPANY ID	NAME	TITLE
001099	00300	Bill Smith	Buyer
001100	00300	Frank Edward	Comptroller
001102	00300	Joe Peterson	Foreman
001101	00300	Susan Fowler	President

Company Table

COMPANY ID	COMPANY	REC	FREQ	MON
00300	XYZ Inc	2/10/98	6	$5,200

Business-to-business marketers have always had a greater challenge in creating a solid database design, and they always will. However, the design should be a practical reflection of the type of relationship they have with the companies and people that buy from them.

Blank Customer Numbers

Blank customer numbers, or any other blank *key field*, are problems for relational databases. They multiply answers if the person looking up information is not aware of them, because tables are joined by matching key fields, and blank matches blank.

For example, assume one customer in the customer table has a blank customer ID, and two invoices in the invoice header have a blank customer ID. If customers are compared with invoices based on the key field customer ID, the customer with the blank customer ID will match two invoice records.

Another example: Assume two customers have a blank customer ID and there are two invoice records with a blank customer ID. Both customers will match both invoice records, for a total of four matches, not just two (two matches for each customer with a blank customer ID).

If 10,000 customers have blank customer ID fields and 10,000 invoices have blank customer ID fields, this is a real problem. Each customer will match all 10,000 invoices, for a total of 100 million matches! This sort of matching certainly results in absurd answers and contributes to bad decision-making, as well as possibly filling up the hard drive and crashing the system.

Marketers often need to keep data that is not complete, however, and this can include the customer ID fields. Consider a survey table that is matched against the customer table by customer ID. If a survey cannot be matched because you don't know which customer filled it out, should it be left out of the survey table?

Of course, you want all the data you can get in the survey table. This is because surveys are often analyzed by themselves, not as a part of a larger database. Rather than omit records not assigned to a particular customer from the survey table entirely, it is better to include all responses and match only the records that do not have a blank customer ID when comparing survey data to other tables. Although this is not correct normalization, it does work. And it meets the needs of marketers.

No Transaction Detail

The invoice detail table is usually the largest table in the database. In a few extreme cases, where individual item purchases are very small and may not be significant (an example might be groceries) the invoice detail table is left out. Only summaries of each transaction, from the invoice header, are stored.

The problem with leaving out the invoice detail is that there is no way to tell who bought what. When someone bought or how much they paid is kept, but not which product. This omission leaves out many possibilities for cross-selling, upselling, and periodic repurchase offers. In truth, if making the invoice detail table part of the database is not practical, odds are good that having a marketing database at all is not practical.

Deleting Customer with Transactions

A relational database is made up of tables related by key fields. If an invoice record has a customer ID that does not match any of the records in the customer table, it is called an orphan record. *Orphan* is a term that can be applied to any record in a table that used to, but no longer does, relate to records in another table.

If a customer's record is removed (entirely) from the customer table, it could result in incorrect reporting of sales. Here is an example. A recent customer's record has been removed from the customer table, and this customer spent $100 during the past month. If a report is created showing last month's revenue *by customer*, the report will underreport revenues by $100. Remember, the report is based on a match of customers and transactions, and the omitted customer did not match even though the revenue is in the transaction table. As a result, the $100 in purchases cannot be included in the revenue by customer report. Similar problems occur when records are removed from other tables.

Example: A customer dies and you are notified of that fact. You need not remove the entire record. Leave the customer record in the database, with the key field intact.

Remove the name, address, and other information such as phone number, which is not a key field. Without causing a database problem, this will prevent an attempt to contact the customer in the future. Better yet, create a "do not contact" field and mark the customer's record.

Business-to-business marketers have to deal with people who change jobs, leave their jobs, or even appear at other companies that already buy and are in the database. It is important not to delete a person and lose company data, but it is also important not to keep trying to contact people who are at a new job. Keeping up-to-date with company names and addresses is one thing, but keeping up with personnel changes in different buying and influencing positions is a challenge.

In a case where a person goes from one customer company to another, the company ID field, along with name and address, can be changed in that person's customer record. However, to avoid creating an orphan company and orphan invoices, at least one person at the old company must have the company ID assigned to his or her customer record.

If people leave a customer company and are no longer to be contacted, remove the company ID from their record and reassign it somewhere else, perhaps to the replacement or to the position title. It may be necessary to add their replacement to the customer table to do this, if the new person was not there before. In no case should a person's customer record simply be deleted.

Gift Recipients

If a business sells products that are gift items, the ability to track who gave gifts to whom is a powerful marketing tool. Gift recipients may not be customers yet, but they tend to be excellent prospects. Clearly it is important to store the information about the customer, but it is also important to store information about the gift recipient.

The database should be able to store data about who gave what to whom, including gift recipient's data. One way to do this is by adding each new recipient to the customer table, with a customer ID, and adding a gift recipient field to the invoice detail table. Gift recipients are people, and you will want to store all people who are customers or prospects in the customer table. Storing each recipient's customer ID in a recipient field in the invoice detail table allows tracking of multiple gifts per order. This arrangement also allows for a customer giving a gift to an existing customer.

No Source ID, No Offer Table

If a database such as the one described in Chapter 5 does not track source ID with transactions and does not have a table like the offer table, it is not a marketing database. It might be an accounting database or a sales database, but it is not a marketing database. Determining what was sold, who sold it, and how many of a given item are left may be possible, but it is not a marketing database.

Without tracking the origin of each sale and each response, determining which offers work and which do not is not possible. Did the customer buy from the spring catalog, the newsletter, or as the result of a sales call? Without a source ID, you will never know. Without a source ID, it is impossible to tell which mailing lists work the best, which magazines have the best response, or which offers customers prefer. It is impossible to analyze sales from a particular catalog when you don't know from which catalog the customer placed the order.

Tracking the source of each transaction and each new prospect inquiry is not only what makes a marketing database different from an accounting database. It is what enables marketers to learn from their mistakes and their successes and to market smarter in the future because of them. No effective marketing database ever has been or ever will be designed without some means for tracking the source of each transaction.

Science, Art, and Practice

Designing a marketing database is both a science and an art. If this chapter seems difficult to grasp, don't be discouraged. Come back to it later, once you've read more of the book, and review it again. The rules of normalization are complex and difficult to understand, and just when they start to make sense, along comes denormalization.

Those who understand the concepts presented in this chapter will be able to do far more with a marketing database than will those who do not. Anyone who plans to be in charge of a marketing database must understand how and why the database is the way it is, or it is sure to be something less than it could be.

Using Data Storage Tools

A worker may be the hammer's master, but the hammer still prevails. A tool knows exactly how it is meant to be handled, while the user of the tool can only have an approximate idea.

Milan Kundera (b. 1929), Czech author and critic

Database Tools: Hardware and Software

In this chapter, we look at the functions of the database itself. That is, what does database software do (and not do), and what does database hardware do (and not do)? A database can do certain things very well, other things not so well. Knowing these strengths and limitations will be a great help to understanding what is practical and impractical in building a marketing database.

Storage Software

The purpose of a database is to store and retrieve data for future analysis. Storage and retrieval of information are its two key functions. The more useful the data that can be stored and the faster it can be retrieved, the better.

Most database software on the market is very good at storing large volumes of data. Inexpensive software packages, such as FoxPro, allow for the storage of as many as a billion records. They can store and retrieve data relatively quickly, even with a million or more records. Of course, if you really have a billion records, getting information will take a bit longer.

Some database software is geared toward very large databases. Sybase, Oracle, SAS, and Red Brick make software to operate large databases that have millions (or even billions) of records. With modern, large-scale software and hardware, there is virtually no limit to the size of the database that can be built and operated. It is now simply a matter of the user's need, the value of the information, and practical cost limits.

Robust is a key word in describing database software and hardware. A robust database stores information in such a way that it is not easily damaged or lost.

73

Updates must be saved as they are made, and backup files must be maintained, to make certain data is not lost. (Better to wait for data than have no data at all.) Ultimately, a slow but robust database is better than a fast but inaccurate database.

Indexing

Indexes are lookup files that the computer uses to find data very rapidly. Just as a phone book is sorted by last name for quick lookup, indexes are a sorted list that the computer uses to find data in the data file. Indexes are an important component of any relational database.

Indexes are stored as separate files. That is, a data file, such as the customer table, is one file. Another file, an index file, is an index of customer ID numbers. Each of the relational tables from Chapter 5 has a separate index file. These files make information retrieval much easier.

One index file will store all the indexes for each indexed field in a database file. That is, if the customer table is indexed on customer ID and ZIP code, the index file for the customer table will contain the indexes for both fields, ID and ZIP. If the customer table is indexed on customer ID, ZIP code, and original source code, the index file will contain the indexes for all three fields: ID, ZIP, and source code. Each index for other tables in the database, for example the invoice header table, will have its own index file.

Customer Table Contains customer data	**Invoice Header Table** Contains transaction data
Customer Index File Index on customer ID	**Invoice Header Index** Index on customer ID, invoice number, source ID, salesperson ID
Invoice Detail Table Contains by-unit transaction data	**Salesperson Table** Contains salesperson data
Invoice Detail Index Index on invoice number, SKU (item #)	**Salesperson Index** Index on salesperson ID
Product Table Contains product data	**Offer Table** Contains data on offers (promotions)
Product Index Index on SKU (item #)	**Offer Index** Index on source ID

Indexing makes databases run fast. Key fields are indexed so that the computer can rapidly compare and match the key fields in two or more different tables. Indexing can make data retrieval literally hundreds or thousands of times faster. At the same time, indexing can make storing data several times slower. Why?

Assume you have 500,000 names in your customer table. Finding the 25 or so that might live in ZIP code 66208 might take about two minutes if the table is not indexed by ZIP code. That is, if you ask for ZIP code = 66208 and there is no index for the ZIP code field, it will take about two minutes to get the output. When asking for the same information, ZIP code = 66208, if you have indexed the file on ZIP code you would expect the output in less than $1/10$th of one second! Indexing the file dramatically speeds data retrieval.

Now assume you want to append 10,000 names to your customer table. To *append* means to create new records by adding data onto the file. Once the data is added, a process that should only take a few seconds, it must be reindexed. The process is much like adding names to the phone book. Simply adding more pages won't work, as each new name must be placed in the correct "sorted order." This process of reindexing will take several minutes for each field that is indexed.

Notice that you are not placing the names in the customer table itself in a particular order (nor do you need to). You are, however, placing the indexes in order (see Exhibit 7-1). Just as the customer file at the phone company is not sorted the same way the phone book is, neither is the customer table sorted like the customer index file.

Be aware that the more fields being indexed, the longer it takes to reindex when data is added (or deleted). One could index on last name, for example, and make very

Exhibit 7-1

REINDEXING, BASED ON LAST NAME

Data Table

Joe	Smith	101 Main St	Chicago	IL	60610
Patty	Davis	200 S 5th St	St Joseph	MO	64501
Tony	Green	1501 Waverly Dr	Los Angeles	CA	90212
Betty	Allen	PO Box 215	Denver	CO	80202

Index File

Allen	Record 4
Davis	Record 2
Green	Record 3
Smith	Record 1

fast lookups to find a person with a certain last name. However, adding or deleting groups of names will take longer when you reindex the file, as you must wait for the last name field to be reindexed.

It can take hours or days for the various files in a large, relational database to accomplish something like a monthly update (adding large volumes of records to several files at once). When this becomes the case, the time trade-off between fast lookups and fast updates is important. Normally, this is a major problem only when millions of customers are on the database.

Indexes must be used for all key fields. Relational database software depends on having indexes when two or more relational tables are joined together and output from each table is needed (see Exhibit 7-2). The indexes are used to "point" to the data being compared and to access the data being used for output. The indexes themselves, however, are not part of the output.

As a general rule of thumb, indexes should be applied to any nonkey fields that require frequent lookup. For example, if mailing lists are pulled or sales are calculated by ZIP code, indexing the ZIP code field makes sense. If a field is seldom used as a basis for lookup, then it should not be indexed.

Exhibit 7-2

INDEXES

Query: Customers who bought in July
Fields: Name, address, date

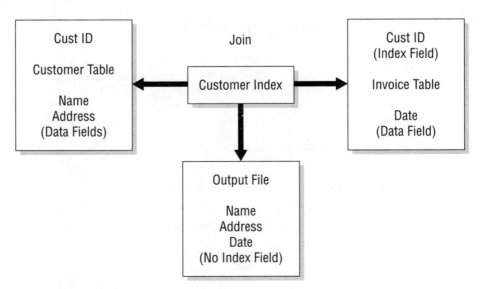

Hardware

PC-based relational databases store information on a hard drive. A hard drive is a set of flat, magnetic disks that provide fast data storage and retrieval. If you could look inside the box, it would resemble a miniature stack of old-fashioned phonograph records. The disks spin, passing a mechanical arm that moves in and out to reach the correct points to read or write information on the disks.

The software retains the location on the hard drive where information is kept (which disks, what point on the disk, etc.). The hardware stores the information in bits and bytes. A bit is simply a "1" or a "0." A byte is a string of eight bits. A byte can represent any letter of the alphabet, numbers 0 through 9, and many common symbols such as =, +, and %.

A one-megabyte hard drive can store 1 million bytes (or 8 million bits) of data. A one-gigabyte drive can store 1 billion bytes of data. A typical mailing list of 10,000 names requires about 1 million bytes of data storage.

Using a hard drive is much faster for retrieving data than using magnetic tape. The hard drive can find information in 10 milliseconds or so, whereas the tape must run to the point the data can be found. Tapes work well for flat files but are not practical for relational databases.

Hard drives make a relational database possible, but they are also the most severe constraint. This is because 10 milliseconds is a very long time when thousands of lookups are being done. Looking up information stored in memory is very fast, but moving the mechanical arm of a hard drive to thousands of different locations, one after the other, can be extremely time consuming.

This problem is compounded by the fact that lookups are primarily what databases are used for. They are looking up data to either copy it, report it, or change it. This is not a severe constraint for smaller, PC-based relational databases. It is, however, a severe constraint when tens or hundreds of millions of records are being stored.

Because databases place most of the strain on storage and retrieval devices, the amount of random access memory (RAM) or the speed of the main processing chip is less critical than with some other applications. A Pentium 90 with 16 megs of RAM and a fast hard drive could give better performance than a Pentium 150 with 32 megs of RAM and a slower hard drive. The main processing chip and the amount of RAM will be much more critical when used with statistical software than with database software. The exception to this rule is when the database can be entirely loaded into memory; this will make processing *very* fast.

For the same reason, doubling the number of processors does not double the speed at which the database will operate. The speed may improve, but not in direct relationship to processing power alone. To double the speed, both the hard drive and the processor must work twice as fast.

When a hard drive starts to fill up—that is, when more than two-thirds of the available space is used—performance goes down. This is particularly true when certain database operations (e.g., copying a file) are being done. The hard drive can be quickly filled, forcing the operation to be stopped.

As a rule of thumb, always have available at least one-third of the hard disk or at least twice as much free space as the size of the largest file (whichever is more). That is, if the largest file is the invoice detail table at 100 megs, you need at least 200 megs free. If there are (or will be) 670 megs of data in the database, you will need at least one gigabyte of space to store the database.

Reliable operation, being "robust," is just as important for hardware as for software. In some operations, it is so important that two identical sets of hard drives are used together in case one set fails. In every commercial application, maintaining backups, whether on tape or disk, is absolutely necessary.

SQL

SQL (pronounced either *see-quill* or *S-Q-L*) stands for structured query language. A query is a question, posed to the database, to extract or count data. Structured query language is the basis for almost all relational databases. Most database software packages use SQL.

SQL is a simple set of 36 commands that are relationally complete: with the use of these 36 commands, any data can be output from any database. Here are examples of SQL commands:

Select	And
Distinct	Or
From	Group by
Where	Order by

Notice that, rather than being bizarre computer syntax, these commands are relatively plain English. When used together in a command, they look like Exhibit 7-3, which shows the syntax for retrieving all customers in ZIP code 66208.

Exhibit 7-3

SQL COMMAND

```
SELECT DISTINCT name, address;
city, state, zip code;
FROM customer;
WHERE zip code = "66208";
ORDER BY name
```

To manipulate a large relational database, one must at least be familiar with SQL. Several database software packages have a SQL window that displays the SQL syntax when a query is created. Creating queries and then reviewing the corresponding SQL commands are an easy way to become familiar with SQL. It is much better to spend an hour or two becoming familiar with SQL than years trying to avoid it!

Changing Data

Data in a database can be changed, added to, or deleted. Data can be viewed in a "change" or "browse" window when it is necessary to modify the information in a record or set of records. When new records are added to a database, this change is referred to as appending. When certain records are not wanted, they are deleted. These records are then packed (permanently removed) from the database as a separate operation. This makes it more difficult to accidentally remove information.

These basic housekeeping functions are an important part of the overall database operation. Some databases will be designed to make many small changes at once, and others will make the occasional large change rapidly. To make best use of its strengths and avoid the weaknesses, be familiar with how your database software handles these jobs.

Screens and Controls

Most database software is geared more toward developers (programmers who create database packages to sell) than for end users. As a result, they have extensive capabilities to create custom input screens, menus, and controls. These capabilities bundled together into stand-alone programs are referred to as applications.

Although it is not necessary to develop an application to use a marketing database effectively, it is important to be aware of the possibilities. Less sophisticated users can be given simple screens that offer a choice of only certain, preset commands. More sophisticated users can have more control and can even work directly from the database software controls.

Screens and controls and the ability to create custom screens and controls are built into database software to make using the database easier. The user does not have to make input screens to use the database, but having the ability to do so makes it easier for some users.

Making screens and controls is what developers do with database software—unlike managers, who use database software to get at data. But, a database software package can be popular with, and useful to, both end users and developers. As a user, be aware that the ability to create custom layouts is there and that most database software offers this capability.

Programs

Being able to write programs (sometimes called scripts) is an important feature of database software. The need to write simple programs to manipulate data is common with a marketing database. An example of a simple program appears in Exhibit 7-4. This program adds region to a record in the customer table, based on a ZIP code match.

Marketers often need to code customers as being in one group or another, to make changes such as adding or deleting the dash (-) in the phone number field or to mark whether or not a customer has been contacted. To be effective with a marketing database, the software must allow for these ad hoc programs when needed.

What Databases Do Poorly

The key weakness of most database software is that finding what is not there is difficult. In other words, it is very fast and easy to query out every customer who does live in California and bought a widget. However, it is very slow and difficult to query out every customer who lives in California and did not buy a widget. You have to mark every customer who did buy, and then take only the ones who are not marked!

Taking two tables, joining them together based on a key field, and looking for "matches" yields a fairly rapid answer. This kind of join is called an *inner join*. An example of an inner join would be all the customers in the customer table who have a transaction in the invoice header table.

Looking for key fields that do not match can take a very long time. This kind of join is called an *outer join*. An example of an outer join would be all the customers in the customer table who do not have a transaction in the invoice header table. Again, you are forced to mark all the matches and then take only the ones that are not matched.

Outer joins can also take up a tremendous amount of hard drive space as they work through all possible combinations. This can fill up the hard drive and crash the computer. It is very similar to what happens in a comparison of two or more tables, each with a large number of blank key fields. Blank matches blank in all cases, making a potentially huge number of blank-to-blank matches.

Databases rely on their indexes for fast lookups and for joining tables together. Complicated queries, based on parts of a field (if the first four characters = "1234," for example, or "soundalike" comparisons), slow the database down. Without a well-thought-out index and query strategy, very large (several million records) relational databases will just be too slow to be practical.

Database software and hardware are normally designed with these trade-offs in mind. Some are well suited for one-at-a-time lookups by several operators at once; an example of this is an order-taking application. A data warehouse, on the other hand,

Exhibit 7-4

A SIMPLE PROGRAM

```
clear
set safety off
close all

select 1
use c:\REGION.DBF

select 2
use c:\CUSTOMER.DBF
set order to ZIP_CODE

select 1
do while not eof()
      store ZIP_CODE to Z1
      store region to R1

      select 2
      seek Z1
      do while Z1=ZIP_CODE
            replace region with R1
            if eof()
                  exit
            endif
            skip 1
      enddo

      select 1
      skip 1
enddo

close all
```

performs large but relatively infrequent changes, queries, and updates, usually by only a few operators, and so must be set up with these constraints in mind.

MAKING CHOICES

It is important to have hardware and software that fit the intended needs of the marketing database. No combination is perfect, but some are far better than others. Take the time to make sure that both the software and the hardware can handle the size and required uses of the database being planned.

When in doubt, choose the software first. Once the application, or program, that the database will run on is selected, picking hardware is much easier.

8 Using Statistical Tools

Telling the truth to people who misunderstand you is really promoting falsehood.

Sir Anthony Hope Edwards (1863–1933), British author

Statistical software is distinctly different from database software for two reasons. First, statistical software is designed to analyze data, whereas database software is designed to move and store data. Second, statistical software reports are based on statistics—clusters, averages, and so on. Database software reports are based on records, summaries, and occasionally a calculation between two fields.

Before looking too closely at what software is available, it is important to review why the software is useful in the first place. Rather than attempt to explain statistics in general, this chapter will be a review of what is relevant to marketers.

STATISTICAL USES

Making a Prediction

The real reason to use statistics is to make predictions: to try to determine, based on some past set of occurrences, what the odds are that some other occurrence will take place in the future.

The occurrence one is trying to predict is described by the *dependent variable*. For marketers, the dependent variable is the thing they are trying to change, control, or improve. The dependent variable is usually the likelihood of making a sale or the likely amount of the sale—or both.

The *independent variables*, or predictor variables, are the things that affect the dependent variable (the variable being predicted). Examples of typical independent variables that affect purchase behavior include

- past buying behavior/recency-frequency-monetary-product (customers)
- neighborhood, age, income, family size (consumer)

♦ Standard Industrial Classification (SIC) code, years in business, annual sales, number of employees (business-to-business)

The way the prediction is made depends on what type of occurrence is being predicted. If the goal is to determine what percentage of prospects will respond to an offer, the prediction may be expressed as odds, or as an odds ratio. A 2 percent response, for example, is the same as 1 to 49 odds, or as a probability of 0.02. An estimated expected amount of the sale cannot be expressed as odds or a percentage. It must be expressed as an amount, such as $50. An expected sale amount could be anywhere from $0 to infinity (at least from a statistical viewpoint). This type of prediction (a monetary amount) requires a different formula than does one that calculates likelihood. The likelihood of an occurrence is expressed as a probability of 0 (no chance) to 1 (perfect likelihood) or from 0 to 100 percent. It cannot be less than 0 percent, nor more than 100 percent.

By now you've probably realized that you need to predict both the expected response and the expected sale. Normally, this is done in three steps:

1. Determine expected response (the odds of a response, or percentage response rate).
2. Determine expected sale amount (average dollars per order).
3. Combine the formulas, in a one-two order.

For example, assume you have 100,000 prospects targeted for an offer. Based on past response data, you expect a 2 percent response. Based on past sales data, you expect a $50 average order. Total sales can be determined this way:

$$100{,}000 \text{ prospects} \times 2\% \text{ response} \times \$50 \text{ average order} = \$100{,}000$$

or $1 per offer being made.

Painting a Picture

Sometimes statistics are used not to make a prediction but to describe what is going on, who the customers are, or what those customers are like. This is usually done through "grouping" techniques that place like groups of companies or individuals into distinct clusters. This technique is called *cluster analysis.*

Unlike predictions, cluster analyses have no dependent variable. Nothing is being predicted, only described, and the description is based on a combination of variables. The object is either to put like groups together (cluster analysis) or to keep unlike groups apart (*factor analysis*).

Cluster analysis helps describe different groups of buyers rather than just describing averages. Imagine, for example, a business that caters to grandparents and grandchildren. The average age might be 35, and the average income for each customer might be $20,000 per year. Of course, there are really at least two groups. There are grandparents, average age of perhaps 60 and an average income around $40,000 per year. There are also grandchildren, average age of 5 and no earned annual income (or very little). A cluster analysis helps describe these two groups.

Statistical Precision

Database marketing is based on testing: analyzing different offers, different products, and different target customers. It is important to understand both how to test and how much to test. Creating tests that are large enough to be statistically valid (based on acceptable statistical precision) but not so large as to waste resources is an important part of testing successfully.

As sample size increases, the precision of predicting how the population as a whole will respond increases. To be twice as accurate, one must increase the size of the sample four times. The desire is to have "enough" accuracy without having samples that are too large (and too expensive to test).

Testing involves three basic measurements:

1. What will the response rate be?
2. What will the sales per order be? If there is a low response rate, it may be necessary to test more names because the validity of prediction is based not on the number mailed but on the number who bought.
3. Are the lists being tested statistically different from one another? In other words, if one list has a 2.1 percent response and another has a 2.0 percent response in a test, is that a valid difference?

As a general rule, marketers want sample sizes to be large enough to achieve results that are at least 95 percent statistically accurate as predictors. This requires a test group (a portion of all prospects or customers) large enough to predict how the population (the entire group) would respond to the same offer. The desired statistical precision has two parts:

◆ The expected range the response of the population will fall into. For example, 2 percent plus or minus 0.4 percent, which means future response rates are expected to be between 1.6 percent and 2.4 percent.
◆ The percentage of time the results are expected to fall within the range specified. For example, a 95 percent likelihood that the response of the population will be between 1.6 percent and 2.4 percent means that the response rate should be in the specified range 95 percent of the time.

This is expressed as: "The predicted response of the population is 2 percent, plus or minus 0.4 percent, with a 95 percent confidence level." In practical terms, if a mailing of 5,000 names gets a 2 percent response, the expected rollout response should be between 1.6 percent and 2.4 percent 95 percent of the time. Of course, if a list is mailed over and over again, it becomes possible to predict the response level more accurately.

To determine the validity of a given sample, first compute the standard deviation. For a probability, use the formula shown here. For a 2 percent expected response to a 5,000-piece mailing, use this formula:

$$\text{Standard deviation} = \text{Square root } \{[0.02 \times (1.0 - 0.02)] \div 5{,}000\}$$
$$= \text{Square root } [(0.02 \times 0.98) \div 5{,}000]$$
$$= .002, \text{ or } 0.2 \text{ percent}$$

Once the standard deviation (SD) is computed, use it as a plus or minus amount to determine the confidence level. Here are examples using the standard deviation plus or minus 1, 2, 3, or 4 times, based on the above example:

> 1 SD: 2% + or − 0.2 %, has a 68.3% confidence
> 2 SDs: 2% + or − 0.4%, has a 95.5% confidence
> 3 SDs: 2% + or − 0.6% has a 99.7% confidence
> 4 SDs: 2% + or − 0.8% has a 99.997% confidence

As an exercise, vary the numbers in the formula for standard deviation (expected response, number mailed) and adjust this for samples you normally use when testing.

If all of a list is being contacted, none of this applies. If mail is sent to a whole list, whatever you get is, in fact, what you get. Statistics do not apply.

The only reason to use statistics, or to have large samples at all, is to accurately predict from mailing part of a list what the entire list would do under the same circumstances. Of course, you can mail fewer than 5,000 names if you are willing to accept greater risk on a rollout to, for example, 250,000 names or if you are willing to retest before rolling out to the entire list.

STATISTICAL TOOLS

Statistical tools are the specific techniques (not the software) used to make statistical predictions or create descriptions of differing groups. Different techniques are best suited for different uses and situations. Here is a brief review of several popular techniques. Consider this as a guide in determining which techniques to use or not use in different situations.

Descriptive Statistics

Descriptive statistics are the starting point when you look at data, particularly for the first time. Statistical software packages make taking a "quick look" at data easy. This quick look is often done by reviewing the descriptive statistics of the data.

Descriptive statistics include several basic means of describing the data. Using a hypothetical example, analyze the ages of seven children. Here is the breakdown:

Age	Number of Children
1	1
5	2
6	1
9	1
11	1
12	1

The *mean* is what most people commonly call the average. The average age for this group is seven years old. It is the total $(1 + 5 + 5 + 6 + 9 + 11 + 12 = 49)$ divided by the number of children (seven).

The *median* is the middle value. If the children are put in order by age, the fourth child (the one in the middle) is six years old.

The *mode* is the most common value. Since there are two children age five and no more than one child of any other age, the mode is 5.

The *minimum* age is 1, and the *maximum* age is 12. If the minimum were less than zero or the maximum were more than 18, you could assume there is a problem with the data (incorrect data, or an adult's data, is included with the children's data).

The *standard deviation* is a measure of variability. It measures deviation from the mean, as compared to sample size. If the standard deviation is large (relative to the mean) you can assume there is a large amount of variation in the data. If the standard deviation is small, you can assume the data is relatively similar. Larger samples will tend to have smaller standard deviations.

Skewness is a measure of deviation from a bell-shaped curve (see Exhibit 8-1). In the example of seven children, the ages are skewed to the left. That is, because of the two five-year-olds a graph of their ages would peak below the middle because the mode, age five, is less than the median. It is possible for a graph to be "bimodal,"— have two peaks. An example of this would be a graph of the ages of children and grandparents in the cluster analysis example, mentioned above.

Some software offers other basic statistics for descriptive purposes. However, mean, median, mode, maximum, minimum, standard deviation, and skewness are good tools with which to begin any statistical analysis.

Regression Equations

Regression equations are designed to predict either a probability or the degree of an expected outcome (for example, the expected sale amount). *Linear regression* is often used by marketers to predict how much customers will spend. A simple linear regression equation has the following components:

Exhibit 8-1

EXAMPLE OF SKEWED GRAPH

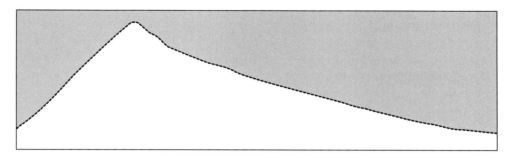

$$Y = A + (B \times X)$$

where Y is the dependent variable, or thing being predicted, A is a constant, B is also a constant, and X is the independent (predictor) variable.

An example of a simple linear regression equation would be to predict the amount of the next purchase based on the amount of the last purchase. Assume most customers' purchases are approximately equal to $10 plus 0.8 times their last purchase. The equation would look like this:

$$Y = 10 + (0.8 \times \text{Last sale amount})$$

Multiple regression is like simple regression with the addition of more X (independent) variables. If the prediction for the next sale were based on past sale amount and number of previous purchases, the equation would look like this:

$$Y = A + B_1X_1 + B_2X_2$$

There are two main drawbacks to linear regression. First, because of the constant, A, the prediction does not start at zero. In the example (see Exhibit 8-2), it would take a past sale of minus $10 to predict a sale of zero in the future. That is, with no predictor input, the prediction starts at $10, not zero. Second, linear regression is linear; it predicts with a straight line. Rarely in life or in marketing do things follow straight lines rather than curves. Linear regression ignores this reality.

Loglinear regression is most commonly used to predict the probability of an outcome. Similar to but more complex than linear regression, loglinear regression computes the "log odds" that an outcome will occur. This is expressed as a probability between zero (no chance) and one (100 percent chance).

Exhibit 8-2

EXAMPLE OF LINEAR REGRESSION

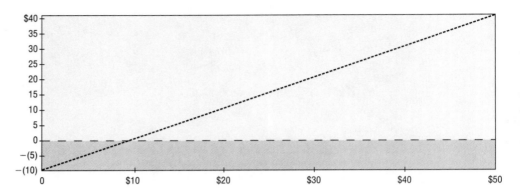

Loglinear regression has two advantages over linear regression. The first is that loglinear regression is a curvilinear function—the graph is a curve, not a straight line. This often "fits" better in making predictions, because it is generally a more accurate reflection of what actually happens in marketing. The second is that linear regression does not work well when the predictor variables are interdependent. (An example of interdependent variables would be height and weight.) This is a drawback to marketers, who normally try to isolate one variable at a time.

Chi-Square Automatic Interaction Detector (CHAID)

CHAID is a relatively new technique based on the chi-squared test for statistical independence. Like regression, CHAID starts with a dependent variable (likelihood of purchase/response rate) and finds the one variable that best predicts the dependent variable.

Once the best predictor variable is chosen, the data is broken into cells that are statistically different. For example, if household size is the best predictor, CHAID may break the sample into groups based on households with one person, two persons, three or four persons, and five or more persons.

One-person households may have a different response based on income, two-person households may be different based on whether or not they have a bank card, three- or four-person households may be different based on age, and the five- or more-person households may not be different based on any remaining predictor variables.

Each group is mutually exclusive. That is, no household can be in more than one group. Every group is created based on the interaction of variables, which can make for different predictions than with regression. For example, younger one-person households may respond better than older one-person households, and older two-person households may respond better than younger two-person households. This interaction of age and household size presents no difficulty for CHAID, but would be a problem with linear regression.

Cluster Analysis

Cluster analysis is a statistical grouping technique that minimizes the statistical "distance" among the members of each group. In the example with grandparents and grandchildren, there were two distinct clusters based on age. If another descriptor variable were used (e.g., gender), there would be four groups: grandmothers, grandfathers, granddaughters, and grandsons.

Cluster analysis works just as well with many descriptor variables (age, gender, income, past purchases, etc.) and with thousands or even millions of records. However, cluster analysis is often the most difficult technique to employ because the clusters must be interpreted (explained).

To use clustering techniques effectively, it is necessary to normalize the data before creating clusters. (Each predictor variable should have approximately the same mean.) If clusters are based on age and income, for example, and income is from $1,000 to $100,000 and age is from 1 to 100, the clusters will be based on income. Income must be divided by 1,000 to give both age and income equal weight in the analysis. This is one of the reasons cluster analyses are usually done by professionals who specialize in statistics.

To create and use clusters involves four steps:

1. Preparing data
2. Creating clusters
3. Describing clusters
4. Using clusters to reach target segments in an appropriate manner

There are companies that create predefined clusters of consumers or businesses. They can take customer and prospect data from client companies and fit the data into these predefined clusters. This is sometimes called a *passive cluster analysis*.

An *active cluster analysis* creates new, unique clusters based on the data being analyzed. This "custom fit" approach to cluster analysis is more labor intensive but can be very effective. It is particularly useful for analysis of opinion data such as surveys.

The Latest, Greatest Thing

Many new techniques are being developed for marketers to use. Neural networks (sometimes called artificial intelligence), tree analysis, logit regression, and other techniques promise advantages over more traditional techniques. In reality, they all compare in some degree to established techniques, and no technique can compensate for an inexperienced user (although some try).

Although some techniques are better than others, the most important thing is to have good, clean data. The next most important thing is to use an appropriate technique for what is being either described or predicted. Despite the claims that are made, which technique is used doesn't really matter as long as it is used properly.

List Enhancement: Adding Data

A 747 airplane is better than a DC-3; a luxury car is better than an economy car; and a steak-and-lobster dinner is a lot better than a burger and fries. On the other hand, a lot of flights would be impractical if all we had were 747s; not everyone can afford a luxury car; and who has the time or money for a fancy meal every day?

Since statistical models are typically made by professionals, garden-variety marketers don't need to know how to make one. But marketers do need to know what a model will do for them and what kind of model will work best for a specific situation. Just as ordinary drivers don't need to know how to build a Buick, they do need to know if they need a four-wheel drive vehicle, a van, or a sports car.

Household-level models are usually better than ZIP code (area-level) models at identifying or describing potential new customers. But that doesn't mean they are always practical, affordable, or desirable. You wouldn't use a 747 to occasionally fly small loads to small airports. You wouldn't use a DC-3 to get across town. Costs and benefits are associated with each model and vary from situation to situation. It is as important to know when to use one or the other as it is to know when not to use either one at all. So it is with household and ZIP models.

To use either household or ZIP code models, the customer and prospect files must first be enhanced. *Enhancing* means adding information to the file, outside of the things we already know such as purchase history or list source. The customer file is enhanced to profile its demographics, in the hopes that the information can be used to find prospects who are similar to existing customers and who should respond at a higher rate than dissimilar prospects will.

There are basically two ways to enhance a customer file. You can add information specific to where a customer lives, or you can add information specific to that individual customer's household.

Most modelers agree that household-level data is generally more accurate for making predictions than area-level data is. On the other hand, it costs more to enhance a file using household-level data than ZIP-level data. Per thousand names matched, household-level data can cost $30 to $50 or more, depending on the size of the file and type of data being added. By comparison, census-based ZIP-level data can be purchased on a CD-ROM database for under $1,000 and added for very little per name.

Either or both methods are likely to produce a certain amount of lift in response rates if used in a predictive model. There is no guarantee, however, that either method will provide enough lift to be cost-effective. To decide which to test, it is important to look at estimates of how each type of model should perform. Testing the models in actual use and measuring the results are crucial for long-term success.

Types of Enhancement Data

Household-level data includes information such as income, age of each resident, home value, type of dwelling, presence of children, and type and number of vehicles. The data is specific to each household and can be quite detailed in terms of lifestyle information, financial information, and whether or not they are direct-response buyers. Usually, however, the more detailed particular pieces of information are, the lower the percentage of households that will be matched.

Area (ZIP code)–level data can be based on the five-digit ZIP code or on smaller areas such as ZIP+4, census tract, or block group. Area-level data includes information such as average home value, percentage of adults who have a college degree, type of jobs and industries in the area, and average income.

Area-level data paints a broader picture of what type of people live there. It cannot be used to determine such things as the age of each buyer, but it can be used to clearly distinguish Manhattan Island from Buffalo, Wyoming. Whether you're selling saddles or theater magazines, you will probably find area-level data to be a big help. Particularly when the consumer buying the product is "keeping up with the Joneses," area-level data tells what profile the Joneses are likely to have.

Using Enhancement Data

To use any type of enhancement data effectively, a marketer must first do two things:

1. Add the enhancement data to each file being used.
2. Create a statistical model, using the data for scoring, selecting, or deselecting names.

In the case of ZIP code–level information, you should expect nearly 100 percent of your customer file to be enhanced. The remainder are likely to have bad ZIP codes. Household-level data, depending on the source, may not match anywhere from 15 percent to 40 percent of your file. Nonmatching records will not have enhancement data, and the model may treat them as one group.

If you are using household-level data, first append the information you want to the entire file, then select only the names the statistical model scores high enough to mail. To put it another way, you append data to every name, then use only a portion of the names. You have to append the data whether you use the name or not.

A low match rate by household will often force the model to default to area-level data. For example, if household data is available on only 45 percent of the file and the other 55 percent has only ZIP+4–level data, most households will (obviously) not be modeled on household-level data. Nonmatching names must, by default, be modeled either on area-level data or not at all.

A low match rate using a household model is perhaps the worst of both worlds. After all the fixed costs of enhancing the file and creating a household-level model, the choices are to (1) create what amounts to a second model for area-level data, (2) not market to nonmatching households, or (3) not use any model on all household-level nonmatching names.

One way to avoid this situation is to enhance a sample of the data first, to determine what sort of match rate the supplier enhancing the data can achieve. If the match rate is low or if a review of the data gives the appearance that a household-level model will not be a good investment, stop! Do not proceed with either the supplier of the enhancement data or with a household-level model. Find a source that will have a higher match rate, or consider an area-level model instead. If the problem is that the names not matching are outdated or incorrect, clean the list first. Only then will match rates be as high as possible.

Practical Limits on Using Data

When you are modeling customers, purchase information will in all likelihood be of great value, and enhancement data will be of little value. Plan from the start to do a good job with recency-frequency-monetary (RFM) when marketing to existing customers, and forget about enhanced data.

The exceptions to this are cross-selling and up-selling when customer groups or product offers/channels are substantially different. Enhancement data can be of great value in deciding which retail buyers should receive a catalog or which buyers of insurance are likely to buy investments.

A model cannot select more names than it is given and it is of no value if it consistently selects all the names it can select from. All names, whether selected or deselected, must be enhanced at some cost prior to being used. This adds to every mailing a fixed cost that must be more than covered by increased profits from higher response rates or higher sales per catalog.

A partial exception to this rule applies only to lists where the names are already enhanced. In this case, some sort of household model must be applied to select any names at all.

A *compiled file* normally has some kind of household-level information available with each name, but a *response file* usually does not have such demographic data available to select. Catalogers normally mail only to response lists, as known previous direct-response buyers are more profitable to market to than are compiled names whose likelihood of buying through the mail is unknown.

According to Don Pelley, director of marketing for DMSI, modeling beyond the ZIP level is usually impractical for direct mailers. For retailers who want to target their mailings, however, a household-level model based on compiled lists is nearly essential. The key is to match the type of model to the offer and lists available.

The Need to Model

Models based on either area-level or household-level data cannot replace good circulation planning, accurate source code tracking, and RFM modeling. Indeed, if these three things are not in place first, any prospect model is likely to fail. The fact that no model is being used does not mean that making one should be a company's top priority. Models should be judged only by what they make or save a company relative to what they cost. If modeling doesn't improve the bottom line, it shouldn't be used.

Sometimes the best way to get from point A to point B is by airplane, sometimes it is by car, and sometimes it is by just walking. By the same token, sometimes the best model is based on household data, sometimes it is based on area-level data, and sometimes the best model is no model at all. It all depends on the offer, the data, and the situation.

SELECTING STATISTICAL SOFTWARE

Many functions of statistical software, such as descriptive statistics and regression, can be performed with spreadsheets such as Excel. However, spreadsheets cannot handle the large number of records marketers tend to analyze. If a marketer never needs to review more than a few thousand customers or prospects at a time, spreadsheets may be adequate. However, with tens of thousands or even millions of records, statistical software is a must.

The two largest companies offering statistical software are SPSS and SAS. Both offer excellent products for PCs, midranges, and mainframes. Both offer easy, Windows-based point-and-click interfaces. And both are going after a different market niche. SAS is used by over 90 percent of the Fortune 500 companies and offers enterprise-wide solutions to statistical, database, and reporting problems. SAS is in the "information delivery" business and specializes in solving both statistical and database problems. SPSS is used by many firms, universities, and researchers for statistical analysis. It is less focused on multiple-user, cross-platform solutions and more focused on single users and smaller networks. The software is very up-to-date, offering the "latest and greatest" along with the tried and true.

Statistical software is an investment, starting at around $2,000 and rocketing up from there. SAS and SPSS (and others) offer demo versions, which should be tried before you buy. Both are excellent products, relatively easy to use (provided users know what they are doing statistically) and very fast. In SPSS, for example, it is possible to run a CHAID model with 500,000 prospects and data from 29,000 ZIP codes on a PC in less than 10 minutes.

Many marketers have used one or the other in a college class, and the preference tends to be for whichever they are most familiar with. However, SPSS has clear advantages (not the least of which is price) for PC users, and SAS has clear advantages for larger corporations.

Statistical software is not something to simply load into every manager's computer and expect to see it used. Although training with the software itself is minimal (no harder than Excel, for example), it is useless without an understanding of statistics. It may require appended data to be useful, and some modeling (e.g., cluster analysis) is often better left to professionals. However, statistical software can be a very powerful tool and can offer a real advantage when used effectively in-house.

CHAPTER

9

Examining and Reporting Data

Our work . . . is to present things that are as they are.

Frederick II (1194–1250), king of Sicily, Holy Roman emperor

CREATING USEFUL OUTPUT

To be useful to marketers, databases must do more than store and maintain data. Indeed, if the information in a database could not be examined, reported, and ultimately communicated, there would be no reason to store the information in the first place.

Because asking questions in the database (with queries) and communicating information stored in the database (with reports) is so important, they should be examined apart from the other workings of the database. Since queries and reports are so closely related (making a report requires information from a query), they should be examined together.

Queries and reports add tremendously to the capabilities of database software. Indexes, structured query languages (SQL) (discussed in Chapter 7), and proper normalization (discussed in Chapter 6) are important database components that make queries much faster. Report writers (the software component that makes reports) can summarize data, perform spreadsheet-like calculations, and allow the user to format output in an attractive manner.

One of the most important capabilities that queries in a relational database offer is the ability to combine information from more than one table into a single output. That output can be a new file. An example would be a file with a customer's name and address (from the customer table) along with the name of the salesperson (from the salesperson table), which could be used for a personalized letter to each customer from his or her salesperson.

Reports can also be created with information from more than one table. An example would be a report with each customer's name from the customer table and the sum total of that customer's purchases last month from the invoice header table.

The customer's name and purchase summary can be reported together, without having to repeat the name for each sale or to show each individual sale amount.

Querying Data

A query is a database operation that takes a prescribed set of information from a database (from one or more tables) and moves a copy of that information (not the original information itself) to another place. There are three basic outputs from a query:

1. Browse windows and counts
2. A new file
3. Printed output (reports/labels)

Browse windows produced from a query look like the browse window used for changing data described in Chapter 7. The difference is that query browse windows are "read only," which means users can look but can't modify the data they see. A query browse window makes sense to use when all that is needed is a quick look at the output or to know how many records will match a certain criterion.

Suppose, for example, the question is, How many customers are in Vermont? Sending the output to a browse window would answer the question. It also shows what the requested data looks like, so it is easy to see if there are any obvious problems. When a browse window created by a query is closed, the data is no longer stored. (This can be a real benefit, as unwanted data that is not stored does not take up hard drive space!)

Queries can create a totally new file, which is usually done for outputs such as mailing lists or call sheets for salespeople. The new file can contain information from several tables if required. The output is not called a new table unless it will be a component of a relational database.

Queries can send the data output to a report, which can summarize the data and define the layout of the printed output. Since reports are so important, they will be discussed separately from queries. However, queries and reports must work together: in order to make the right printed output, a report requires the right information in the right fields in the right order to be produced from a query.

Running a Query

Most database software offers a query-by-example interface that helps users run queries in a relatively simple manner. (Not that long ago, it required programming.) Virtually any information in a relational database can be extracted using these kinds of tools.

See Exhibit 9-1 for an example of what a query-by-example tool looks like. The window says "RQBE - by state" at the top. This example is from FoxPro, and RQBE

Exhibit 9-1

QUERY BY EXAMPLE

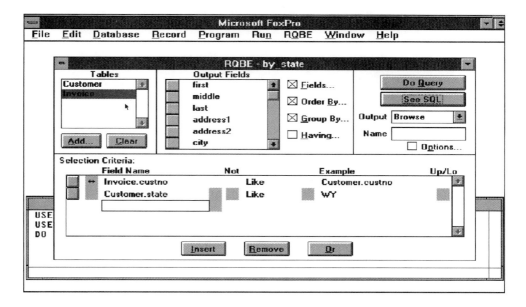

stands for relational query by example. The query is by state. A query can be saved (and named) just like any other file. This allows the user to use the same queries over and over, as well as to write programs that use previously created queries.

In the upper left section of the window is a box labeled "Tables," with "Customer" and "Invoice" inside it. This is a listing of the tables being used in the query. This query is "joining" the customer table and invoice header table. The "Add" and "Clear" boxes allow for tables to be added or removed from the query.

The upper center section lists the fields being output from the query. Clicking the mouse on the top check box (labeled "Fields") to the right of the output fields will display a selection window to add or remove fields. Clicking on the "Order By" box will display a selection window to set the order of the output. A typical output order would be by postal code or alphabetic by name. Clicking on the "Group By" box displays a menu that allows the user to describe what groups should be unique in the output. For example, a query that is "grouped" by last name will have one and only one of each last name available in the output. (No duplicate data within the fields is included in "Group By.")

The lower portion, "Selection Criteria," is where the output from the query is prescribed. The first line, with the ↔ symbol, is where the criteria for the join of the tables are described. These two tables are joined on customer number (custno), so "Invoice custno" is like "customer custno." If three tables were included in this query, there would be another join line, preceded by a ↔. If a third table is added, it can be joined to either of the first two tables. The second line is the selection criteria for this query. In this case, the query is for all customers in the state of Wyoming (WY). It is possible to have many more such criteria as required, and the selection does not have to be "like" something. The criteria can be:

- Like
- Exactly Like
- More Than
- Less Than
- Between
- In a Specified List

For example, anyone with the last name Smith could be excluded with the criteria "Last name is NOT like Smith," postal codes in a certain range can be specified with "Between," or transactions above or below a certain amount can be used with "More Than" or "Less Than."

"Do Query" (in the upper right) starts the query and makes it run. Just below is "See SQL." Clicking on this pops up a window that displays the SQL code for this query. Exhibit 9-2 shows the SQL code from the example query.

Most "serious" database software will allow the user to see the SQL and other codes generated through point-and-click interfaces. This is important for advanced users who want to use the code in their own programs. Even more casual users can benefit from being able to "see what's going on" when they are learning.

Optimizing Queries

Indexes are an important part of what makes relational databases work. They are also an important tool for making queries as fast as possible. Query optimization is a way of making full use of indexes, as well as some other "speed tricks," to make queries run with a relational database perform better.

Several techniques will make queries run faster. The first is to use the indexes. Although this may sound obvious, it isn't always. Assume that a query is needed to extract all the customers in Wyoming. If the database is not indexed on state, this may be a time-consuming query. On the other hand, if the database is indexed on postal code, the query can run very fast. By querying for postal codes in the correct

Exhibit 9-2

```
SELECT Customer.first, Customer.middle, Customer.last,
Customer.address1, Customer.address2, Customer.city, Customer.state,
Customer.zip;
FROM Customer, Invoice;
WHERE Invoice.custno = Customer.custno;
  AND Customer.state = "WY";
GROUP BY Customer.custno;
ORDER BY Customer.zip
```

range, the software can use an indexed field (postal code) rather than a nonindexed field (state) to search. The result is a much faster answer.

Some queries are not "optimizable" and will never be as fast as possible. One example is *string searches*. This is when the desired information could be anywhere in the field. An example is looking for "FRED" anywhere in a field. Possible correct answers are "ALFRED," "FREDERICK," and "ELFREDA," in addition to "FRED." Another example is searches based on soundalikes (yes, most software does this). Soundalikes are good for certain matches, particularly with people's names.

Different brands of software have different algorithms for optimizing queries. Users should become familiar with how the software they use can be optimized if they want to create fast queries for large databases.

Running Queries Successfully

The real key to running queries successfully is knowing what is in the database and what output is desired. If users know what they want and how to describe it (with More Than, Like, etc.), using almost any query tool will be relatively easy. However, if users don't know what they want or how to describe it, no query tool will be easy to use.

When running queries, knowing what data is stored in which fields and in which tables is important. As with the sample tables from Chapter 5 (Exhibit 5-3, page 46), the user needs to start out with a "map" of what data is where. When the user knows where the data is stored, constructing a query is relatively easy. If the user does not know, constructing a query that will create the correct output is next to impossible.

The best way to learn is to practice on real data by sending the output to a browse window. This shows the user the output without overwriting files or filling up memory. Running queries is what people with databases want to do; without queries, databases are not much use.

Reporting Tools

Presenting information in a practical manner, so that managers can make sound decisions based on reliable data, is the purpose of database marketing. Making useful, meaningful reports is the single most important function of any database. Without the ability to effectively communicate that which can be learned from a database, the other functions (storage and retrieval) are irrelevant.

Reporting tools take the data output from queries and turn it into printed output. This output can be on paper or on screen. Reports are not limited to printing out data in rows and columns. Reports can summarize data, present it in any order (up or down and right to left), and combine different data fields into an output that looks as if it came from a single field. An example of this would be combining the first- and last-name fields without unnecessary spaces in between.

Report writer software allows users to control the format of the output. They can show the information in the order they choose, as well as select fonts and type sizes and add graphics. Most report writers allow for not only lines and shapes but also many kinds of pictures and graphics.

Spreadsheet-like calculations can be done in the report writer, making the output more useful. A common example would be displaying sales in one column, cost in another, and a calculated field listing sales minus cost (profit) in another. It is not necessary to have a profit field stored in the database.

Parts of a Report

A report being created is begun with the fields from each record that is being output from the query, going into the detail band of the report. In other words, if 100 names and addresses were output to a report, the report would be 100 lines (rows) long. It would look very much like browse window output.

Above the detail band is the page header. This is where the user can insert, usually by typing, the name of the report and other relevant information about the report. Below the detail band is the page footer. This usually contains summary information from each page, or it can be left blank. Look at Exhibit 9-3 to see how this appears with a typical report writer.

Information can be summarized in summary bands in a report. The summary band can be above or below the detail band (or both), depending on what is desired. Totals and averages from groups, such as by salesperson, by state, or by department, can be shown here. Exhibit 9-4 adds these additional bands to the report.

In addition to summary bands that are created for groups of data, data can be summarized for the entire report. This is particularly useful when a report is several pages long. There can be an initial title band, as well as the final summary band for the total report (see Exhibit 9-5).

A report can have more than one level of summary band. Summaries can be shown by, for example, salesperson, region, and department.

Calculations in Reports

Calculations can be made on numeric fields in any band of a report, and counts can be made with numeric or character data (words, names, etc.) as well. Two or more fields also can be combined in a mathematical equation to produce an output.

In very few situations should it be necessary to take the output from reports, enter it into a spreadsheet, and perform calculations to get a desired answer. This is because most features available in a spreadsheet are available in a good report writer.

The real importance of creating reports with calculations as opposed to working with spreadsheets is that reentering data is not necessary with reports. All that is necessary is to rerun a query. It is much easier to start a query than to enter hundreds of

Exhibit 9-3

REPORT WRITER SCREEN

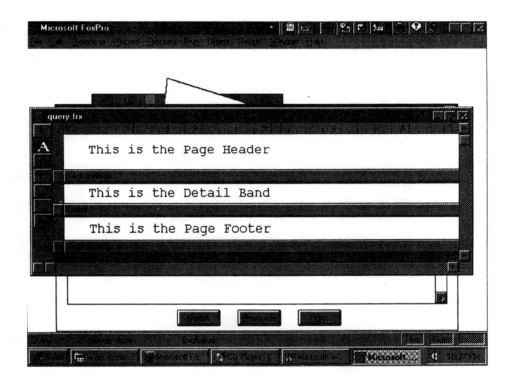

numbers, and the output will be 100 percent in line with current information in the database.

Setting up the calculations in a report should take no longer than setting the same calculations in a spreadsheet. The real dividends, however, come when the report is used again. Getting an updated report takes practically none of the user's time. Even if the query takes several minutes to run, that's several minutes of valuable time that the user can be doing something else while the computer does the work.

Designing Reports

Most normal managers are not looking for ways to get more reports. No prize is given for producing the most, the biggest, or the most comprehensive reports. It is particularly foolish and wasteful to make detail reports (e.g., every transaction, line by line) when nobody reads them, and anyway, the data is on-line if anyone needs to look something up.

Exhibit 9-4

EXPANDED REPORT WRITER SCREEN

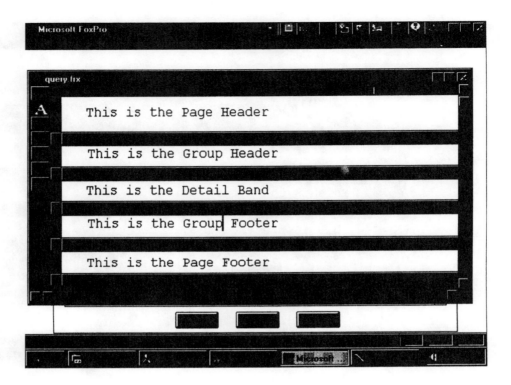

Reports must have meaning to be useful. They must compel the reader to action, inform, explain what they describe, or all of these. How information is displayed and summarized and what calculations are shown are crucial to a report's usefulness.

Reports are where the understanding of the manager and the abilities of the programmer traditionally collided. The manager knew what he or she wanted and the programmer knew how to program, but they didn't communicate with each other as effectively as they needed to. Fortunately, reporting tools are becoming much easier to use. As a result, managers are able to make their own reports without becoming programmers. This is a tremendous benefit, especially when managers use these tools to show information in a more effective manner.

Databases Versus Spreadsheets

Many jobs done now by managers with spreadsheets could be done more efficiently with queries and reports. Examples of these are reports that are created regularly,

Exhibit 9-5

MAXIMIZED REPORT BANDS

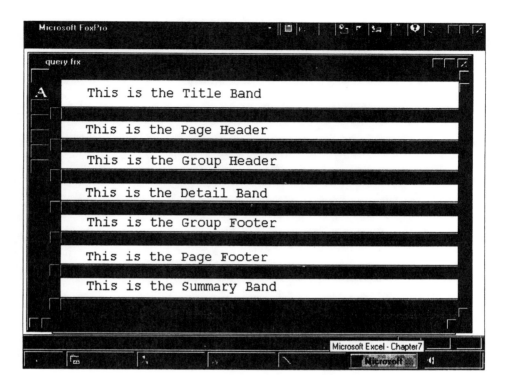

based on recent data, and used for making decisions on a regular basis. Commonly, a change from spreadsheet sales and commission reports to reports from the database can eliminate 20 percent or more of some office worker's workload!

Reports, however, are limited to reporting what is in the database. They are not as flexible as spreadsheets at what-if calculations, particularly when the information being used is hypothetical. Planning and forecasting, for example, are usually better done with spreadsheets than with reports.

Both spreadsheets and reports are needed in a modern business. However, managers should look at what type of spreadsheet work is being done and ask what can be replaced by reports from the database. Improved accuracy and less staff time can be the payoff in many cases.

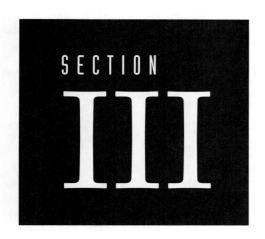

SECTION

III

Developing Your Database Strategy

10

Customer Loyalty and Relationship Marketing

Brand loyalty today means you stick with a brand only until you find a better deal.

Jeffrey Hill, Meridian Consulting Group, as quoted in *USA Today*

Defining Customer Loyalty

These days, there seems to be a great deal of confusion about what customer loyalty means and how to deal with it. Marketers use a number of terms, some of which mean the same thing and some of which are quite different. So here's a short glossary of terms to take into this important chapter.

Brand loyalty is customer allegiance to a specific branded product, such as Tide, Budweiser, or Mercedes-Benz. Each of these is a specific brand that its owners try desperately to build and protect through promotions, advertising, and word of mouth.

Brand equity occurs over time when a particular brand builds strength and undying customer loyalty and when the brand has real worth. When we think of brand equity, names such as Hershey's, Hallmark, L'eggs, Radio Shack, Kodak, or Xerox come to mind. In direct-marketing companies, names such as L.L. Bean, Lands' End, Spiegel, Harry and David, and Omaha Steaks are quickly thought of.

Customer loyalty is the process of building repeat purchase activity with one's customers. Some advertisers call it "top of mind," the idea that your company is the first one customers think of when they initiate the shopping process for a product or service.

Relationship or loyalty marketing is the method of using prospect and customer database information to initiate regular, consistent, and thorough communication to convert prospects to customers and to build regular, repeat purchase activity with customers. It is the process of nurturing your top customers and converting average and good customers to best customers.

Many people feel database marketing is synonymous with relationship marketing and that building ongoing affinity with one's customers will almost always lead to success. Usually it does. In this chapter we will examine the whole concept of loyalty or relationship marketing and see what marketers can learn.

How Do Customers Choose?

Why does a customer choose you over the competition? This is the age-old question, and the answers are often elusive. Generally, loyalty is associated with faithfulness, but maybe it's more than just blind faithfulness. Look at this checklist of reasons that people give for being loyal:

- They make me feel good when I buy/shop with them.
- They have an atmosphere that I like.
- They make me feel comfortable.
- They consistently give good value.
- They recognize me by my name.
- They always have a good selection of product.
- They are always coming up with new products.
- They make me feel appreciated and always say thank you for my business.
- They have the best customer service anywhere.

Whether the reason is physical or intrinsic, real or psychological, building a competitive edge through better products and service and dealing with the customer on a one-on-one basis are what loyalty and relationship marketing are all about.

Loyalty Programs

Understanding the Need for Loyalty Programs

The continuum shown below can help explain when loyalty programs are needed and when they may be a waste of money.

Totally		Product
Unique		or Service
Product or Niche		Is a Commodity

On this continuum, the further to the left you are, the less a special loyalty program is needed. In fact, it may be a waste. Possible examples include membership in Mensa, a fly-fishing trip with the world champion fly-fisher, a one-of-a-kind vegetable such as Vidalia onions, or collectibles such as Limoges boxes. On the right side of the continuum, every product or service is commonplace, almost a commodity. A seat on an airplane, a hotel room, long-distance telephone service, and a Visa or MasterCard credit card are examples of commodities that use every promotional concept and gimmick to attract and build customer loyalty.

Examples of Relationship/Loyalty Programs

Exhibits 10-1 and 10-2 list a few of the thousands of loyalty programs available in the world today. Exhibit 10-1 shows the wide range of loyalty programs from the first American Airlines frequent-flyer program, started in 1981, to a frequent-eater program at the local deli or Subway fast-food shop. Of particular interest is greater use of loyalty programs by direct marketers, particularly catalogers; Exhibit 10-2 demonstrates how both consumer and business catalogers are using unique techniques of offers, premiums, and services to reward loyal customers.

Six Keys to Building a Successful Loyalty Program

If you're thinking about any type of loyalty program, here are several tips that might be helpful.

1. *Integrate Any Loyalty Efforts into Your Existing Marketing and Communication Program.* It makes no sense to have separate programs and not have every type of prospect or customer communication tied together.

2. *Ask Your Customers to Help You Build the Loyalty Program.* No one can help you design the program better than your existing (and usually your best) customers. Critically you need to know and understand

- what customers want in a loyalty program
- what will motivate them to regular purchase activity
- what the "no-nos" or disincentives are

3. *Target Specific Messages to Specific Target Audiences.* Targeting is where the database comes in. Potentially five or six different messages must be targeted to unique prospect or customer groups. Some messages, such as "We miss you," are to reactivate inactive buyers or older inquiries who have never purchased. Other messages (e.g., "We want you as a preferred customer") are important to persuade one-time buyers to come back. Messages such as a special loyalty offer can be targeted to top buyers. Seldom will one message be appropriate to everyone.

4. *Set Realistic Goals.* Don't expect a loyalty program to be your marketing panacea. By starting with modest goals and carefully tracking results, you will be far

Exhibit 10-1

RANGE OF RELATIONSHIP/LOYALTY PROGRAMS

Type of Program	Company Offering Program	Type of Perquisites/ Benefits to Customers	Cost to Join Program
Airline frequent flyer	American Airlines	Free flights, seating upgrades	No cost
Air Miles	American Express credit card	Earn air miles for use of credit card	$50 annual card fee
Travel Plus	Visa credit card	Earn air miles for use of credit card	$50 annual card fee
Phone card with air miles	MCI, AT&T, Sprint	Earn air miles for use of phone card	No cost to join
Personalized credit cards	General Motors	Earn points toward a new auto by using the credit card	May be annual credit card fee
	Colleges and universities	Make a donation to your college by using the card	May be annual credit card fee
	Charities	Make a donation to a charity by using the card	May be annual credit card fee
Hotel frequent visitor	Most major hotel chains	Air miles, free nights, room upgrades	No cost
Gasoline credit card	Most major oil companies	Charge purchases; no need to carry cash	No cost
Retail revolving charge cards	Most department stores	Pay for purchases over time	No up-front cost Finance charge for extended payments
Catalog revolving credit	Spiegel, Fingerhut, Hanover House	Pay for purchases over time	No up-front cost Finance charge for extended payments
Regular credit cards	Visa, MasterCard	Charge purchases; no need to carry cash Pay for purchases over time	May be annual fee, depending on card Finance charge for extended payments
Discover Card	Discover Card	Charge purchases; no need to carry cash Pay for purchases over time; annual rebate of 1 percent	No up-front fee Finance charge for extended payments
Debit cards	Various banks (very popular in Europe)	Charge purchases; no need to carry cash Direct debit to one's checking account	No fee
Frequent eater	Various fast-food and Subway-type restaurants	Varies with each program (e.g., make 9 purchases and get 10th free)	No fee
Frequent retail shopper	Various retail outlets where repeat purchases (e.g., birdseed) are common	Varies with each program (e.g., make 9 purchases and get 10th free)	No fee

Exhibit 10-2
CATALOG LOYALTY PROGRAMS

Type of Program	Company Offering Program	Type of Perquisites/ Benefits to Customers	Cost to Join Program
Consumer Catalog Loyalty Programs			
Frequent buyer	Sharper Image	Earn points toward future purchases	No fee
Co-op/rebate	REI	Annual rebate based on purchases	$15 one-time fee
Silver Rattle Club	The Right Start	20 percent discount on all purchases and special offers	$25 fee
Birthday Club	Fingerhut	Special gifts and offers with birthday	No fee
Hannadowns®	Hanna Anderson	10 percent off value of used clothing returned Used clothing given to needy families	No fee
Special member pricing	Winterthur, Smithsonian, and other not-for-profit	10–15 percent off regular pricing	Modest initial membership fee
Preferred buyer club	Damark	First opportunity to buy specials, new remainder merchandise	$49.99 per year
Newsletter	Gooseberry Patch, Wolferman Muffins	Quarterly (or periodic) newsletter offering product news and special offers to preferred buyers	No fee
Magazine	Marks & Spencer (UK)	Quarterly large magazine to communicate with credit card holders	No fee
Business Catalog Loyalty Programs			
Special delivery services	Paper Direct	Next-day delivery for $1.00 more	$1.00 extra shipping and handling
Preferred buyer concept	South Hills Datacom	Three levels: platinum, gold, and silver, with all benefits tied to customer service	Variable, based on number and dollars of purchases in last year
Delivery service	Quill	All products shipped second-day air	No fee
Business (and personal) gift giving	Harry and David Cushman Fruit Co. Dessert of the Month	Customers who gave gifts the previous year receive a catalog with a personalized list of previous year's gift recipients	Customers must have given multiple gifts in the previous year
Personalized imprinting of product	Hallmark Business Expressions	Personalized imprinting of message on business Christmas cards	Included in price of cards

ahead. Each additional marketing dollar needs to pay for itself with additional sales and profits, or the program won't last long.

5. *Measure Results and Capture Database Information.* Every change in marketing or communication strategy needs to be tested, measured, and tracked. One common pitfall of any new marketing program is the inability to track results. Without detailed, careful tracking of source codes, the sales and profit contribution of each campaign, and each list segment, your grand ideas will be lost. Recommendation: don't even consider an elaborate loyalty program until you have your database and fulfillment process under control.

6. *Consider Longer-Term Consequences.* Most marketers are very *good* in initiating and testing new concepts. They are very *bad* in thinking about an "exit strategy" for a program. Loyalty programs are probably easier to start than to quit. Do you think the airlines would discontinue the frequent-flyer programs if they could? What happens when you cease or discontinue a loyalty program? Loyalty programs are much like the use of sweepstakes in that they can

- give your promotions a lift in response and even average-order value
- be difficult and expensive to administer
- be disastrous to quit

Pros and Cons of Successful Customer Relationship Marketing

In a successful relationship or loyalty marketing program, a number of things are happening:

- Customer purchase history is being actively tracked through a database.
- Suspects, prospects, inquiries, catalog requesters—all those nonbuyers who have expressed some interest in your company's products or service are also tracked and maintained by date.
- The customers react to communications and loyalty efforts. They have a high response to promotions, surveys, and so on. In effect, they are really interactive with you, as in a partnership.
- Customers feel good about the relationship, that it is a win-win situation for them and the company with which they are dealing.
- Sales and profits are increasing because your company can be more selective about to whom it mails, can increase the frequency with which it communicates with its better customers, and can get higher response and higher dollar levels in orders.
- Your company can truly target its promotions with more personalized messages about past items or categories customers have purchased or about special offers. Reliance on general, mass communications is a thing of the past.
- All orders are expertly tracked and maintained on the company database.
- The database is used to drive marketing, using segmentation of the prospect and customer lists.

- The company is able to apply research and statistical modeling techniques to understand better who the elite customers are and to find others who match their profile.

Are there negatives, or "pitfalls," to a relationship marketing program? Definitely! Here are a few that should be recognized:

- The company goes to a great deal of time and effort building its database and developing elaborate loyalty programs and incentives, only to find that it is getting the sales that it would have gotten anyway. One retail company aptly described this phenomenon as "deflection," or taking sales from one channel (i.e., retail stores) and moving them to mail order (another channel) without increasing the overall sales. It's trading dollars.
- Without adequate systems, staff, and operations, the company cannot maintain total control of customer and prospect communication and purchase history.
- There can be a lack of commitment from the entire company for a database-driven marketing effort.
- You may assume that customers really desire a relationship when in fact they couldn't care less.
- The proper benefits for customers may not be defined. In effect, the question that must be continually answered by putting oneself in the customer's shoes is "What's in it for me?"
- Goals in terms of schedules, sales, and profit growth may be unrealistic.
- The program may not be keeping it simple in terms of concept, offers, or communication.
- Measurement of results and tracking of actual data by customer may not be adequate.
- Personalized information may be mishandled by your not getting the right message to the right person, by fouling up spelling of names, or by promoting persons who have already responded to a promotion. Nothing makes a program look worse than erring in such critical information.
- The final pitfall is a classic. It is building an elaborate database operation, history, and mechanics and then not using it or integrating it into the day-to-day, month-to-month marketing communications program.

USING THE DATABASE TO MANAGE LOYALTY PROGRAMS

Successfully managing a marketing database to improve customer loyalty centers around measuring one key factor: *profitability*. In the most general terms, measuring profitability for loyalty programs requires that the following four areas must be tracked and monitored with the database:

- **How much is each customer (or customer group) spending in total?** Does the loyalty program cause customers to buy more and/or buy more often?

- **What effect does the loyalty program have on profit margin, per sale?** Is the profit margin—that is, percentage profit per dollar in sales—higher or lower as a result of the loyalty program? If it is lower, is it more than offset by higher total sales?
- **How much is spent marketing to customers in the loyalty program, and how much is spent marketing to customers *not* in the loyalty program?** Does the loyalty program add to the cost of marketing to a customer? If it does, is the cost more than offset by higher sales or higher margins, or both?
- **What effect does the loyalty program have on customer attrition?** Are customers in a loyalty program less likely to stop buying than those who are not? If the program is working, there should be lower customer "churn."

To communicate the program effectively, it is usually necessary to mark which customers are in a loyalty program and which are not. You will need to track

- when they became customers
- when they joined or became a part of a loyalty program
- how much each group spends—and report it on a regular basis
- what profit margin each group is generating, both in total and as a percentage of sales—and report it on a regular basis
- how much it costs to administer a loyalty program, in total and per customer, and how that compares to the total and per customer cost of marketing to other customers
- the retention rate by group, or how many repurchasers (both in total and as a percentage) are rebuying each month/quarter/year—and report it on a regular basis

Measuring the cost of acquiring customers and measuring the cost of keeping the customers you have already are of great importance when judging loyalty programs. The key is to keep more of your own customers without driving down the profits you earn from them.

The simplest way to track customers in a loyalty program is to mark them as members in the customer table. Mark which program they are in and store the date that they entered the program. With a database such as the one described in Chapter 5 and a simple loyalty program, these may be the only changes required.

A more complex program may take on a life of its own. Tracking bonus points, flyer miles, and other activities can require an entirely separate database. At the very least, they would require a separate transaction file (similar to the invoice header or invoice header/invoice detail combination) to track each customer's behavior.

Small businesses do best to keep it simple. Some things, such as giving a free sub sandwich after 10 purchases, may not even be worth tracking with a database (as long as paid sandwiches outnumber free ones by more than 10 to 1!). Before creating any loyalty program, consider the four areas in question: sales, profit margin, marketing cost, and attrition. Make sure, before the program starts, that you can monitor each area.

Realistic Tracking

Be sure to track the effects of the loyalty program. This includes tracking results before as well as after it begins. For example, suppose a small shoe repair shop decides to offer a loyalty program to all its best customers. The shop offers a free resoling for every sixth pair a customer has resoled, and they offer the program to only their best customers. Several things are likely to be true about customers in the program:

◆ They come in more often than those who are not in the program.
◆ They spend more than those who are not in the program.
◆ They are less likely to go to another repair shop.

Of course, all these things were true *before* the program started. Possibly, the program's only effect is that customers who normally paid for all their repairs now get every sixth one free! If the shop's before and after sales were tracked in the database, this could be measured. How could a program like this work? It could have positive value for the shop either by persuading infrequent customers to come in more often or by encouraging loyal customers to repair their shoes more often.

As suggested above, offering such a program to customers who already do all their shoe repair business at this shop will make them less profitable as customers. However, if this loss *is more than offset* by the additional profits resulting from less loyal customers coming in more frequently, the program as a whole can be profitable. The key to knowing the difference is being able to measure customers *before*, *during*, and *after*.

Building a "Discount Database"

Using the database primarily to offer discounts is a classic problem with database marketing programs. If 80 percent of a company's profits come from 20 percent of its customers, it cannot afford to lose the profit margin from that 20 percent. When the database loyalty program only gives discounts to the most profitable customers, these customers become marginally profitable or unprofitable.

A successful loyalty program should do one or both of the following:

◆ Sell more product without decreasing profit margin
◆ Increase the profit margin

Without increasing the profit margin the company earns from customers who are part of the loyalty program, you have nothing to pay the cost of the program.

It is essential to calculate the effects a loyalty program will have on the lifetime value (LTV) of a customer. Will the program increase LTV or decrease LTV? Any loyalty program that decreases lifetime value is worth *less than nothing*. To be profitable, a loyalty program must increase the LTV of the customers in the database by more than the cost of the program. (How to measure LTV is discussed in detail in Chapter 12.)

CASE STUDY

ADOLPHSON'S WOMEN'S READY-TO-WEAR (A)

INTRODUCTION TO THE COMPANY

This is a hypothetical case of a small, midwestern retail chain of stores. The company is family owned and managed by husband and wife Les and Vera Adolphson and run by professional store managers at each location. Here are other pertinent facts about Adolphson's:

◆ The company was founded in 1976 by Les and Vera Adolphson. Both owners had previous experience in retail sales and management and, in particular, in women's ready-to-wear with large retail firms, including J. C. Penney, Saks Fifth Avenue, and Dillard.

◆ The two owners have a clear division of labor within the company. Vera, as the merchandiser and buyer, is responsible for all product selection and for forecasting initial and rebuy quantities. Les is responsible for store management, the company's single distribution center, and all financial operations for the stores.

◆ Starting with an initial store in Kansas City, the company has expanded to 12 stores located in the following cities:

- Greater Kansas City metropolitan area (Missouri and Kansas) (5 stores)
- Topeka, Kansas (1 store)
- Wichita, Kansas (1 store)
- Tulsa, Oklahoma (1 store)
- Oklahoma City, Oklahoma (1 store)
- Omaha, Nebraska (1 store)
- Lincoln, Nebraska (1 store)
- Springfield, Missouri (1 store)

A central distribution center is located in North Kansas City, Missouri, and stores are serviced with a small fleet of company-owned trucks and vans.

◆ Adolphson's is positioned to service a moderate-to-upscale female clientele in a four- to six-state area. The store's niche is "classic design"; it carries a full range of better clothing catering particularly to working women and to women involved in not-for-profit activities within their communities. The product includes a complete line of women's wear:

- suits and blazers
- dresses
- sweaters
- skirts and slacks
- blouses and shirts
- sportswear
- sleepwear
- lingerie
- shoes
- hosiery
- a full line of accessories

◆ The North Kansas City central distribution center also serves as the company's headquarters and office. Besides warehousing, a small pick-and-pack operation, and shipping facilities, this building houses the computer and MIS function, accounting and financial management, a merchandising/product-buying group, an advertising manager, and a human resources manager.

◆ Although the primary channel of selling is through the retail stores, the company has maintained a small mail-order business to serve good customers who work and typically cannot shop during store hours and those outside the immediate retail marketing areas. The distribution function services these customers. A hallmark of the company is outstanding customer service.

◆ In 1980, the company began offering revolving credit by issuing its own credit card. This has been an attractive feature in retaining good customers who may wish to pay for their purchases over time. In addition to its own credit, the stores and mail-order unit offer the use of MasterCard, Visa, American Express, and Discover credit cards. Monthly statements to customers include several mail-order offers for seasonal product specialties.

◆ Adolphson's has 350,000 customer names on its database. *Active* store credit card holders are those who have used their store charge in the last 36 months. Other buyers' names have been collected through various name-gathering efforts, hand-entering of names from checks, nonstore credit cards, and customer phone numbers. An estimated total of 1.5 million people have shopped at Adolphson's in the past 12 months. Buyers recorded in the database are broken down as shown in the chart below.

◆ The company is thinking about expanding its mail-order business by bringing out a catalog that would have two major issues (spring and fall/holiday) and several smaller supplements during each season. As the catalog business grows, additional specialty catalogs will be planned. Use of the mail-order channel has several objectives:

• To expand store traffic by highlighting retail locations in each catalog
• To build a separate mail-order business, especially to serve busy working women
• To expand the stores' reach beyond the immediate four- or five-state marketing area
• To give customers the choice of how, when, and through what media to

shop (e.g., at the store; via telephone, fax, or e-mail; during their lunch hours, in the evening from home, or before they go to work)

◆ Management feels a number of the company's assets will aid it in entering the mail-order business:

• The financial stability and resources to launch the business
• The house database of 350,000 present or previous buyers
• A strong name recognition in a six- or seven-state marketing area
• A reputation for unparalleled customer service
• A strong retail base from which to launch the business
• Modest experience in mail order and pick, pack, and shipping of individual orders

BUILDING CUSTOMER LOYALTY

How has Adolphson's built customer loyalty, and what additional customer relationship techniques might it consider?

1. *Adolphson's credit card.* The retailer has already taken one very positive step in customer loyalty by issuing its own revolving-charge credit card. The card allows good customers to spread purchase payments over a number of months. The fact that the company has 130,000 "last 24 months" credit card buyers is an excellent testament to the fact that women are happy to use the card. Adolphson's needs to rein-

Buying Record	Credit Card Holders	Other Buyers
Last 6 months	60,000	10,000
Last 7–12 months	20,000	5,000
Last 13–24 months	50,000	7,500
Last 25–36 months	40,000	5,000
More than 36 months	100,000	52,500
Total buyers	270,000	80,000

force the benefits of card ownership and continue its new-card acquisition program.

2. *Personal shopper.* Initiating a personal shopper concept is a technique used by a number of upscale retailers who want to provide better, personalized customer service. This idea is especially well positioned for the older, more affluent customers. Targeted groups (selected from the database) are offered the use of a personal shopping representative who, by appointment, will preselect items (e.g., a blazer or suit) for the woman to preview in a comfortable, specially designed lounge supplied with coffee and "nibbles."

3. *Preferred-customer designation.* Based on customers' annual purchases, Adolphson's database can identify customers it wishes to target as special preferred customers. They would be notified of their elite status and the benefits, such as first opportunity to shop the special sales, a preview of new mer-

chandise, and first chance at other special events, programs, and so on sponsored by the stores.

4. *Assigned personal salespersons.* Every customer who makes a certain number of purchases or reaches a designated dollar level of purchases can be assigned a specific salesperson with whom they can communicate or shop. This idea is much like the personal-shopper concept but done at a slightly lower level.

Each of these ideas has potential challenges and pitfalls. Obviously, then, every new customer-loyalty or special-customer relationship program must be well thought through. Exit strategies must be considered when the program is being conceived. Retailers are notoriously poor at managing special programs, such as a loyalty program, on the basis of long-term customer value.

RFM

One's past is what one is. It is the only way by which people should be judged.

Oscar Wilde

What Is RFM?

RFM stands for recency-frequency-monetary value, and measures how long ago a customer's last purchase was made (**Recency**), how many purchases a customer has made (**Frequency**), and the total amount a customer has spent on all past purchases (**Monetary value**).

Many direct marketers use RFM to create a score to help them determine which customers are most likely to buy. (For example, a good customer might be "scored" a 50; a marginal customer might be scored an 8.) In this chapter, however, RFM is defined simply as recency-frequency-monetary, not as any formula or equation to generate a score from the data.

Each part of RFM will be defined as follows:

◆ *Recency* is the number of days, weeks, months, or years since the customer's last purchase. For example, a customer with "90-day recency" has made a purchase in the last 90 days. Recency is based on the last purchase, not the first purchase. Unless a customer has made only one purchase, recency is different from the length of time that person has been a customer.

◆ *Frequency* is the number of times a customer has purchased. It may be one, two, three, or more times.

◆ *Monetary* is the amount of money a customer has spent on all purchases. A customer who made three different $25 purchases has a monetary of $75.

RFM is based on a simple logic:

◆ Customers who have purchased recently are more likely to buy again than are customers who have not returned to purchase for a long time.

- ◆ Customers who have made frequent purchases are more likely to buy again than are customers who have made infrequent purchases.
- ◆ Customers who have spent a large amount in the past are more likely to spend money in the future than are those who have spent a small amount.

To put it another way, customers who are "good customers" are likely to be good customers!

Using RFM

RFM uses past purchase behavior to target customers. While using RFM effectively should improve lifetime value and make gathering more prospects profitable, it is of no use in targeting prospects who have never made a purchase. Prospects have no RFM data (or they wouldn't be prospects) and must be targeted in other ways.

RFM is sometimes expanded to RFM-P. The *P* can be either product category or profitability. *P* information adds a logical dimension to RFM, particularly when very different products are being offered with very different profit margins. Certain customers may typically buy only low-margin items, others may buy a mix, and still others may buy mainly the most profitable items. For some companies, *what* a customer buys is as important as *how much* a customer buys.

In many cases, a company may offer product lines so different that customers who buy from one line are quite unlike customers who buy from another. In this case, it may be best to treat buyers of different product lines differently, even if their RFM is the same. This is particularly true when one product line is a consumable (e.g., gas or oil) and the other line is a durable (e.g., cars or houses) or when one line appeals to consumers and the other to businesses.

A business that sells to both other businesses and consumers usually needs to treat the two groups separately. Businesses may buy at a lower margin, even if the product is the same. They are also likely to have a higher average order. Whether a customer is a business or consumer should be clearly marked in the database of a company that sells to both.

In addition to use in identifying *which* customers are the best targets for new offers, RFM can be used to identify *with* customers appropriately. For example, customers who buy frequently but in small amounts can be targeted for offers to increase their average order. Customers who have not purchased for some time may receive a "we miss you" message. High-volume, frequent buyers can be treated with the special care they deserve. Knowing how, based on RFM, to respond to a customer can be as important as knowing whether or not to respond at all.

How much a customer spends, either in total or at one time, is important knowledge to have when planning offers. For example, assume an insurance agent has a new, low-cost $50,000 term life insurance program to offer. Likely customers to contact will be those who have relatively lower coverage. They may consider adding to their coverage or, if it is less than $50,000, increasing it. A customer with a $1 million policy won't be very interested. On the other hand, if the agent had a low-cost million-dollar program, the customer with $50,000 in coverage probably won't be interested. The ones who already have $1 million in coverage, though, may consider doubling their insurance.

Seasonality can have a big effect on how RFM should be used. For example, a sporting goods store wants to have a late fall promotion featuring basketball gear. Their most recent customers, however, may have bought mostly football gear. Are they the best prospects for basketball equipment? Rather than targeting recent football equipment buyers, it may work better to send a flyer to all the buyers of basketball gear from last fall. The same pattern could be true for summer buyers of swimwear, and winter buyers of skiwear.

Statistics can be used with RFM data to make predictions and contact/no contact decisions. It is entirely possible to create a statistical formula that will predict, with greater accuracy than most human judgments, who will buy and at what level. However, although these formulas may do a better job of identifying *which* customers are likely to buy, they are of little use in understanding or identifying *with* those customers.

The emphasis here is not on creating the ultimate computer program to make predictions. The emphasis is on providing marketers with the information they need to make the best possible decisions. It is easy to overestimate the capabilities of the computer and underestimate the capabilities of human beings.

In the end, a human being must create the strategy, devise the tactics, and carry out the marketing program. Computer assistance in these functions is usually good. When computers take over the process, relieving humans of some of the understanding, it can be bad. Better to use the best system you can understand and manage than to be too concerned with whether or not you're using the best statistical technique.

The Historical Perspective

In the past, companies that used RFM had large, mainframe computers and stored their customer lists on tape in a flat-file format. This limited their ability to study different buying patterns, to change data retroactively (e.g., changing the purchase of a product from one category to another), or to easily determine when each buyer made each purchase.

As a result, many RFM formulas were designed to use the summarized data available in the customer flat file. All of these methods, although far from ideal, worked far better than not using RFM at all.

Using the sample RFM program outlined in Appendix 11-A (pages 130–32), recoding RFM with a PC does not take long. In a few minutes or hours RFM can be updated with two years', three years', or just one year's data and it can be run for certain products or product categories. With a mainframe tape update, this was not so easy. Often the invoice records were discarded after a few months, making this kind of change impossible. In any case, it might literally take days to run a complete update, if the information were available at all.

This lack of flexibility forced companies to summarize product purchase history by category for each customer. However, what happens when one item in a category, such as a small infant seat, may lead to the purchase of another item, such as a large infant seat? Having both seats lumped together makes it difficult to target offers for one seat to buyers of the other.

Nevertheless, most of the logic behind RFM that is being applied to database marketing has grown out of the RFM pioneered on mainframe computers. However, companies need to realize when it can be done a better way on modern PCs, so they don't imitate a technique that can be easily improved upon.

Putting RFM into the Database

The simplest way to "code" RFM into the database is to store recency, frequency, and monetary as fields in the customer table. The contents of each field will be these:

- Recency—a date stored in a date field
- Frequency—a number (1, 2, 3, etc.) stored in a numeric field
- Monetary—a dollar amount stored in a numeric field with two decimal places

Working with RFM in a simple format such as this is much easier than attempting to "code in" a score. For example, if buyers who purchased in the last 90 days have a recency score of 5, they will need to be rescored frequently, as when recency exceeds 90 days. On the other hand, with recency stored as a date, determining who bought fewer than 90 days ago is simple.

A database with "basic" data (as opposed to scores) is easier to manage, especially when a special effort is being created. If a company wants to contact all 30-day buyers, it is much easier if recency is a date than if recency is a number that could be anywhere up to 90-days recency. If a company does plan to use statistical modeling to determine whom to contact or not to contact, the RFM in the database can be converted to a score when the model is used.

The sample RFM program in Appendix 11-A (pages 130–32) is a simple one that updates the RFM fields in the customer table, based on information in the invoice header. This is a working example of an actual RFM update program. When used to update a 50,000-record customer table, using information in a 150,000-record invoice header table stored on a Pentium PC, it runs in about 30 minutes.

For larger databases, rather than starting at the beginning each time (for example, counting up frequency from zero, using all invoices), it is practical to update based only on the invoices from the past week or month. This could cut the 30-minute update time to less than a minute, making it practical to update 1 million– and 2 million–customer databases relatively quickly.

The same logic can be used to calculate returns. Returns should be kept separate, as customers do not always return everything they buy from a single transaction. For example, if a customer buys a blouse and slacks, and then returns the blouse, frequency should still go up by one. To say that one sale and one return yields a frequency of zero is incorrect because the customer still has the slacks.

Another reason to keep returns separate is that the effect on future buying behavior varies from company to company. For some, customers who make a return, particularly if it is their first purchase, are far less likely to buy again than those who do not return. For others returns seem to make little difference. The result may depend on the product, the market, or the quality of customer service the company provides. Companies with excellent customer service lose less future business after returns than do companies with poor customer service.

A Simple RFM Strategy

Without a strategy to use RFM, it is just three more pieces of data in the database. RFM must be used to segment the database, allowing more profitable customers to be contacted more often and unprofitable customers to be contacted less often or not at all.

One simple way to use RFM is to divide buyers into several groups based on RFM. For example, assuming a three-year buying history, a cataloger that mails customers for four, five, or more years will have more groups based on recency (see Exhibit 11-1). Customers with a purchase in the past year are put into two groups, 0–6 months and 7–12 months, because of a likely large difference in buyers' response; previous years are in 12-month groupings: 13–24 months, 25–36 months, and 37–48 months.

The next groupings are based on frequency. In many businesses, 50 to 60 percent of their customers have made only one purchase. Based on this, customers are divided into two frequency groups: one-time buyers and two- (or more) time buyers.

The last groupings divide customers with a monetary below the average order into one group and customers with a monetary above the average order into another. Assuming the average order is around $50, the two groupings would be under $50 and over $50.

Based on this RFM segmentation strategy, the total number of groups is 20, one for each combination of RFM. The likelihood of each group making a purchase varies, depending on RFM. Exhibit 11-1 shows each cell and the likely response outcome.

RFM can be effective only if it is put into practice. Using the simple methods outlined, businesses can get a good start in finding who the best customers are, which customers are marginal, and which customers are unprofitable.

Visual Approach to RFM

One way to manage with RFM is to create a report that graphically shows what customers are doing and provides enough information to make a decision. Being able to

Exhibit 11-1

LIKELY RESPONSES OUTCOME IN SIMPLE RFM DESIGN

	FREQUENCY = 1		FREQUENCY = 2 OR MORE	
	$0 TO $50	$51 OR MORE	$0 TO $50	$51 OR MORE
0–6 months	Good	High	High	Best
7–12 months	Good	Good	Good	High
13–24 months	Fair	Good	Good	Good
25–36 months	Poor	Fair	Fair	Good
37–48 months	Worst	Poor	Poor	Fair

look at a chart, see what responses are likely to be, and know how many are in each group make using RFM easy.

The visual RFM method charted in Exhibit 11-2 is an expansion of the simple RFM described previously. Customers are segmented, using each of the three RFM criteria. It is important not to make segments too small as that can overcomplicate the chart.

◆ *Recency* segments are based on how quickly responses decline. If 0- to 30-day buyers respond differently than 31- to 90-day buyers, they should be separate. Research the data to find natural breakpoints and use them as segment boundaries.
◆ *Frequency* is broken into three groups that work for many businesses. Most buyers (50–60 percent) have made only one purchase, 20–25 percent have made only two purchases, and 20–25 percent have made three or more purchases. This varies greatly from company to company but does describe a surprising number of businesses.
◆ *Monetary* is broken into three roughly equal groups of spenders. This often approximates the natural breakpoint in response based on monetary.

Each segment on the chart in Exhibit 11-2 is described by the number of customers in that cell (number mailed), the dollars per mailing (book), and the response rate of those customers (% response). Each customer can be in one and only one place on the chart.

The chart shows that 1,350 customers spent $49 or less and made only one purchase, which was 30 days or less prior to being recontacted with a new offer. Once the new offer was made, 10.9 percent of them (147) responded and made a second purchase. The 147 buyers spent a total of $7,357.50 (an average order of $50), which equals $5.45 for every promotion mailed.

There are 1,016 customers who spent $100 or more and made only one purchase, which was four to six months prior to being recontacted with a new offer. Once the

Exhibit 11-2

VISUAL RFM SEGMENTATION (Assumes $50 Average Order Value)

RECENCY		FREQUENCY = 1 MONETARY VALUE:			FREQUENCY = 2 MONETARY VALUE:			FREQUENCY = 3+ MONETARY VALUE:		
		0–$49	$50–$99	$100+	0–$49	$50–$99	$100+	0–$49	$50–$99	$100+
0–30 days	Number Mailed	1,350	450	360	675	338	321	293	899	1,347
	$/Book	$5.45	$6.10	$7.45	$8.18	$9.16	$11.18	$13.63	$15.27	$18.62
	% Response	10.90%	12.21%	14.89%	16.35%	18.31%	22.34%	27.25%	30.52%	37.23%
31–90 days	Number Mailed	2,612	871	697	1,306	653	620	568	1,179	1,724
	$/Book	$4.10	$4.59	$5.60	$6.15	$6.89	$8.40	$10.25	$11.48	$14.01
	% Response	8.20%	9.18%	11.20%	12.30%	13.78%	16.81%	20.50%	22.96%	28.01%
4–6 months	Number Mailed	3,811	1,270	1,016	1,906	953	905	828	845	1,057
	$/Book	$3.60	$4.03	$4.92	$5.40	$6.05	$7.38	$9.00	$10.08	$12.30
	% Response	6.80%	7.62%	9.29%	10.20%	11.42%	13.94%	17.00%	19.04%	23.23%
7–9 months	Number Mailed	3,916	1,305	1,044	1,958	979	930	851	869	1,086
	$/Book	$2.95	$3.30	$4.03	$4.43	$4.96	$6.05	$7.38	$8.27	$10.08
	% Response	5.90%	6.61%	8.06%	8.85%	9.91%	12.09%	14.75%	16.52%	20.15%
10–12 months	Number Mailed	4,002	1,334	1,067	2,001	1,001	950	870	888	1,110
	$/Book	$2.55	$2.86	$3.48	$3.83	$4.29	$5.23	$6.38	$7.15	$8.72
	% Response	5.10%	5.71%	6.97%	7.65%	8.57%	10.45%	12.75%	14.28%	17.42%
13–18 months	Number Mailed	7,950	2,650	2,120	3,975	1,988	1,888	1,728	1,764	2,204
	$/Book	$2.05	$2.30	$2.80	$3.08	$3.45	$4.21	$5.13	$5.75	$7.01
	% Response	4.10%	4.59%	5.60%	6.15%	6.89%	8.40%	10.25%	11.48%	14.01%
19–24 months	Number Mailed	8,120	2,707	2,165	4,060	2,030	1,929	1,765	1,801	2,252
	$/Book	$1.70	$1.90	$2.32	$2.55	$2.86	$3.48	$4.25	$4.76	$5.81
	% Response	3.40%	3.81%	4.65%	5.10%	5.71%	6.97%	8.50%	9.52%	11.61
25–36 months	Number Mailed	7,653	2,551	2,041	3,827	1,913	1,818	1,664	2,198	1,622
	$/Book	$1.45	$1.62	$1.98	$2.18	$2.44	$2.98	$3.63	$4.07	$4.96
	% Response	2.90%	3.25%	3.96%	4.35%	4.87%	5.94%	7.25%	8.12%	9.91%
37–48 months	Number Mailed	15,347	5,116	4,093	7,674	3,837	3,645	3,336	2,404	2,255
	$/Book	$1.25	$1.40	$1.71	$1.88	$2.11	$2.57	$3.13	$3.51	$4.28
	% Response	2.50%	2.80%	3.42%	3.75%	4.20%	5.12%	6.25%	7.00%	8.54%
49–60 months	Number Mailed	14,391	4,797	3,838	7,196	3,598	3,418	3,128	2,192	1,990
	$/Book	$0.70	$0.78	$0.96	$1.05	$1.18	$1.43	$1.75	$1.96	$2.39
	% Response	1.40%	1.57%	1.91%	2.10%	2.35%	2.87%	3.50%	3.92%	4.78%
60 months +	Number Mailed	16,302	5,434	4,347	8,151	4,076	3,872	3,544	2,616	2,520
	$/Book	$0.55	$0.62	$0.75	$0.83	$0.93	$1.13	$1.38	$1.55	$1.89
	% Response	1.10%	1.23%	1.50%	1.65%	1.85%	2.25%	2.75%	3.08%	3.76%

new offer was made, 9.25 percent of them (94) responded and made a second purchase. The 94 buyers spent a total of $4,998.72, which equals $4.92 for every promotion mailed.

The buyers in the three columns under "Frequency = 2" have made two purchases prior to the new offer, and buyers in the three columns under "Frequency = 1" have made only one prior purchase. In this example, purchase history goes back beyond 60 months. The chart contains counts, response rates, and sales levels for every segment in the database. By seeing how customers responded in the past, it is possible to predict quite accurately how customers will respond in the future.

For a planned mailing, there is no response information. However, where each customer falls on the chart can be determined, as well as how many are in each segment. By planning to market to each segment, based on that segment's responses in the past, it is simple to determine who will or will not be contacted, how many will receive which offer, and how many will be targeted in total.

Assume that the company must generate sales of $2 per mailing to make a profit. In Exhibit 11-3, all the unprofitable segments are shaded dark. Marginal customers—those on the verge of being in a segment below $2—are shaded gray. Notice how customers who have either spent more or purchased more often in the past remain profitable to recontact longer than those who spent less or less often. In this example, small, one-time buyers are unprofitable to recontact after just 18 months. (This is not uncommon.) On the other hand, customers who have spent a large amount and who have made several purchases are much more loyal. They can be marketed to at a profit for up to five years after their last purchase. (Again, not uncommon.) Customers in the gray band bordering the unprofitable customers are perfect targets for retention offers. "We miss you" and "we want you back" offers are appropriate here. Better to make an effort here than to wait until customers are less likely to respond.

Look down the chart and notice how response rates and dollars per mailing drop the longer it is since the customer's last purchase. Now look across from left to right and notice how they go up with frequency and monetary! In Exhibit 11-4, recent buyers in the $50–$99 monetary range are shaded dark. Notice how response rate jumps from 12.21 percent to 18.31 percent to 30.52 percent for, respectively, one-, two-, and three-time buyers. Now look at how quickly the one-time buyer response rate drops from 12.21 percent to 9.18 percent to 7.62 percent (nearly half) in only six months!

Many companies waste marketing efforts trying to regain customers who are not profitable and fail to convert enough one-time buyers into two-time and three-time buyers. It makes far more sense to attempt to move buyers who are responding at 12 percent from one-time into two-time buyers than to try to reconvert five-year-old buyers who respond at 1 percent.

The more people the company can move into the two- and three-time buyer columns, the higher future sales will be. Using the chart effectively to target

Exhibit 11-3

VISUAL RFM: MARGINAL AND UNPROFITABLE SEGMENTS

RECENCY		FREQUENCY = 1 MONETARY VALUE:			FREQUENCY = 2 MONETARY VALUE:			FREQUENCY = 3+ MONETARY VALUE:		
		0–$49	$50–$99	$100+	0–$49	$50–$99	$100+	0–$49	$50–$99	$100+
0–30 days	Number Mailed	1,350	450	360	675	338	321	293	899	1,347
	$/Book	$5.45	$6.10	$7.45	$8.18	$9.16	$11.18	$13.63	$15.27	$18.62
	% Response	10.90%	12.21%	14.89%	16.35%	18.31%	22.34%	27.25%	30.52%	37.23%
31–90 days	Number Mailed	2,612	871	697	1,306	653	620	568	1,179	1,724
	$/Book	$4.10	$4.59	$5.60	$6.15	$6.89	$8.40	$10.25	$11.48	$14.01
	% Response	8.20%	9.18%	11.20%	12.30%	13.78%	16.81%	20.50%	22.96%	28.01%
4–6 months	Number Mailed	3,811	1,270	1,016	1,906	953	905	828	845	1,057
	$/Book	$3.60	$4.03	$4.92	$5.40	$6.05	$7.38	$9.00	$10.08	$12.30
	% Response	6.80%	7.62%	9.29%	10.20%	11.42%	13.94%	17.00%	19.04%	23.23%
7–9 months	Number Mailed	3,916	1,305	1,044	1,958	979	930	851	869	1,086
	$/Book	$2.95	$3.30	$4.03	$4.43	$4.96	$6.05	$7.38	$8.27	$10.08
	% Response	5.90%	6.61%	8.06%	8.85%	9.91%	12.09%	14.75%	16.52%	20.15%
10–12 months	Number Mailed	4,002	1,334	1,067	2,001	1,001	950	870	888	1,110
	$/Book	$2.55	$2.86	$3.48	$3.83	$4.29	$5.23	$6.38	$7.15	$8.72
	% Response	5.10%	5.71%	6.97%	7.65%	8.57%	10.45%	12.75%	14.28%	17.42%
13–18 months	Number Mailed	7,950	2,650	2,120	3,975	1,988	1,888	1,728	1,764	2,204
	$/Book	$2.05	$2.30	$2.80	$3.08	$3.45	$4.21	$5.13	$5.75	$7.01
	% Response	4.10%	4.59%	5.60%	6.15%	6.89%	8.40%	10.25%	11.48%	14.01%
19–24 months	Number Mailed	8,120	2,707	2,165	4,060	2,030	1,929	1,765	1,801	2,252
	$/Book	$1.70	$1.90	$2.32	$2.55	$2.86	$3.48	$4.25	$4.76	$5.81
	% Response	3.40%	3.81%	4.65%	5.10%	5.71%	6.97%	8.50%	9.52%	11.61%
25–36 months	Number Mailed	7,653	2,551	2,041	3,827	1,913	1,818	1,664	2,198	1,622
	$/Book	$1.45	$1.62	$1.98	$2.18	$2.44	$2.98	$3.63	$4.07	$4.96
	% Response	2.90%	3.25%	3.96%	4.35%	4.87%	5.94%	7.25%	8.12%	9.91%
37–48 months	Number Mailed	15,347	5,116	4,093	7,674	3,837	3,645	3,336	2,404	2,255
	$/Book	$1.25	$1.40	$1.71	$1.88	$2.11	$2.57	$3.13	$3.51	$4.28
	% Response	2.50%	2.80%	3.42%	3.75%	4.20%	5.12%	6.25%	7.00%	8.54%
49–60 months	Number Mailed	14,391	4,797	3,838	7,196	3,598	3,418	3,128	2,192	1,990
	$/Book	$0.70	$0.78	$0.96	$1.05	$1.18	$1.43	$1.75	$1.96	$2.39
	% Response	1.40%	1.57%	1.91%	2.10%	2.35%	2.87%	3.50%	3.92%	4.78%
61 months+	Number Mailed	16,302	5,434	4,347	8,151	4,076	3,872	3,544	2,616	2,520
	$/Book	$0.55	$0.62	$0.75	$0.83	$0.93	$1.13	$1.38	$1.55	$1.89
	% Response	1.10%	1.23%	1.50%	1.65%	1.85%	2.25%	2.75%	3.08%	3.76%

Exhibit 11-4

VISUAL RFM: MOVEMENT OF RESPONSE RATES

		FREQUENCY = 1 MONETARY VALUE:			FREQUENCY = 2 MONETARY VALUE:			FREQUENCY = 3+ MONETARY VALUE:		
RECENCY		0–$49	$50–$99	$100+	0–$49	$50–$99	$100+	0–$49	$50–$99	$100+
0–30 days	Number Mailed	1,350	450	360	675	338	321	293	899	1,347
	$/Book	$5.45	$6.10	$7.45	$8.18	$9.16	$11.18	$13.63	$15.27	$18.62
	% Response	10.90%	12.21%	14.89%	16.35%	18.31%	22.34%	27.25%	30.52%	37.23%
31–90 days	Number Mailed	2,612	871	697	1,306	653	620	568	1,179	1,724
	$/Book	$4.10	$4.59	$5.60	$6.15	$6.89	$8.40	$10.25	$11.48	$14.01
	% Response	8.20%	9.18%	11.20%	12.30%	13.78%	16.81%	20.50%	22.96%	28.01%
4–6 months	Number Mailed	3,811	1,270	1,016	1,906	953	905	828	845	1,057
	$/Book	$3.60	$4.03	$4.92	$5.40	$6.05	$7.38	$9.00	$10.08	$12.30
	% Response	6.80%	7.62%	9.29%	10.20%	11.42%	13.94%	17.00%	19.04%	23.23%
7–9 months	Number Mailed	3,916	1,305	1,044	1,958	979	930	851	869	1,086
	$/Book	$2.95	$3.30	$4.03	$4.43	$4.96	$6.05	$7.38	$8.27	$10.08
	% Response	5.90%	6.61%	8.06%	8.85%	9.91%	12.09%	14.75%	16.52%	20.15%
10–12 months	Number Mailed	4,002	1,334	1,067	2,001	1,001	950	870	888	1,110
	$/Book	$2.55	$2.86	$3.48	$3.83	$4.29	$5.23	$6.38	$7.15	$8.72
	% Response	5.10%	5.71%	6.97%	7.65%	8.57%	10.45%	12.75%	14.28%	17.42%
13–18 months	Number Mailed	7,950	2,650	2,120	3,975	1,988	1,888	1,728	1,764	2,204
	$/Book	$2.05	$2.30	$2.80	$3.08	$3.45	$4.21	$5.13	$5.75	$7.01
	% Response	4.10%	4.59%	5.60%	6.15%	6.89%	8.40%	10.25%	11.48%	14.01%
19–24 months	Number Mailed	8,120	2,707	2,165	4,060	2,030	1,929	1,765	1,801	2,252
	$/Book	$1.70	$1.90	$2.32	$2.55	$2.86	$3.48	$4.25	$4.76	$5.81
	% Response	3.40%	3.81%	4.65%	5.10%	5.71%	6.97%	8.50%	9.52%	11.61%
25–36 months	Number Mailed	7,653	2,551	2,041	3,827	1,913	1,818	1,664	2,198	1,622
	$/Book	$1.45	$1.62	$1.98	$2.18	$2.44	$2.98	$3.63	$4.07	$4.96
	% Response	2.90%	3.25%	3.96%	4.35%	4.87%	5.94%	7.25%	8.12%	9.91%
37–48 months	Number Mailed	15,347	5,116	4,093	7,674	3,837	3,645	3,336	2,404	2,255
	$/Book	$1.25	$1.40	$1.71	$1.88	$2.11	$2.57	$3.13	$3.51	$4.28
	% Response	2.50%	2.80%	3.42%	3.75%	4.20%	5.12%	6.25%	7.00%	8.54%
49–60 months	Number Mailed	14,391	4,797	3,838	7,196	3,598	3,418	3,128	2,192	1,990
	$/Book	$0.70	$0.78	$0.96	$1.05	$1.18	$1.43	$1.75	$1.96	$2.39
	% Response	1.40%	1.57%	1.91%	2.10%	2.35%	2.87%	3.50%	3.92%	4.78%
61 months+	Number Mailed	16,302	5,434	4,347	8,151	4,076	3,872	3,544	2,616	2,520
	$/Book	$0.55	$0.62	$0.75	$0.83	$0.93	$1.13	$1.38	$1.55	$1.89
	% Response	1.10%	1.23%	1.50%	1.65%	1.85%	2.25%	2.75%	3.08%	3.76%

customers is as much a matter of knowing whom to contact as it is knowing whom not to contact. Better to send two offers to one recent one-time buyer than to send one offer to two four-year-old, one-time buyers. This is why new customers often receive several offers immediately after their first purchase. The company knows they are the best prospects for becoming loyal multibuyers!

Using RFM to Market Smarter

RFM is not about treating all customers equally. It is about identifying and cultivating customers who are likely to be the most profitable in the future. Using RFM effectively will usually involve the following efforts:

- More marketing emphasis is placed on new customers to entice them to make a second purchase.
- Retention offers are directed toward marginal customers. This also prevents sending too many retention offers or sending them to the wrong people.
- Less effort is wasted on unprofitable customers. Without a very good offer or enticement, there is no point in directing contacts to them at all.

It is important to understand and manage this process. If a company has only 20,000 promotional pieces to send, a computer model may do the best job of predicting which 20,000 customers are most likely to buy. But what if 30,000 customers could be mailed profitably, or only 10,000? Someone managing the process has to decide how many promotional pieces to print. The computer model will not decide this for the company.

Sending the right message at the right time can be tremendously effective. Some "We miss you" offers increase response rates 30 to 60 percent! Personal letters, phone calls, catalog cover wraps, and special messages can have a great effect. These kinds of efforts must be based on knowledge, understanding, and creativity. Nothing will make the customer feel that you understand and care about them like understanding and caring about them!

Appendix 11-A   Sample RFM Program

```
SET SAFETY OFF
CLOSE ALL

SELECT 1
USE C:\database\customer.dbf

SELECT 2
USE C:database\invheadr.dbf
SET ORDER TO custno
* Use the customer number index in the invoice header

SELECT 1
DO WHILE NOT EOF()
  * Go through the customer table one record at a time
  STORE custno TO custno1
  STORE recency TO recency1
  STORE 0 TO freqncy1
  STORE 0 TO monetary1
  * Recency, frequency, and monetary are fields in the
    customer table
  * Start from 0 for frequency and monetary on a complete
    update

  SELECT 2
  SEEK custno1
  * Find the matching customer IDs in the invoice header
  DO WHILE custno = custno1

    IF extprice>0
      * If a sale was made (not a return)
      STORE extprice + monetary1 TO monetary1
      * Add the sale amount to the monetary amount
      STORE 1+freqncy1 TO freqncy1
      * Add 1 to the frequency

      IF invdate > recency1
        * Use the most recent date for recency
        STORE invdate TO recency1
```

```
        ENDIF
     ENDIF
     if eof()
     exit
     endif
     * Stop if at the end of the file

     SKIP 1
      * Go to the next record in invoice header
      * Continue to update as long as there are customer ID
        matches
   ENDDO

   SELECT 1
   *Go back to the customer table, update RFM
   REPLACE recency WITH recency1,freqncy WITH freqncy1,;
     monetary WITH monetary1

   SKIP 1
    * Go to the next customer record
 ENDDO

 CLOSE ALL
 * End
```

Lifetime Value

For tribal man, space was the uncontrollable mystery. For technological man, it is time that occupies the same role.

Marshall McLuhan (1911–1980), Canadian educator and author

What Is Lifetime Value?

Lifetime value (LTV) is the value today of future profits from customers. It measures the value of making an investment in gaining new customers, based on what future sales (and profits) from those customers are likely to be.

One of the basic assumptions in any lifetime value calculation is that marketing to repeat customers is more profitable than marketing to first-time buyers. For most businesses, this is the case. Catalogers, retail stores, and many other businesses find that their most profitable business comes from customers who have purchased from them in the past.

Compared to prospects who buy for the first time, repeat buyers usually either spend more, have a higher response rate, or both. If this were not true, it would make much more sense to constantly acquire new customers than to market to existing ones. That might be the case for hot-dog vendors on a beach in a resort community, but even they are likely to have a few loyal customers, such as local souvenir vendors.

Another basic assumption needed to make lifetime value useful is that there is a return on investment *over time*. LTV is not based solely on what happens today or on one transaction, such as profit margin on a single sale. It is the value today of the profit margin(s) that will be earned over time.

In all, lifetime value involves four basic assumptions:

1. Marketing to repeat buyers is more profitable than marketing to prospects.
2. An investment (advertising, signage, coupons, etc.) is made to acquire the customer.
3. There is a return on the investment.
4. The return occurs over time.

In a case where customers are acquired at a profit and more customers can be acquired, the company should step up its effort to get more customers! This is particularly true when money spent gathering new customers is returned immediately. If a company can spend $1 today and get back $2 today, it should do so as much as possible. (However, this is rarely the case.)

Another key concept in understanding lifetime value is time value of money. *Time value of money* simply reflects the fact that a dollar today is worth more than a dollar will be one, two, or three years from now. *Net present value*, the value today of some amount in the future, is based on the time value of money.

Assume that a company can earn a 20 percent return (the same as getting paid interest at 20 percent) by investing in new equipment. If this company is going to invest in something else, it will demand at least a 20 percent return to do so. For a company that requires a 20 percent rate of return, here is the value today of $1 one, two, and three years from now:

> One year from today: 83.3 cents ($1.00 ÷ 1.2)
> Two years from today: 69.4 cents ($1.00 ÷ [1.2 × 1.2])
> Three years from today: 57.9 cents ($1.00 ÷ [1.2 × 1.2 × 1.2])

For this company, a dollar in profit each year for the next three years is not worth $3 today. It is worth $2.106 (83.3 + 69.4 + 57.9 cents).

Lifetime value is based on profits, not sales. It is not uncommon to hear that since the typical consumer spends $1 million or so in his or her lifetime, a baby's lifetime value is $1 million. (Of course, they won't spend much for at least 20 years, and some of their future purchases could be 75 years away.) However, that $1 million is based on sales, not profits. The merchandise they buy may cost the sellers $800,000, not to mention the cost of the ads they will see, catalogs they will get, and commissions that will be paid as a result of their purchases.

Making a useful LTV calculation requires three basic sets of information:

1. The amount the customer has spent
2. The cost of the goods the customer bought (to determine margin)
3. The cost of marketing to reach the customer

Determining how much a customer spends is simple. Establishing cost of goods sold, which may include transaction costs (commissions, cost to deliver, etc.), is critical to determining the profit margin accurately. The most easily overlooked (and often forgotten) cost is the cost of marketing. If the expected margin (sales minus cost of goods sold) from customers next year is $1 per customer and each customer will be mailed two catalogs that cost 50 cents each, the expected profit is zero!

PREREQUISITES FOR CUSTOMER LIFETIME VALUE

Broadly speaking, calculating lifetime value requires the following inputs:

- Repeat customer purchases
- Greater profit and/or lower cost (per sale) from repeat customers than from initial customers (converting prospects)
- Other benefits from customers, such as referrals

Narrowly speaking, calculating lifetime value requires the following inputs:

- Customer records
- Transaction records (summary and detail)
- Products and product costs
- Marketing and transaction costs
- Response rates to marketing/advertising efforts

Fortunately, you have already reviewed (in Chapter 3) a marketing database that makes it possible to gather the inputs required for lifetime value. The tables in this marketing database contain the following:

- *Customer records:*
  - Original source code (where the customer came from)
  - Date the customer first entered the database (became a customer)

- *Transaction records* (header and detail):
  - Transaction source ID (which offer the customer responded to)
  - Date of transaction (when the transaction occurred)
  - Amount of the transaction (sale amount)
  - Number of items sold (for cost of goods sold and transaction costs)
  - What was sold (to tie to product table)
  - Sales ID (who sold it and where)

- *Product records:*
  - Product description (category of purchase, transaction cost)
  - Product cost (to be subtracted from sale amount)

- *Marketing records*, from offer table:
  - Marketing cost to make each offer
  - Description of each offer (number sent, discounts, etc.)

Ideally, the database should contain enough transaction and marketing (offer) information to provide a "moving window" of transactions—that is, to analyze customers who first purchased one year ago, two years ago, and so on. Having enough information to determine what buying behavior has been, as well as for how long lifetime value should be measured, is desirable.

In actual practice, some data is better than no data. One, two, or three years' worth of customers and transactions is better than none. It is far better to start with what is available, make educated assumptions (instead of wild guesses), and use what you've got than to use nothing at all.

FINANCIAL IMPORTANCE OF LIFETIME VALUE

A solid prediction of lifetime value gives a company the ability to compare marketing to acquire more customers and other alternatives. For example:

- Does the company need to advertise more or to buy new equipment?
- Should it send out more catalogs or get a new computer system?
- Should it borrow or sell stock to get more money to attract new customers?

Lifetime value helps companies make these kinds of decisions. It gives marketers the "ammunition" they need to justify an additional push when a push is, in fact, justified.

Risk plays a big part in how businesses view investments. If an investment is risky, a higher rate of return is expected. If an investment is not risky, a lower rate of return may be acceptable. When the market is changing rapidly, such as when new competitors are entering the market, it is harder to predict what repeat customers will do in two or three years. Companies often require a high projected rate of return before they will invest in a volatile market.

Companies determine the level at which they will invest in new customers in one of three basic manners:

1. Maximizing profit margins (as a percentage of sales)
2. Maximizing net profit (total short-term profit amount)
3. Maximizing the net present value of profit

The first method, maximizing profit margin, practically invites competition. Unless a company occupies a small and protected market niche, it is just a matter of time until competition arrives. This is because the company is selling only to the most profitable customers and ignoring less profitable customers. A competitor that aggressively goes after the entire market is likely to gain enough profitable customers to be a serious threat.

Maximizing net profit, the second method, maximizes profit in the short term. Under this strategy, every customer who can be sold to at a profit, right down to the last penny, is targeted. Although this method will maximize profits for a quarter or two, it still allows competitors with "deep pockets" to invest in customers who will pay them back with future profits.

The third method, maximizing the net present value of future profits, maximizes the return on investment over time for the company's owners or shareholders. It also discourages competition, as a company using LTV calculations to acquire new customers tends to have, or to get, a large market share. That makes it very difficult for new competitors to build a profitable business in the short term.

Most people buy stock and investments based on expected returns over at least several years. Companies using a long-term outlook to acquire customers usually make better investments than do those with only a short-term focus. When a company suddenly shows higher short-term profits but has fewer new customer sales and more repeat customer sales, it may mean they will have lower profits in the future. Why?

Possibly, they may be trying to "look good on paper" by cutting back on prospecting. Companies for sale often do this, with sometimes disastrous results for the new owner, who thought the profits would continue. If new customers are not brought in to replace old ones that leave, the company is headed for trouble.

Strategy and Budgeting Based on Lifetime Value

Lifetime value is a tool used in creating marketing strategy, which then affects marketing tactics. Strategy is long term and big-picture focused, as is lifetime value. Tactically, it may not be possible immediately to carry out the perfect marketing plan based on LTV. Over time, however, tactics can meet strategy.

For example, assume a company is acquiring customers with a very high lifetime value and would like to acquire twice as many. However, the sales force is at full capacity and cannot handle any more leads. What to do? In the short term, giving the sales force more leads than they can handle makes no sense. Any effort to do so is wasted. In the long term, however, the company should build a larger sales force. Then the strategy of acquiring more customers can meet the tactics of gathering more leads.

The mix of fixed and variable costs in the company's budget can affect how aggressively it "needs" to gather new customers. A company with extra capacity can drive down fixed costs (as a percentage of sales) by selling more. A company with a factory operating at 50 percent of capacity can double sales without drastically increasing fixed costs. A company at full capacity, one that would have to build a new factory to accommodate more business, will be less eager to increase sales in the short term.

The need to increase sales by increasing the number of the customers in the database is especially obvious in business start-ups. A new catalog company, for example, still has the fixed costs of creating a catalog, administrative salaries, and warehousing products. To be profitable, the new company must reach a minimum level of business. There is no profit until both fixed and variable expenses are covered.

Establishing Measurements of Lifetime Value

Before you use lifetime value to determine strategy, an appropriate measurement needs to be created. Two basic things must be determined through judgment and research:

◆ Return on investment (ROI) goal, reflecting both risk and time value of money

◆ A realistic time frame, reflecting the number of months or years future buying behavior can be reasonably predicted

Usually, the ROI goal is *at least* as high as the company's return on equity. Thus, if a company is earning a 20 percent return on investment for the owners or shareholders, it is ill advised to plan to acquire customers at less than a 20 percent rate of return. If the market is volatile, technology is changing, and customer loyalty is likely to shift, then a higher rate of return is required to make the investment worthwhile. A stable market, where the company has a patent or is in a protected niche, does not require the same "risk premium."

How long is a customer likely to be a customer? If a company sells high school athletic wear to individual students, probably not more than four years. However, if a company sells high school athletic wear to schools, it could be a very long time.

For most consumer products, three to five years may be a sufficient time frame. Beyond that, customer attrition and the time value of money are likely to reduce the present value of future profits to a negligible amount. For a product such as an automobile or a major appliance, however, five years may be too short. This is especially true if the product requires maintenance parts.

One key to deciding how long is too long is to look at customer attrition. For many companies, 50 to 60 percent of all customers buy only once. If 95 percent don't come back after three or four years, for example, there is little point in using sales to five-year customers on which to base a decision.

CALCULATING LIFETIME VALUE

How is lifetime value calculated? The following example walks through the calculations step-by-step, detailing each calculation as it occurs. This example is based on gathering new customers through catalogs, but the calculations work for all kinds of selling. Simply vary the figures to suit the situation.

The first step is to determine how much acquiring a new customer costs. In this example, it costs $0.60 per catalog (total cost in the mail, with list rental and postage) to reach a prospect, and the response rate from rental files averages 1.1 percent.

Advertising cost to acquire a customer =
Cost to reach a prospect ÷ Average response = $0.60 ÷ .011 = $54.55

Next, determine how much profit margin is earned on the average initial sale. Subtracting this amount from the cost to acquire a customer will show how much is initially invested in a new customer. Assume an average initial order of $70 and an average margin of 40 percent after fulfillment cost (the cost to take and ship the order).

$$\begin{aligned} \text{Profit margin on} \atop \text{initial sale} \quad &= \quad {\text{Average initial order} \atop \text{repeat sales}} \quad \times \quad \text{Average margin} \\ &= \quad \$70.00 \times 40\% \quad = \quad \$28.00 \end{aligned}$$

$$\begin{aligned} \text{Initial investment} \atop \text{per customer} \quad &= \quad {\text{Advertising cost to} \atop \text{acquire a customer}} \quad - \quad {\text{Profit margin on} \atop \text{initial sale}} \\ &= \quad \$54.55 - \$28.00 \quad = \quad \$26.55 \end{aligned}$$

Thus, the initial investment to acquire a new customer is $26.55.

To determine what future profits are likely to be, subtract for the cost of recontacting the customer and for the required rate of investment return, which we will call the *time value of money discount factor*. This lifetime value example is based on three years' purchases and four catalogs per year to existing customers, at $0.50 each (a lower cost than prospect catalogs, as there is no list rental expense). Response rates are based on the response rate of customers during each of the past three years. (Note, this is not based on the most recent purchase [recency], it is based on the amount of time since their *first* [original] purchase.) A group of customers who made their first purchase in the past year responds at a rate of 16 percent to each of the four offers, a customer group who made their first purchase two years ago responds at 13 percent, and the three-year customer group responds at 11 percent. The numbers drop off because customers tend to drop off over time and fewer are recent buyers.

Based on the information given in the preceding paragraph, the annual marketing cost can be calculated:

$$\text{Annual response rate} = \text{Number of mailings} \times \text{Response per mailing}$$
$$\text{Year 1 response rate} = 4 \times 16\% = 64\%$$
$$\text{Year 2 response rate} = 4 \times 13\% = 52\%$$
$$\text{Year 3 response rate} = 4 \times 11\% = 44\%$$

$$\text{Annual marketing cost} = \text{Number of mailings} \times \text{Cost per mailing} =$$
$$4 \times \$0.50 = \$2.00$$

With the cost per year of reaching an existing customer (the annual marketing cost) and the responses expected from existing customers (the annual response rate) known, the math can be simplified. Look at each year as if it were a single $2 catalog mailing, with a 64 percent response rate for one-year customers, 52 percent for two-year customers, and 44 percent for three-year customers.

Now consider the required investment return, or time value of money discount factor. Assume this is 20 percent per year (which is the same as paying interest at 20 percent per year to investors). The time value of money discount factor for year one is 1.2 (the principal amount plus 20 percent). For year two, it is 1.44 (1 + 20 percent for two years, or 1.2 squared); for year three, it rises to 1.73 (1 + 20 percent for three years). This is the opposite of calculating what an investment would be worth with interest, because it is dividing by one plus the interest rather than multiplying; it is calculating what a future dollar amount is worth today, not what a dollar amount today will be worth in the future. It is also necessary to determine the margin on *repeat* sales, which may differ from the margin on *initial* sales but is calculated the same way. These are the values needed for the calculation:

◆ 20 percent time value of money discount factor
◆ $75.00 average repeat order
◆ $30.00 margin on repeat sales (average repeat order $75.00 × Average margin 40 percent)
◆ $2.00 per year marketing cost
◆ 64 percent response in year one, 52 percent in year two, and 44 percent in year three

$$\text{Profit per year} = (\text{Margin on repeat sales} \times \text{Response}) - \text{Marketing cost}$$
$$\text{Year 1 profit} = (\$30.00 \times 64\%) - \$2.00 = \$17.20$$
$$\text{Year 2 profit} = (\$30.00 \times 52\%) - \$2.00 = \$13.60$$
$$\text{Year 3 profit} = (\$30.00 \times 44\%) - \$2.00 = \$11.20$$

$$\text{Present value of future profit} =$$
$$(\text{Year 1 profit} \div \text{Time value of money discount factor}) +$$
$$(\text{Year 2 profit} \div \text{Time value of money discount factor}) +$$
$$(\text{Year 3 profit} \div \text{Time value of money discount factor}) =$$
$$(\$17.20 \div 1.2) + (13.60 \div 1.44) + (11.20 \div 1.73) =$$
$$\$14.333 + \$9.444 + \$6.474 = \$30.25$$

Finally, subtract the initial investment to acquire a customer ($26.55) from the present value of future profit to determine if the investment goals are met or exceeded:

$$\text{Lifetime return on investment} = \text{Present value of future profit} -$$
$$\text{Initial investment to acquire a customer} = \$30.25 - \$26.55 = \$3.70$$

In this example, acquiring new customers not only covers a 20 percent return on investment but also shows additional profit. It is possible to vary the time value of money discount factor to make the end figure zero so as to determine the exact projected return on investment. It is also possible to vary the time period to determine how long it takes to recover, with interest, the initial investment in the customer.

The figures here work well for determining how much effort to place on attracting new customers. They can also be used to market to existing customers. For existing customers, lifetime value should *always* be positive, and the object is to make the value as high as possible. To use these calculations, simply start with an acquisition cost and initial sale of $0.00 (past profits are not being measured). Then adjust the marketing effort to make the lifetime return on investment as high as possible.

To consider customer referrals, assume the rate is the same (mathematically) as an increased response rate. That is, if 16 out of 100 customers respond (a 16 percent response rate) and 5 out of 100 customers bring in a new customer as a referral (5 percent of the customers), this is the same as a 21 percent response rate. This enables you to estimate the effects of investing in referral programs.

COMPARING LIFETIME VALUE

Understanding lifetime value is especially important when you compare one method of marketing to customers with another. As discussed in Chapter 10, it is very easy to create a customer loyalty program that loses money in the long run. It is just as easy to "leave money on the table" by not marketing to customers frequently enough.

Using the LTV formula from this chapter, compare three different customer marketing strategies:

- Method A: three contacts per year
- Method B: four contacts per year
- Method C: four contacts per year, with 10 percent off all repeat orders over $60

Each method will have a different effect: method A will have the highest response per contact, method B will have the highest annual response, and method C will have the highest average order. Method B will have the lowest cost per contact, as method A will have lower economies of scale, and method C will require explanation of the 10 percent offer.

This example compares programs among existing customers to avoid having to consider the acquisition cost. You are simply interested in increasing future profits. Exhibit 12-1 shows a set of likely results if you were to try these three ways of marketing to customers.

In this example, contacting each customer four times, with no discount, produces the most profits over time. If the discount offer had produced a substantially higher average order or if the response rate had increased, it would have been more profitable. In this case, however, giving margin dollars away simply lowered profits. Notice that reaching customers less often is more profitable when response rates are low (as in year three). This points out why it is important to segment the customer base and contact some customers more frequently than others.

MEASURING SUCCESS WITH LIFETIME VALUE

A successful effort to increase customer lifetime value brings several benefits:

Exhibit 12-1

LIKELY RESULTS OF MARKETING STRATEGIES

	METHOD		
	A	**B**	**C**
Number of mailings per year	3	4	4
Response rate per contact			
Year 1	12%	10%	10%
Year 2	9%	8%	8%
Year 3	6%	5%	5%
Average order	$75.00	$75.00	$80.00
Profit margin (%)	40%	40%	37%
Cost per contact	$1.00	$0.95	$1.00
Annual marketing cost	$3.00	$3.80	$4.00
Profit per year			
Year 1	$7.80	$8.20	$7.84
Year 2	$5.10	$5.80	$5.47
Year 3	$2.40	$2.20	$1.92
Present value of future profit			
Year 1	$6.50	$6.83	$6.53
Year 2	$3.54	$4.03	$3.80
Year 3	$1.39	$1.27	$1.11
Lifetime return on investment	**$11.43**	**$12.13**	**$11.44**

- ◆ Increased return on investment
- ◆ Increased customer loyalty
- ◆ Increasing profits from existing customers
- ◆ Steady, predictable growth
- ◆ Increasing value of the database

Any effort that succeeds with lifetime value will help make the company more profitable. In all likelihood, a successful effort will result in greater customer loyalty. Increasing customer lifetime value is very difficult when fewer customers repurchase!

Another measure of success is the value of the database itself. For many companies, the database is their most valuable asset, more valuable than buildings, equipment, or inventory. A solid measure of lifetime value is also a solid measure of the value of the database itself.

Selecting Internal Data

Get your facts first, and then you can distort them as much as you please.

Mark Twain (1835–1910), author

Marketing databases act like warehouses to store information. And like warehouses, they "ship" and "receive" information. This chapter focuses on information received from within the company. From where can needed information be received, and how can the database receive that information?

Much of this chapter builds on Chapter 5. The main focus is to find the data required to assemble the basic building blocks, then to look for additional data that will increase the effectiveness of the marketing database. Note the use of the word *effectiveness*. There is no reason to attempt to increase the size, complexity, or capabilities of your database unless you can increase the effectiveness of the database in the process.

Internal Data Defined

Internal data is information that a company captures (and hopefully stores) while it conducts business. Companies generate information about sales, customers, products, personnel, taxes, equipment, and so on, on a continuous basis. Not all this information is stored on a computer; nor is all of it useful for marketing. Marketing does not require information about healthcare plans or depreciation methods, for example, but marketing does require knowledge of

- what was sold
- who bought what
- when a sale occurred
- where a sale occurred (which store, by mail, by phone, etc.)

Generally, all this data is either available within the company or not at all. A company that does not know who buys its products will not find out by researching at the library. It must either start tracking customers itself or bring someone in to do the job. Either way, the data cannot come from some external source.

WHERE TO LOOK FOR GOOD DATA

Where data is stored and how it can be brought into the marketing database depend on the company and type of information system(s) it uses. Factors such as whether a company sells from one location or several or whether it manufactures what it sells or buys finished goods to sell can have a great effect on the information systems that company is likely to have.

This chapter will review each of the building blocks described in Chapter 5 and discuss where the data can be found and how to retrieve it. Different parts of the marketing database require different kinds of updating and preparation, so each can be covered more or less separately.

Customer Information

The customer table contains information about people. People's names, their addresses, and so on, along with a unique ID, are stored in this table. Summary information, such as how much they have spent in total, is also stored in the customer table.

Start by breaking the customer table into two parts. Part 1 contains only information that comes directly from the customer, such as name, address, and phone number. Part 2 contains information about the customer that is summarized from other data in the database. The information in part 2 is not gathered; it is created, normally with a regular update program (more on the update program later). Examples of parts 1 and 2 are shown in Exhibit 13-1.

In addition to the names, addresses, and phone numbers of the customers, part 1 of the customer table also contains the information about where the customers came from (initial source code) and when they first entered the database. All this customer information is entered directly into the database.

The information in part 2, including the customer ID, is created by the computer. The information either comes from another table and is summarized, or it requires a lookup to another table.

Ideally, customers will be assigned unique customer IDs at the time of their first purchase. If a company has a transaction processing system that already assigns IDs, gather customer IDs as in part 1. If not, a unique customer ID must be created for each customer. New customers will receive a new ID when added to the database. Repeat customers must be matched by either name and address or phone number (in some combination) to assign the correct customer ID to their new purchases.

Customer information must be amended in two ways during each update:

1. New customers must be added (appended)
2. Old customers whose data has changed must be updated

Exhibit 13-1

THE TWO PARTS OF A CUSTOMER TABLE

CUSTOMER Part One
Mr/Ms
First Name
Middle Initial
Last Name
Title
Company
Address 1
Address 2
City
State or Province
ZIP or Postal Code
Phone #
Initial Source Code
Date Entered in the System

CUSTOMER Part Two		
Customer ID ↔ Key Field		
Do Not Rent		
Change of Address		
Cash		
Charge		
Phone		
Mail		
First Purchase Date		
Last Purchase Date	**R**	
Total # of Purchases	**F**	
Total $$ of Purchases	**M**	
Last Return Date		
Total # of Returns		
Total # of Exchanges		
Total $$ of Returns		
Last Cancellation Date		
Total # of Cancellations		
Last Mailing Date		
Total # of Mailings		
Gift Giver		
Product Classification 1		
Product Classification 2		
Product Classification 3		

Normally, deciding which customers just made their first purchase is relatively easy. New customers have new (recent) customer numbers, or their customer identification number doesn't match any of the old customers. Keeping up with customer changes, however, can be a challenge.

One of the problems with multiple databases, which then becomes one of the problems of data warehouses and marketing databases, is keeping different databases in sync. Ideally, updates to the customer information will be made in the transaction processing system and flagged as changes. The records flagged as changed can then be updated.

This is difficult for a company with many systems. Customer service and sales may be totally separate, and a change sent to customer service may not filter back to either sales or marketing. If a change of address, for example, is sent to marketing, that department may update the marketing database but not the transaction processing system. This may result in a new customer record (old customer, new address) being added to the database. If it is, past purchase history will be assigned to a different customer ID than future purchases.

Business-to-business marketers have an even tougher job, particularly if several people at a "customer" company make purchases or play different roles in making a purchase. (People change jobs, and titles, faster than they move to different homes.) When things become this complex, you may need to have a *company customer* and a *person customer* table. When a company has many contacts, with many different decision-making abilities, they must be tracked not only by name and address but also by company, title, and buying influence. It is often easier to have customer companies in one table, with a company (customer) identification, and people who buy at those companies in another table, with both company identification and customer identification numbers. This enables you to assign all of a company's purchases to that company accurately and to determine who made which purchase for that company.

Duplication errors are as much management issues as database issues. One area should be responsible for making changes and informing other areas (sales, service, billing, marketing, etc.) what changes have been made. The more emphasis on strategy and planning, the better—and the less effort will be needed to clean up messes!

Customer information can be gathered from several locations. Some of the most likely sources are

1. billing and accounting
2. order processing (fulfillment) systems
3. systems (point-of-sale/cash register systems)
4. sales reporting systems (salesperson laptops, etc.)
5. parts/service/warranty systems

When customer IDs, names, and addresses come directly from billing and accounting or from fulfillment systems, getting the information into a marketing database is usually a straightforward task. Duplication and updates are likely to be handled in some manner already, and often the name and address format is adequate.

Some billing systems do not store names and addresses in a manner that works well for marketing. A name might be stored in a last name–comma–first name format (e.g., "Doe, John" instead of "John Doe"), the address fields may be too short (forcing data to be truncated or to run into the next field), and the name/company name/address fields may have data entered into the wrong fields. Unfortunately, this can affect the quality of data being entered. Inexpensive software is available that corrects address formats, puts data into the correct field, and puts names into a useful format.

A simple piece of software, however, cannot add information that is not there. No contact name means either bad data or additional effort to get the contact name. The better the information is when it is gathered, the better it will be in the marketing database.

Transaction Information

Transaction information, defined as the invoice header and the invoice detail, is normally found together. That is, if a system creates one table, it creates the other, or at least the parts needed to assemble the other.

Two fairly common problems that arise with transaction data must be overcome when converting the data and putting it into the marketing database. They are:

1. Customer data is in the invoice header.
2. There is no header file, only a detail file.

The problem with putting customer information (name, address, etc.) in the transaction file is that the name will be repeated (usually differently) every time the customer buys something. Usually, then, no unique customer ID is assigned by the transaction processing system. Customer and transaction data must be split apart, and the customer information "cleaned" during each update.

Often there is no header file. Instead, each item the customer buys creates a record in the transaction file, and information such as method of payment and salesperson gets repeated with each record. No record summarizes the entire transaction. Fortunately, this is a relatively easy problem to solve with the computer. An invoice header record can be created and information inserted, summarizing all the related transactions. Even if no unique number was assigned to each item record, they can usually be grouped in some way. For example, all items bought by one customer on one day may be considered one transaction. (It usually is.)

Reliable and useful transaction information can normally be found either in a billing and accounting system or in a transaction processing system. Building this data from scraps of paper in salespeople's briefcases or from e-mail comments is not advisable. It should be based on hard, factual information.

It is important to gather information that not only reflects when the sale occurred but also shows the exact sale amount. Is the sale amount with or without discounts? What about freight and taxes? Does the sale occur when the order is taken, when the product is shipped, or when it is billed? The information in the marketing database must reflect the "correct" reality.

Shipping and handling should be a separate field so they are not confused with the sale amount. Otherwise, accurately determining profit margins is difficult. Direct marketers, who ship every order, need to track shipping cost versus revenue, as well as to test shipping charges to determine how the market reacts to different shipping charges (e.g., does a higher shipping charge lower sales overall and hurt profits?).

Transaction data should match, as closely as possible, sales figures used elsewhere in the company. Marketers commonly forget to include a field, such as a discounts field, when assembling their database. Naturally, this will cause sales to be overstated. Assemblers need to look at each field in the transaction processing system to make sure all necessary data is being captured.

If the marketing database is consistently different from the management information system or transaction processing system in stating what the sales level is in a given period, it probably is consistently wrong. Unless there is no need for credibility (we haven't seen this yet), it is important to make sure the correct data is being captured.

Most transaction processing systems, particularly those that tie into an accounting system, do not change past invoices. If an invoice made yesterday, for example, is found to be incorrect today, a new invoice is made to show a return, credit, or additional sale to "cancel out" the prior mistake. In a case like this, invoices can be added each day, week, or month to the marketing database, and changing or updating an old invoice will never be necessary. Changes will be made, in effect, by adding new invoices.

In some cases, invoices are "held open" in case a return is made, a credit is given, or a product is not shipped. When this happens, changed invoices must be updated, in addition to adding new invoices to the marketing database. If invoices are not marked as changed, sales figures and customer information will become incorrect.

Normally, the hard facts of what was sold for how much and when are easy to find. The challenge is getting the right data into the marketing database. Correct sales totals, correct sale dates, and so on, go a long way toward making the marketing database a credible source of information.

Product Information

The information in the product table is usually the easiest to find and update. Normally, product cost, retail price, description, and so on are found in either the billing and accounting system or in the fulfillment system. In cases where a company sells only a few products, this file can even be updated manually.

The key item to get for the product table, along with product ID and description, is an accurate unit cost. This is needed for determining profit margin and return on investment after promotion costs. Since costs tend to change, keeping this table up-to-date is important.

When updating the marketing database, database managers often simply replace the entire product table with new data. The accounting department tries to keep costs as up-to-date as possible, so using their information is usually more practical than manually updating cost information.

Manufacturers often have a far more complex unit-cost tracking system than marketers need. This is because a finished product can be made up of thousands of components and subassemblies. If the cost of one bolt in a subassembly changes, the cost of the finished product changes. Just as with transaction data, finding the right data (usually the cost that matches what is in the accounting system) to put into the marketing database is important.

Salesperson Information

Salesperson information, like product information, is relatively easy to maintain in a marketing database in most cases. It is usually practical simply to enter new people and update old ones manually. A company would have to have hundreds or thousands of salespeople before updating the salesperson table became much of an issue. While getting cost and sales information right may be difficult, it usually doesn't take a wizard to figure out who the salespeople are!

Do not delete salespeople when they leave (even if you really, really want to), as this will cause their sales information not to show up in reports using both the salesperson and transaction tables. Also, do not reassign salesperson ID numbers when salespeople change; this will also cause incorrect reporting.

Offer Information

Offer information should be entered into the database when the promotion is planned. Once the substance of the offer is determined—costs, quantities, and source codes—that is the time to enter the information into the offer table. Often, unfortunately, it is not entered until the first few responses with a new source code appear and they don't match anything in the database. Unless offer information (which catalog, which list, which discount offer) is stored in the fulfillment system, it is time to go through the file cabinet and rummage through papers! For accurate tracking, source code (offer) information should be in the database before the offer reaches the customer.

Although storing a source ID in each record of the invoice header table is necessary to properly track purchases by offer, that does not mean information about the offer will be in another system.

For updating purposes, offer information should be added directly to the marketing database, not brought in from another source. Offer information includes

- a description of the offer (spring catalog, newspaper ad, etc.)
- the quantity mailed, called, or reached
- the cost of each contact ($1 catalog, $5 phone call, etc.)

This information should be findable, though that may require some digging. It may be in accounting records (look through old advertising bills if you have to); it may be buried in the filing cabinet. But it should be available *somewhere*. To effectively run a marketing department without having this stuff is darned hard, although that doesn't always stop people from trying.

Converting Data for Input

Different systems run on different software. The accounting system could be running in UNIX, the billing done on DOS, while marketing may be running on Windows. This may seem to be an insurmountable problem, but it is not. Many software applications are available that move data from one platform to another. The most difficult problem with converting data tends to be with establishing business rules and making the data conform to those rules. For example:

- Customers can buy in any of three locations, and each has a different system.
- There is no invoice header file; it must be created from the detail file.

What to convert and when to convert are usually more difficult to determine than how to copy data and move it from point A to point B. Occasionally, retrieval of data from one format and conversion to another may be difficult, but only until the right software is found (and used).

Keep in mind that converting data is not a matter of just taking data from one system and copying it into another. To begin with, only certain pieces of data will be copied from other systems. In addition, summary data will be created, addresses will be standardized to match postal regulations, and various quality checks should be performed. You are not just copying data.

Cleaning and Removing Duplicates

Quality checks must be built into periodic database updates. Can the addresses be postal coded, or are they incorrect? Are names in the right name fields? Are names in the address (street) fields? Do the sales being added for last week add up correctly? Are a customer's name and address already in the database? These questions must be answered at each update to be sure the database is as accurate and useful as possible.

Here is an example of "cleaning" a customer record. It may come in looking like this:

Name	Address	City	State	ZIP
Doe, John	101 Main Street, #200	Salem	Oregon	97355

It needs to look like this:

First Name	Last Name	Address1	Address2	City	State	ZIP
John	Doe	101 Main St	#200	Salem	OR	97355

In addition, the company may need to add postal codes (e.g., carrier route and delivery point), check that the phone area code is correct, and so on. Blank addresses, blank names, and large numbers of addresses that do not match the postal database should send up a red flag. Cleaning and standardizing all records *before* seeking duplicates greatly improves the odds of matching correctly.

Duplicates can be removed several ways, usually in combination. "Matches" can be found by name and address, address only (household), phone number, and sometimes name of business and postal area. (To find two businesses with the same name in the same area would be unusual.)

The difficulty with duplicates is finding and eliminating them. When two records are duplicates but each has a different customer ID and each has purchase history assigned to it, you have a problem. The record being kept will need to include the transactions of the record(s) being eliminated. This requires updating both the customer and invoice header tables.

WHEN TO UPDATE

Marketers have very different database needs than sales or customer service does. Marketing does not need to know if the item ordered at 10:00 A.M. by Mrs. Jones has shipped yet or not in case she calls to check at 3:00 P.M. Marketing does need to know who bought last month and who should receive target offers next month.

Most marketing systems are updated on a weekly or monthly basis. Day-to-day information is usually taken from the transaction processing system, which is typically quite adequate for this type of data. Rarely is updating a marketing database each day worth the effort, unless you're someone who loves to sit in front of the computer.

The timespan between updates should match the company's management style. Some companies manage based on weekly periods; management meets once a week to review the last week, discuss the current week, and plan for future weeks. Other companies manage by the month. Reports and updates should reflect the corporate style.

Reports themselves should reflect the time periods by which a company manages itself. Most people think a month begins on the 1st and ends on the 30th or 31st. To a company, however, the last day of the month may always be a Sunday. "March" might begin March 2 and end on March 30. In such a case, a report that covers the calendar month (March 1 to March 31) will simply confuse people. Sales totals won't match other reports, unit sales will be different, and so on.

Weekly updates make sense for companies who use a lot of space advertising, television direct response, radio, or other fast-changing media with short lead times. If a company finds itself asking questions such as "Do we want the remnant space in the *New York Times* next week?" weekly updating is a good idea.

For many companies, monthly updates are sufficient. If information doesn't change fast enough each week to affect longer-range decisions, a weekly update serves no purpose. Examples of things that can be dealt with using data updated monthly include decisions such as "How many catalogs should we order?" or "Which magazines should we sign a contract with next year?" In truth, most companies can update monthly.

The other advantage to monthly updates is that it prevents reports from coming too fast and too often. Changes tend to be big enough to be interesting, which means the reports are more likely to actually get read! Remember, unless people read them, reports are a waste. Think about how often reports will actually be wanted, and try not to make reports more often than needed.

How to Know It's Right

To be certain their database is working as it should, marketers can make several benchmark "quick checks":

- 95 percent – plus transactions with source ID (not blank or unknown)
- 95 percent – plus postal-coded addresses
- No blanks in state or province field
- No blanks in primary address field
- Sales total matches accounting *to the penny*
- 100 percent of the invoice headers match one and only one customer record (each)
- 100 percent of the invoice headers match *at least one* invoice detail record
- 100 percent of the invoice detail records match one and only one product record (each)
- 100 percent of the invoice detail records match one and only one invoice header

When checking for transaction amount, join the invoice header, invoice detail, product, and salesperson tables together and see if the total remains the same. If not, at least one matching ID number is missing from at least one table. Trying different combinations of tables in this manner is a quick way of finding which table is incomplete or incorrect.

ADOLPHSON'S WOMEN'S READY-TO-WEAR (B)

Assembling Internal Data

The first order of business for Adolphson's is to assemble the customer list in one place and then relate customers to their purchase information. Once this is accomplished, product and promotion data will be added.

The first source of name and purchase data is credit card information. This is stored on tape in a flat-file format. Names are repeated with each transaction but do have a unique customer ID number. Unfortunately, purchases are summarized for each month. As a result, determining which products customers bought in the past is not possible.

To incorporate this data, Adolphson's intends to take the following steps:

1. Retain customer ID numbers as the master ID numbers.
2. Consolidate duplicate customer names by allowing only one of each unique customer ID in the customer file. The most recent record for each ID will be retained in order to have the most up-to-date information; this will serve as the customer table.
3. Each purchase record will be retained, keeping the customer ID but eliminating name and address data. They will be ordered and numbered in sequence, and the customer ID will become the key field. The customer ID kept when duplicates are consolidated will be updated into the invoice header to avoid any "orphan" records; this will serve as the invoice header table.
4. Unique item purchases will be retained in order to have an invoice detail table. Although these are not available on

transactions older than six months (the data was not kept on file), Adolphson's at least has six months of item-by-item purchase history.

Next, the hand-entered names will be incorporated into the database. The following steps will be covered to bring this new information on line:

1. Customer names and addresses will be compared to those already in the database. Those that match will be given the customer ID number they already have. Those that do not match will be given a new customer ID but will not yet be added to the database.
2. Duplication among the new names will be checked and one customer ID given to each duplicate purchase record. The most recent name and address for each customer will be retained and the others discarded. New customers can now be added to the database.
3. Each purchase record will be given a unique ID, as with the credit card data. Since the products purchased are included with the data, each invoice line will be given a number as well. For example, invoice 100 includes a blouse and slacks. The purchase is invoice 100, the blouse is invoice 100 line 1, and the slacks are invoice 100 line 2. This will create information for both the invoice header and the invoice detail tables.
4. Purchase history will be appended to the invoice header and invoice detail tables.

With customer and purchase data in place, Adolphson's is ready to add product, salesperson, and promotion data, following these steps:

1. Each product is keyed into the product table with the retail price, current cost, description, and product category. In addition, Mrs. Adolphson felt adding the

name of the supplier would help in merchandising. The product ID will match the product ID in the accounting system the store presently uses.

2. A salesperson table including store ID is keyed into the database. This will allow for analyzing who made each sale and where the sale was made. This is important since salespeople may work at more than one store.

3. Only certain special offers were recorded with purchases in the past, but those are entered into the offer table. The table includes their source ID and a description. For upcoming offers and where available for past offers, the data includes the reach and the cost per reach.

With customer, purchase, product, salesperson, and promotion data in a basic relational database, Adolphson's has the beginnings of an effective marketing database. To improve its ability to analyze the data, Adolphson's will add external information, which will be discussed in Chapter 14.

Selecting and Using External and Research Data

It is the unknown that excites the ardor of scholars, who, in the known alone, would shrivel up with boredom.

Wallace Stevens (1879–1955), U.S. poet

External and Research Data Defined

External data is any data that must be bought, rented, or obtained from sources outside a company. Census data, credit reports, and vehicle registrations are examples of external data. Gathering such data is often called *secondary research*, as it is the compiling of data that has already been discovered. *Primary research* is the uncovering of new facts and information. Focus groups and formal or informal surveys, such as those on warranty cards, are examples of primary research.

Answers to marketing questions can come from three basic sources of data:

1. Internal data (secondary research within the company)
2. External data (secondary research outside the company)
3. Primary data (primary research done by or for the company)

The reasons to start with *internal data* are simple: it is already there, it is specific to the company and its customers, and it is available at no cost. For these reasons, most of this book is about using internal data effectively. Using *external data* (data from outside the company) is usually the next step as in most cases it can be obtained faster and for less expense than the same information can be obtained through custom research.

Primary research is usually a "last resort," done only when the required information is not available any other way. Customer surveys about specific products, features, and the type of use to which products are being subjected require primary research.

In a broad sense, renting lists of prospects is using external data, but in this chapter, the discussion of external data will be limited to overlay or enhancement information. Using outside (rented) lists will be covered more thoroughly in Chapter 17, when we discuss how to use them to build the customer database. How outside lists are used is more a part of the communication/media strategy than of the database strategy.

EXTERNAL DATA: TYPES AND USES

Just because obtaining all sorts of information about consumer or business customers is possible does not necessarily make doing so a good idea. If a company already tracks the source of each customer and what purchases each has made, tracking other data (e.g., income, household size, number of employees in the company) will often be of little value in deciding which customers will get the next catalog and which will not.

Frequently, however, companies need to know what their customers are like, where they live, how many prospects are like existing customers, and so on. Overlaying data on the customer file and determining what profiles describe existing customers are a good way to decide how big the company's target market(s) may be.

In most cases, using customer profiles based on external data to market only to those customers is of marginal value. However, using external data to profile good customers, average customers, and even unprofitable customers is often of tremendous value in targeting or avoiding certain prospects. The company can use the information not only to target prospects more likely to respond but to target prospects likely to be more profitable when they do respond.

Consumer Data

A wealth of information is available about consumers, both individuals and households, that can be obtained at a low cost per name. For example, the following household data is only a partial listing of what can be added to a consumer's record for around 5 cents per name or less:

- Age range of adults
- Age range of head of household
- Presence of children
- Age ranges of children
- Gender of each member of household
- Occupation of head of household
- Occupation of spouse
- Estimated household income
- Number of vehicles owned
- Value of vehicles owned
- New car buyer/leased car

- Truck/motorcycle/RV ownership
- Mail-order buyer
- Type(s) of credit cards held
- Homeowner or renter
- Length of residence
- Type of dwelling (single- versus multifamily)

In addition, other data can also be gathered at relatively low cost. Depending on what the company is selling and what type of offers it is making to consumers, some of the following may be useful:

- Actual birth date of the consumer/spouse/child(ren)
- Make, model, and year of vehicle owned
- Indicator of creditworthiness

A company selling gift items (such as jewelry, flowers, or toys) may benefit from targeting offers to consumers about to have a birthday or who have spouses or children about to have one. Auto companies are very interested in who drives what, as are companies that sell unique auto parts and accessories. Credit card companies are very interested in the creditworthiness of consumers they are targeting with offers.

Lifestyle information—what type of likes, interests, and hobbies a consumer may have—is available for many households. National Demographics and Lifestyles (NDL) is one company that specializes in compiling this sort of information. Assembled in large part from warranty card information sent in by consumers, lifestyle data provides a good picture of what type of interests consumers have shown in the past. Lifestyle data can be very useful in determining what type of offers may interest consumers.

Consumer information is available from either single-source or multisource databases. *Single-source databases* are compiled by one company and contain only information that company has gathered. R. L. Polk, Metromail, TRW, NDL, American Business Lists, and others do the primary research required to gather and create single-source databases.

Multisource databases combine information from several compilers into one database. This allows more information and more consumer households to be included. If, for example, information on a consumer's age isn't in one of the source databases, it may be in another. A company having the data overlaid on its customer file is likely to get not only more pieces of data but also data on more consumers. (Nobody has data on everybody.) Infobase (a division of Axciom) and CAS in Omaha, Nebraska, are examples of multisource databases.

Basic data can also be added by phone matching, reverse matching, and credit card matching. *Phone matching* is adding a phone number to a record that has a name and address. *Reverse matching* is adding an address to a record that has only a phone number or both a name and phone number. *Credit card matching* is adding a name and address when the record has only a credit card number.

Matching is a quick way to flesh out a database when only partial information is available. Many companies do phone or reverse matching, often overnight and via modem. Examples include Telematch, CAS and Infobase. Companies such as TRW offer credit card matching, which enables retailers to build a customer list quickly.

Business-to-Business Data

Business data is compiled and made available in much the same way as consumer data. Usually business-to-business information is of more value than consumer information in targeting potential prospects and determining target market size. This is partially because business-to-business selling is often more complex than selling to consumers.

Business-to-business marketers typically target different individuals inside a company, based on each one's role in initiating, influencing, or deciding what to purchase. In addition, businesses buy very different things, depending on what type of business they are in. Using outside data can greatly assist in targeting the right offers to the right people in the right companies.

Basic business-to-business data is likely to include

- Standard Industrial Classification (SIC) code
- contact name(s)
- contact title(s)
- number of employees
- sales volume
- headquarters or branch location
- phone and fax numbers
- years in business

More specialized information is also available. For example, the number of beds in a hospital or nursing home, the number of students in a school, assets of a bank, church denomination, and specializations of doctors, lawyers, and dentists can be gathered from external databases.

One resource not to overlook when gathering business-to-business data is industry associations; these groups often compile company-specific as well as industry-specific data. Another source of data is industry magazines, which are often controlled circulation and require subscribers to fill out a detailed survey to receive the magazine. The information gathered by these magazines can be of great value to marketers.

Census Data

Government census data is a good way to add area-specific data to customer records in the database. In the United States, ZIP code–level census data is available on

CD-ROM for only a few hundred dollars. While the U.S. Census contains literally thousands of variables, not all are useful to marketers. For example, the age ranges of women of Tongan descent in a given ZIP code are likely to have little value. Average household income in a given ZIP code, on the other hand, may be a useful piece of data. Variables likely to be useful to marketers include

- household and per capita income
- relative percentages of occupations (managers, doctors, lawyers, factory workers)
- types of employers (government, education, services, manufacturing)
- home values
- percentage living in single- or multiunit dwellings
- percentage that rents versus owns
- percentage of homes not occupied
- percentage urban/suburban/nonfarm rural/farm rural
- percentage with high school diploma/two-year degree/four-year degree/master's/Ph.D.

Various compilers will use census and other data to make information available at levels smaller than ZIP codes. In many cases, the data can be added at the ZIP+4 level, which is approximately 10–15 households, usually on the same or facing city blocks. For apartments, it may be available for the apartment complex.

The smaller the area that census data is applied to, the less specific the data will be. This is to protect the privacy of citizens who fill out the census. For example, it is possible to find out the total income of Illinois by county or ZIP code during the last census but not what individuals stated as their income. Groupings with complete information are large enough to make it impossible to tell exactly what any one citizen entered on a census form.

One advantage of area-level census data is that it can be applied to everyone, while household information may be available on anywhere from 50 percent to 85 percent of the customer file. (Again, nobody has information on everybody.) Another advantage is the low cost per name for which census data can be obtained. Census data is useful for both consumer and business-to-business marketers because it describes not only the people but also the businesses in a given area.

Mapping Data

The cost of adding location coordinates to an address record and the cost of software that will not only display but also assist in analyzing customers based on purchases and location have dropped dramatically. A company can now buy very effective mapping software packages for only a few thousand dollars.

Mapping is most useful for retailers, restaurants, and other companies that want to target customers in a specific location or within a radius of their site. Profitable areas can be identified in such a way that prospect lists can be selected by using city streets as boundaries.

For opening new stores, mapping software will be useful in site selection. Knowing where the customers are on the map makes deciding whether or where the new store should be on the map much easier.

Premodeled Data

One way to streamline the process and reduce the expense of using external data is to use premodeled data—information that has already been sorted into distinct groups of consumers or businesses based on census, household, or business-level data.

An example of premodeled consumer data is PRISM clusters. PRISM clusters are distinct clusters of consumers based on area-level demographics and lifestyles. Names such as "Shotguns and Pickup Trucks," "Young Suburbia," and "Upward Bound" paint a clear picture of the type of consumers that predominate in a given area.

Ruf Strategic Solutions offers business cluster information for business-to-business marketers. Based on information from a wide variety of sources, Ruf clusters described businesses by SIC code, size, and even creditworthiness.

A field is often added to the demographics table to carry preexisting clusters. This allows marketers to select and analyze customers in their database according to this information, just like any other variable. This can be very useful when selecting a prospect list that matches these premade clusters.

The advantage of premodeled data is that it can be used relatively quickly and cheaply compared to custom models and custom research. The disadvantage is that it may not fit an individual company's customers as well as custom research will.

National Change of Address (NCOA)

Keeping customers' addresses accurate and up-to-date is important. For addresses in the United States, using National Change of Address (NCOA) data is one way of keeping them "clean" without the expense of verifying each address individually.

To do an NCOA update, all customer and prospect names and addresses must be sent to an NCOA supplier. This company takes the list, compares it with the list of consumers and businesses that have moved, and returns the file with both the old and new addresses.

Although not 100 percent accurate, this is far less expensive than relying on returned first-class mail or paying for address correction requested bulk mail. NCOA can be done for 3 to 5 cents per name and does not require data entry, unlike returned-mail corrections. Many companies routinely update their file through NCOA once a year.

Primary Research: Employing Surveys

Normally, what people have done in the past is a far better predictor of what they will do in the future than is what they say they will do. Words may lie, but actions speak the truth. This is partly why marketing to past customers based on their purchase history works so well. However, it does not tell marketers everything they may need to know about the customer.

Certain questions cannot be answered unless the right question is asked. In database marketing, a specific offer is made to specific prospects or customers, and their response (or lack of it) is recorded. This goes a long way in establishing their likes (they bought it, they must like it) and their dislikes (they didn't buy it, they must not like it that much).

Here are specific examples of what certain companies may need to know about their customers to market more effectively:

◆ A clothing seller wants to know how customers feel about the durability of natural-fiber products.
◆ A specialty toolmaker wants to know what other tools its customers own.
◆ A restaurant wants to know what new items customers want on the menu.

These and a whole range of other questions must be asked directly of customers and prospects if the company is going to find out what people want. The survey data can be either added to the database or analyzed on its own.

Although tying the responses back to each customer is useful in order to market smarter to them, a blind survey is preferable at times. In a blind survey, the customer is told (honestly, we hope) that their responses will be kept anonymous. Depending on the information being sought and the intended use of the information, this may be a better way to survey people. In most cases, a blind survey gets a higher response rate than a survey where people know their responses are not private.

To do primary survey research costs far more than to do secondary research by paying for existing data. For this reason, it usually makes the most sense to first do secondary research and then do primary research to answer any remaining valid questions. It is common in business to rush out and do a survey when confronted with new questions. Instead, using existing internal data, existing secondary data, and then primary research, *in that order*, is usually the best approach.

Designing External Data into the Database

With a relational marketing database such as the one described in Chapter 5, adding external data to the database is a relatively easy task. It is a matter of keeping the customer ID with the customer record when new data is added, then creating a table with only the customer ID and the additional information.

Exhibit 14-1 is an example of a consumer demographics table that contains data commonly relevant to consumer marketers.

Exhibit 14-2 shows a business demographics table that contains data commonly relevant to business-to-business marketers.

Keeping the date the information in each record was obtained is important for two reasons. First, overlay data, rather than being sold, is often rented for a one-year period. After one year, the data should be removed from the database. Secondly, data gets old and outdated quickly. There should be a way of removing old data and replacing it with more recently verified information. Having a date in each record makes determining which records to update or delete a simple task.

Exhibit 14-1

CONSUMER DEMOGRAPHICS TABLE

Customer ID ↔ Key Field
Age of Male Adult
Age of Female Adult
Presence of Children
Type of Housing
Own versus Rent
Estimated Income
Mail-Order Buyer
Credit Card
Length of Residence
Type of Vehicle 1
Type of Vehicle 2
Value of Vehicles
Lifestyle Cluster
Information Source Date

Exhibit 14-2

BUSINESS EXTERNAL DATA TABLE

Customer ID ↔ Key Field
Standard Industrial Classification (SIC) code
Number of employees
Sales volume
Headquarters or branch location
Years in business
Business cluster
Information source date

CASE STUDY

ADOLPHSON'S WOMEN'S READY-TO-WEAR (C)

Gathering Data

EXTERNAL DATA

Adolphson's has just assembled a database of all the internal data available that marketing requires. Before it begins analyzing the data, however, management wants to review outside sources of information to enhance its own data where practical and effective.

The first step will be to add outside information to the customer list. This will be done by several methods:

1. Reverse-matching customer telephone numbers to gather address information. Telephone numbers are available for customers who have had items tailored.
2. Sending nonstore credit card numbers gathered from transactions to be reverse-matched to the customer's name and address.
3. Sending all names through NCOA to ensure that each is correct and up-to-date as well as to improve accuracy in removing duplicates.

Additional names and purchase histories (from credit card data) gathered in this manner can be added to the database. They can be inserted in the same manner as the data that was keyed in, as described in Chapter 13.

At this point, Adolphson's has as much data as it can gather about customer names, addresses, and purchase histories. Now management wants to add demographic information to describe who the customers are. No one wants to go to the expense of appending data to all the customers in the database at this point, so management will

overlay a sample of 20,000 customers. The sample includes

- high-, medium-, and low-spending customers
- customers from each store area
- credit card and non–credit card customers

In addition to demographic data, Adolphson's is particularly interested in lifestyle information. Both NDL and PRISM cluster data are added to the file. To facilitate mapping customers geographically, location coordinates are added to each customer record.

Since Adolphson's did a thorough job of cleaning the customer name and address information prior to enhancing it, the store can expect a high match rate. In this case, it matched just over 80 percent of its customer file, which is very good.

INTERNAL (CUSTOMER SURVEY) DATA

Adolphson's has done several surveys in the past. In each case, however, the survey was anonymous. For example, it regularly receives data through mall intercept surveys in which patrons of malls where Adolphson's has a store are questioned about their shopping preferences. However, this type of data is biased in that interviewers tend to stop some people and not others, based on who is or appears to be willing to answer the survey.

Mrs. Adolphson feels her customers are the "busy type," not likely to want to spend time being surveyed while shopping. Mr. Adolphson is concerned that, since the surveys are conducted for only stores in malls, they will not reflect mail-order and other competition that is not present in those particular malls. Nevertheless, both consider it necessary to have a good idea of what their customers' opinions are about the following areas:

- Shopping by mail order

- Shopping at Adolphson's
- Why they buy in stores
- Why they buy through mail order
- What they like and don't like about Adolphson's

Adolphson's feels targeting promotions to different customer types will be easier with this information. Since there is no set program (e.g., warranty cards) in place now, the survey must be conducted as a special project.

To have a valid sample of opinions, Adolphson's plans to survey 1,000 people initially. To ensure the survey is not biased, a random sample of 2,000 customers, representing a variety of purchase histories, will be drawn from the database. Each of these 2,000 will have been overlaid with enhancement data, so both survey and enhancement data will be available for all customers who answer the survey.

An outside telemarketing firm will call the selected customers, making a minimum of three attempted calls (morning, afternoon, evening) until 1,000 surveys are completed. Since this will not be a blind survey, the customer ID number will be in the record that contains each customer's response. This will allow later comparisons of opinions with what customers bought, where they bought, and how much they bought.

Should this information prove valuable enough to make further surveys worthwhile, the survey effort can be expanded. For now, only 1,000 customers will be represented in the survey table. Adolphson's will continue, however, to use blind survey data as it has in the past.

BUILDING EXTERNAL DATA INTO THE DATABASE

The external data comes back to Adolphson's in a flat-file format. The first portion of each record includes the customer ID, name, and address. The remaining portion contains coded variables for each data point added, such as *M* for male or *F* for female in the gender field.

To make this data usable, a field must be created for each variable, and the data appended into the new table. Name and address can be discarded, but customer ID is retained, indexed, and used as the key field. This is why it is important to include customer ID in any file sent out for enhancement.

Where appropriate, some of the variables must be recoded into a numeric format for use either in reporting (to put things in the correct order) or for mathematical analysis in a statistics package. For example, averaging income is difficult when it is coded *A, B, C,* or *D.* These types of variables are stored as numbers.

The same basic procedure is followed for both the enhancement data and the survey data. The survey table and the demographics table are both keyed on customer ID, although the fields of data they carry are quite different.

FROM ASSEMBLY TO REGULAR USE

Adolphson's now has all the data it can gather from past transactions and as much data as it needs from external sources. It is ready to start analyzing the data. The store has one other challenge: how to manage and keep the database up-to-date on a day-to-day basis. A solution to this challenge is presented in the case study at the end of Chapter 15.

Choosing a Database That Fits

There are many paths to the top of the mountain, but the view is always the same.

Chinese proverb

COMPANY SIZE DIFFERENCES

Regardless of company size, the role of the marketing database ultimately is to store and retrieve data in an efficient manner. Size and complexity both play an important role in deciding what type of system should be used, and complexity can arise for more than one reason.

Fortunately, PCs are rapidly becoming more user friendly. Simple-to-use contact manager software can help almost anybody who sells to keep track of clients more efficiently, even when he or she has only a handful of customers. Contact management software works particularly well for a one- or two-person operation or where salespeople operate autonomously. For small companies, starting out with contact management software avoids much of the complexity of dealing with the database itself. Others, who need a more powerful package, have an ever-widening choice of hardware and software.

A database can be complex to create when many users will store and retrieve data, especially when they will do so simultaneously. The task is complicated by data coming from multiple sources, as in a store chain where each store creates unique data. If the company sells through multiple regional offices or if stores all have different systems, the task is even more complex. Even linking two salespeople, each making independent calls, can be a challenge.

A need for frequent updates and rapid queries can complicate setting up a marketing database as well. When minutes or hours are acceptable and last month's data is good enough, updating and querying are relatively easy. However, when last night's transactions on millions of customers must be included, updates must be done not only frequently but quickly. A system that is updated every day and requires 24 hours for an update will never be in use!

With faster and faster PCs, using off-the-shelf PC hardware to create marketing databases is usually practical with up to around 1 million customers. Beyond this point, a midrange or even a mainframe will be in order. In some rare situations, the complexity of updating from multiple sources, multiple users, and rapid updates demands midrange or mainframe power with as few as 10,000 customers.

Both size and complexity are affected by the number of transactions. Consumer catalogers sell an average of 1.6 items per sale, and the typical customer buys once or twice a year. Contrast this with the many items typical grocery shoppers buy and the many trips they make over the course of the year to that same grocery store. Building a marketing database for a grocery store is so difficult that it is almost impractical.

From a computer and database perspective, the number of items sold is rarely a major factor. Most businesses sell anywhere from 50 to 2,000 items, a very small amount of information to store in a database. Although dealing with many products, different offers, different coupons, and different catalogs may seem difficult for people (and often is!), it offers little challenge in database design.

As discussed earlier in the book, indexes make the queries go faster, but they also make updates slower, as each table must be reindexed. Indexes also add to the size of the database. The more indexes, the more storage space the database will require.

Another way to make queries faster is to store summarized data. For example, storing all the information in summarized form for customers in each state, region, or retail store will grow the database tremendously. Of course, analyzing sales by store will be much faster, but the database will be both larger and more complex. This approach also makes updates slower and more complex, as the summary information must be updated each time.

In the case of some data warehouses, three to seven times as much space will be taken up by summarized data and indexes than will be taken up by the original data itself. For example, a database planned to hold three years of data could consume 21 times as much space in total as the space required for one year of data alone. If the company grows or expands the information in the database, the space required will be even larger.

For small businesses, the space required to store summarized data should be of very little concern. When a customer list with 500 names and addresses takes up only $1/20$th of a meg, having seven times as much data about the customer stored in summary fields makes little difference, at least not as far as storage is concerned.

Small businesses do need to be careful in storing "copies" of data. For example, a lawn service might store a list of its customers as of the end of each month into a new file. After a year, 12 old customer lists are sitting somewhere on the computer. Creating regular backup files, copying them to diskette or tape, and keeping them in a safe place are a much better habit. Not only do you provide insurance, you avoid the confusion of having too many files and not knowing what all of them are.

Both size and complexity must be considered when choosing the hardware and software to handle a marketing database. In general, the systems chosen should be adequate for at least five years—any less and the system will be outdated too soon. Planning to build a system for longer than five years tends to lead to overengineered solutions. Remember that computing power that seems expensive today will probably seem cheap five years from now.

Very Small Businesses

Many very small businesses and many people in larger businesses know most customers by name and can tell you what they like, what they don't like, and maybe even how long they've been a customer. What these businesses and businesspeople can't keep track of without some kind of system is what exactly customers have bought and when they will be back.

When a business or a salesperson's customer base grows beyond the point where it can be managed by memory, that is the time to start using a database. One place to start is a contact management software package. These can be bought for anywhere from $50 to $500, and some come included with database software packages. Microsoft Access, for example, includes several pre-setup databases, including an address book, a contact manager, and several others. Contact managers work well if they are used and kept up-to-date, but how well transactions can be tracked without custom programming has limits.

Another option is to use the accounting package as a marketing database. Although this has severe limits, it at least ties customers to their transactions. The important thing is to get access to the information, using a database or report writer tool, and to be sure not to destroy or modify accounting data.

The key is finding a simple, low-cost solution that does a reasonable job of tying customers and transactions together. The financial investment is likely to be minimal for a very small business, and the time to create, update, and modify the database should be minimal as well.

Small Businesses

Small businesses can construct a marketing database and purchase little or nothing in hardware and software. For businesses with only a few hundred or a few thousand customers, particularly those that sell out of one office or location, building a database on a PC with off-the-shelf software is practical.

Businesses using software such as Microsoft Office Professional, which includes both Access database software and Excel spreadsheet software, can build a small but effective marketing database with these tools alone. Other software packages, (e.g., FoxPro, Paradox, dBase) make very effective database tools. FoxPro, for example, can easily handle hundreds of thousands of records, allowing this type of application to be quite large.

Example

A manufacturing business sells from one location directly to consumers. The transaction processing system and accounting system are the same. A separate manufacturing cost system does not directly integrate with the accounting system. Consumer requests for information, generated primarily from space ads, are entered into a third system, which contains their name, address, phone number, and a source ID.

The complexity of running the manufacturing operation and the expense of changing the transaction processing system means that changing either to fit marketing's needs is not practical. As a result, the input from the transaction processing system must be accepted as a given.

The company has 10,000 customers from the last five years and generates another 10,000 new catalog and information requests each year. No customer information older than five years is kept, and no request information is held beyond three years.

The transaction processing system updates nightly, and any information downloaded will be no more recent than the day before. It takes several hours to download new data from the transaction processing system and run an update of the marketing database. The business, however, tends to manage to weekly periods. Because manufacturing wants to be kept as up-to-date as possible by marketing, and because response from space ads tends to come in quickly, monthly updates would be too infrequent. This company will update the marketing database at the end of each week.

With a company this size, data storage is minimal. The whole database, with indexes, will take less than 50 megabytes and so should fit easily on an existing PC. The database is small enough that most statistical analyses can be done in Excel or Lotus; Access, FoxPro, or Paradox can easily accommodate the data and allow for rapid queries. These software packages also contain report writers that are likely to be adequate for most small businesses.

If the company plans to statistically analyze customers and prospects together, however, it may need something more than spreadsheet software. SPSS statistical software will allow the company to perform cluster analysis and other detailed analysis to uncover patterns that might otherwise be missed. Although a relatively expensive ($2,000–$3,000) piece of software at this level, it can be a very useful tool. In this small business case, the requirements are

- an existing PC
- existing spreadsheet software
- database software
- statistical software (optional)

Marketers who are PC literate and already familiar with their companies should be able to assemble a simple database such as this mainly on their own. A degree in computer science is not required, but they should expect to take two to three days of software training if they are not already familiar with database software. Most people take 30 to 90 days to complete such a project, although it can be done in a week or so if you already have the expertise.

Medium-Size Businesses

Complexity is as much of an issue as size when you create a marketing database. Different kinds of businesses have different ways of gathering data, reporting, and running their business day-to-day. Often, software applications are already on the market that cover most of the needs a business may have (depending on your line of business).

Example

A mail-order catalog company reaches the stage at which it employs several people to take phone orders, has a warehouse staff to pick, pack, and ship, and manages thousands of names on its customer list. At this point, it also has very complex database needs.

Many catalogers choose to buy a fulfillment system designed specifically for cataloging. The fulfillment system combines the transaction processing system with the marketing database, with the emphasis on processing transactions. However, the data capturing, storing, and reporting are so good that many catalogers are served quite adequately by this arrangement.

This approach has pros and cons. Like buying a suit off the rack, it fits almost right but never perfectly. If an extensive amount of custom programming will be required to make the system work, starting with a custom program may make more sense. On the other hand, it may fit well enough that altering it, other than perhaps one or two small changes, is not worth the expense.

Several systems of this type are on the market. One is Mail Order Wizard by the Haven Corporation. Mail Order Wizard makes it possible to track offers, catalogs, customers, and products by following simple steps built into the program. Other examples of such software include MOM (Mail Order Manager) and Response. Rather than taking days to learn and weeks to implement, this type of software can be up and running in hours.

As do many fulfillment packages, Mail Order Wizard comes with the following features:

- Has network capability for multiple users
- Allows order entry, including customer lookup features to avoid duplicate entries
- Handles payment types (on-account, charge card, etc.)
- Tracks inventory, including number in stock
- Tracks shipping, including printing labels

- Tracks returns
- Finds and removes duplicate names and addresses
- Allows correction and updates to the customer/mailing list
- Tracks sales by source code
- Reports sales by offer, catalog, list, etc.
- Reports catalog sales by square inch
- Allows for importing and exporting of data
- Adds calculated fields to customer records (recency-frequency-monetary)
- Allows mailing lists to be created and source codes to be added, based on criteria such as RFM

Most businesses will find that some desired features, such as the ability to integrate with their particular accounting system, may be unavailable with a "canned" package like Mail Order Wizard. Certain modifications, such as a screen change or something to adapt to a unique product line, can often be accomplished with small programming changes. These can be done (for an hourly fee) by the software company.

Mail Order Wizard runs on either a single PC or a PC network. Depending on the version, it can handle from 5,000 to 4 million customers. The software costs from $1,000 to $8,000, depending on the version and number of users. In addition, each user will need his or her own PC, and all PCs must be networked.

Compared to custom software, this can be a bargain. It makes little sense to spend many times more making something that resembles Mail Order Wizard. Many companies sell comparable software (e.g., MOM) as well as fulfillment software for larger operations. Several packages (e.g., MACS by Smith Gardner) are designed for midrange computers such as the HP 3000; others are built for the IBM AS400. Some systems handle millions and even tens of millions of customers and cost hundreds of thousands of dollars.

Companies sometimes modify their systems to the point that they no longer resemble the original! In such cases the company often buys the program code from the software company and modifies it when the need arises. The program code (or source code, as it is often called) is the internal computer code that creates the application itself. Many software companies will sell the source code, provided it will not be recopied or sold and the buyer is willing to pay several times more than for the "working version" of the package. Buyer companies taking this approach are likely to need a full-time programmer.

Before embarking on an effort to create a custom-built marketing database, see what is already "out there." Software packages are available that work quite well for churches, repair shops, video stores, and many other types of businesses. At some future point, a business may want to improve upon these types of systems, but they make a great starting point if you are just beginning in business.

Large Businesses

Large marketing databases are typically found not on mainframes but on powerful midrange computers such as the IBM AS400 or the HP 3000. More than one midrange computer may be tied together in a network, which can include 10, 50, or even hundreds of PCs.

Fortunately, most software for large-scale databases is designed to be "platform independent." This means that it will work with mainframes, AS400s, HPs, and other popular hardware. Most large-scale database software is also able to read and write in many different data formats. This means a computer running in Windows NT can retrieve data from a computer running different database software in UNIX without any difficulty.

Unfortunately, very few companies have the expertise to design their own large-scale marketing databases. They may have the computer resources, they may have a staff of programmers, and they may have marketers. However, building a marketing database is very different from building a transaction processing system. It usually requires a specialist to bring needed MIS and marketing skills together to build the database.

One alternative is to use an outside service to build and maintain the marketing database. For many businesses this is a logical choice. The company does not have to recruit or train people to get the skills they need to have a marketing database. The database project is often completed very quickly (in weeks instead of months or years). And results are almost ensured.

Of course there are disadvantages. If the heart and soul of a company's business is its database, it really should have in-house expertise to maximize its own understanding and capabilities. Outsiders simply cannot understand a company the way an insider does, nor can they look at things the same way. Although that can be good or bad, many companies simply do not want to give up control of something as precious as their marketing database.

A large-scale in-house marketing database is likely to have anywhere from 500,000 to 20 million customers along with their transactions. This information is likely to be held on a computer such as an IBM AS400 and linked to 20 or more PCs. Assuming a company takes this route, it will have a number of software choices.

The database software will be specifically designed for a client-server network. The data will be stored on the server, as will the server database software. The PC clients will generate information requests, which will be handled in the most efficient manner chosen by the server.

The database software on the server is quite different from PC database software such as Access. Aside from being able to perform queries very quickly, it is also designed to run updates very quickly. It is not designed for building transaction processing systems or to have a user-friendly interface. (The client PC provides the interface.) Instead, it is built like a race car—simple, stripped down, and fast. Quite often, the database software on the server is specifically designed for data warehousing.

Both Oracle and Sybase offer data warehousing software, as well as Red Brick (for really big databases) and SAS. These are not found in stores in shrink-wrapped boxes. They are usually bought from companies that will assist in setting up and maintaining the database. Along with the software, these companies quite often provide part of the expertise a company needs to create its data warehouse.

SAS is the most likely statistical software for companies to choose with databases of this size. Aside from offering all sorts of analytical capabilities, from time-series projections to clustering to regression, SAS integrates with many other types of software. It can read and write in more than 40 formats, works well with large networks, and is quite fast with large amounts of data. SAS also offers consulting and training, providing another part of the expertise companies need to create their marketing databases.

Much like the canned programs for medium-size businesses, there are specific analytical programs for large businesses in specific industries. Designed to do jobs such as determining stock reorder times and amounts, what to inventory, or how to segment customers, these products do a specific set of tasks quite well. Unlike the programs for the medium-size businesses, however, duplicating or improving upon them with custom-programmed off-the-shelf software is often quite easy. It is important to look at both cost and capabilities before buying specific analytical programs. SAS or SPSS may do the job as well or better for less.

Large-scale marketing databases are expensive. Software and software consulting (at this point, they blend together) are likely to cost at least $100,000. That is in addition to the hardware, which will cost at least $50,000. A company with 5 million customers can easily spend $500,000 building a marketing database.

Having specific marketing database expertise, most likely from a consultant, will also be important. Building a data warehouse is one thing; seeing to it that the data warehouse is a marketing database is another. Building the right data the right way is as important as building the right hardware and software combination. To be a success, the database must serve the purposes that marketing requires.

Growing into a New System

Sooner or later, all systems become outdated. Ideally, the company will be prospering, and its systems will be outgrown. In most cases, the new system will not be much like the old one. The file format may be different, field and field widths may be different, and so on.

Unfortunately, most companies changing from one system to another find importing data from the old system into the new one so difficult that they simply "start fresh" with the new one. Even worse, purchase history is lost, customer records are duplicated between the "old" and "new" systems, and marketing is severely handicapped trying to figure out who bought what when and where.

Whether they use database marketing or not, profitable companies tend to add new customers faster than they lose old ones. Any successful database marketing effort is likely to see constant growth in the size of the database. Therefore, it makes sense to choose a system today that will allow the data to be used in a bigger system tomorrow.

Marketers can track, test, and manage only so many things at a time. It is possible to start with a system that does too many things. If a less expensive system can track all the things that need to be tracked at first, there is no reason to buy a more expensive system to track things that won't be tested for several years anyway. In three to five years, either system is likely to be outdated and could be updated to an even better system, probably for less money than the difference in today's cost between the less expensive and more expensive systems. When in doubt, be conservative in setting up a new system.

From the standpoint of the company buying database software, the database preferably should not be in "proprietary" format. In other words, a database that stores data in a unique manner not compatible with other systems is not as useful as a database that stores data in a format that can be easily shared. Short of this, the best alternative is software that can import and export in generic formats, such as .dbf or ASCII.

Most database applications will import names and addresses relatively easily. However, very few will import invoice header and invoice detail records. When this is the case, item-by-item and purchase-by-purchase data cannot be brought into the new database. Some systems attempt to compensate for this by allowing each customer's source date, source ID, and recency-frequency-monetary data to be included with the customer file. New purchases are added to the past purchase total, and the most recent purchase date is updated in the new system as well. This does work as a partial solution for marketers.

Other systems affecting the marketing database may also be replaced. Information from the transaction processing system, for example, may be in a different format if that system is updated. Better to have a flexible marketing database that can cope with these changes than to be forced to scrap otherwise good software because some other system changed.

For some businesses, outgrowing a system is literally impossible. There are only so many policies an insurance salesperson can sell, only so many lawns one family-owned lawn care service can mow, and only so many clients one attorney can handle. In cases such as these, buying hardware and software that will be supported in the future is important. A perfectly good, useful system could become useless junk if the computer fails and can't be repaired or if the software crashes and can't be fixed.

ADOLPHSON'S WOMEN'S READY-TO-WEAR (D)

Sample Database Solution

Adolphson's has both a large and a complex database. It has 12 stores, 350,000 customer names and addresses, and a separate distribution site, and it is likely to have 1 million to 2 million names in its database eventually.

One of Adolphson's main difficulties, common for a retail store, is gathering name and address information with each purchase. Even Adolphson's credit card holders use their store cards roughly only half the time. The other half of their purchases are likely to go untracked.

One solution Adolphson's has looked at is building one big marketing database to track all of each customer's purchases where name and address or phone number can be captured with the sale. This would require replacing every cash register in every store with a point-of-sale (POS) system and tying to a central database in the headquarters area.

In addition to requiring the purchase of new cash registers for each store at several thousand dollars apiece and creating a wide-area network to hook each store system into a single database, Adolphson's also needs to purchase

◆ one more midrange computer, at $65,000 for hardware

◆ $125,000 of database software and consulting to create a data warehouse

◆ $50,000 of statistical software to analyze customer behavior and product sales

The initial outlay is expected to be enough to get the database put together, but it will require modification as they use it. Estimates run from $75,000 to $125,000 a year in programming costs to improve and modify the system. This is in addition to a full-time programmer to manage updates and keep the system working day to day. Added together, these costs go well beyond the amount of capital and effort Mr. Adolphson planned to commit when he and Mrs. Adolphson decided to launch a catalog. Adolphson's doesn't know everything it would like to know about its retail customers, but the owners are not convinced that the time and effort required to build a data warehouse with retail customers would be worthwhile.

One reason the Adolphsons question the expense of a full-blown database is that they already mail offers to credit card customers and advertise regularly to customers and prospects near the stores. They do not need a new database to continue reaching people they already reach. On the other hand, they must have a database to manage their catalog. Although it is true that store customers are store customers, they remain catalog prospects.

Since the emphasis for Adolphson's is not to build a database but rather to start direct marketing through a catalog, Mr. Adolphson decides to create a database specifically for the catalog operation. This will allow the other areas of the company, including the checkout clerks and MIS department to conduct business as usual. Mrs. Adolphson feels confident that catalog buyers will be sufficiently different from store buyers to make using store purchases as an indicator of catalog purchases a weak link at best.

The Adolphsons want to take what information they already have and use it as efficiently as possible to help launch their new catalog. To get off to a fast start, they take the following steps:

1. All the names they currently have are marked as to source (credit card, tailoring, etc.).
2. Total purchase amount and last purchase date are added to the file.
3. The file is merge-purged to remove duplicates.
4. The file is enhanced with demographic and lifestyle data.
5. A cluster analysis is performed to describe the different buyer groups.

The first three steps are done in-house by Adolphson's MIS department. The enhancement and cluster analysis are done by an outside vendor. No predictive model is done, as no catalog has been mailed and store buying may not be a predictor of catalog buying.

Once these steps have been completed, a survey is sent to 1,000 customers, promising a discount coupon if they respond. This is compiled and reviewed by Adolphson's with the help of an outside consultant.

Now Adolphson's has as much information as it will get about its catalog customers prior to actually sending a catalog. Along with rented lists, it has a "house file" prospect list with demographic enhancements that it can mail to. All it needs now is a catalog—and a catalog database.

Adolphson's will take all calls and ship all product from its North Kansas City location. In addition to getting a dedicated 800 number, the company will rely on fulfillment software to handle its catalog database

needs. Given the expected size of the catalog customer database in five years, Adolphson's feels Mail Order Wizard will work well for the company.

No names and addresses will be pre-loaded onto the catalog database system. Instead, the enhanced and deduped prospect file will remain on a PC. The catalog customer and catalog request names collected as sales are made and request names are gathered will be exported from Mail Order Wizard prior to each mailing (as the catalog house file), and duplicate names found in the prospect file will be removed. Since most store customers will not buy from the catalog, this will be the simplest method overall.

This also allows Adolphson's to gather store customer and credit card holder names and add them to the prospect list on a PC. Comparing the purchase information on the prospect file with the names that match from the catalog customer file will give Adolphson's insight as to who buys in stores, who buys in the catalog, and who buys from both.

This solution provides for the needs of the catalog operation at a relatively low cost, while not hampering or changing other departments in Adolphson's. The problem Adolphson's set out to solve was not that it didn't have a data warehouse. The real problem was that the company wanted to launch a catalog and needed to be able to manage it effectively. This solution solves the real problem without commiting resources to any problems that so far are only imagined.

SECTION

IV

Managing Your Database

16 THE ART OF TESTING

God gives every bird his worm, but He does not throw it into the nest.

P. D. James (born 1920), British mystery writer

Test, test, test, and test some more is the direct marketer's rallying call. At times, testing is almost a crutch that deters action or slows down the process of decision-making. But in the end, testing has a number of very positive purposes in direct marketing. It enables the marketer to

◆ gain knowledge
◆ become smarter in merchandising and marketing efforts
◆ compare one variable or alternative to another
◆ understand better how customers respond to offers and creative techniques
◆ determine which lists or media work best
◆ in the end, improve customer response, average order value (AOV), and sales per piece mailed

This chapter contains a great deal of practical "how to" information on improving your testing and ultimately your bottom line.

THE FIVE PHASES OF TESTING

Five distinctive phases can properly be included in testing. Here we look at each phase in some depth.

Phase 1: Exploratory or Basic Research

Basic research takes place during an investigation of a new product or new venture. If you are contemplating launching a new catalog or repositioning an old one, some basic facts and data need to be understood thoroughly. This phase of testing seeks to better define the marketplace your product or venture is considering entering. The greater your understanding and knowledge, the smarter you can be in product development, creating the mailing pieces, and so on. Here is the type of basic information that typically will be gathered during this phase:

- Complete statistics on the target market segment being considered

    - Market size
    - Growth rates
    - Trends
    - How to leverage the business

- Competitive analysis of who the players in this market are

    - Detailed information on each company's size, growth
    - Niche of each competitor
    - Strengths and weaknesses of each competitor
    - Void in the target market not being met by the competitors

- Target customer (primary, secondary, even tertiary)
- Accessibility of each segment of the target audiences
- Buying habits of the target customers
- Customer needs in the target market
- Problems of entering the target market

Most of this information is gathered at the library, through trade journals, and from trade associations, the Internet, or government statistical sources.

Phase 2: Pretest

Assume that you have a concept for a new venture and have done your "homework" in Phase 1. You have a great deal of theoretical information about the target market and target audience. The next phase concentrates on two things:

1. *Product offering*, including the depth (number of products per category), positioning of the product, price points, key product attributes and benefits, and product categories
2. *Creative concept*, including cover or outside envelope, page/spread concepts or brochure layouts, offers, copy platforms, etc.

Product and creative conceptualization are prepared on physical display boards to give a strong visual sense of the ideas being presented. The ideas are then presented to representative cross sections of the target audience to get their reaction. This method utilizes focus groups, mall intercept interviews, or other in-depth interview techniques. Importantly, this type of testing is highly qualitative, not quantitative, in nature. Such research or pretesting is done in several areas of the country to attempt to read geographical bias or reaction. The information summarized in this phase should refine the merchandise and creative positioning of the venture.

Phase 3: Quantitative Testing

In Phase 3, the company is ready to present the promotion to the prospects and get a real reading of their reactions. This can be done by mail, by telephone, through a magazine or newspaper, or on radio or television. With almost any medium, the following steps are typically followed:

- Source and select final merchandise.
- Determine how the promotion will be organized and, if it contains multiple items, what the pagination will be (what product goes on which page).
- Design the promotion, using information gained from Phase 2 (pretesting).
- Prepare copy to the specifications of the layouts.
- Shoot photography to the specification of the layouts.
- Produce the promotion and the order form.
- Complete color separations and printing.
- Develop the communication plan—determine to whom, when, and how often the promotion is to be mailed.
- Develop the merchandise plan; forecast and commit for product.
- Ascertain how and where the fulfillment will be done (receipt of orders by phone, fax, and mail; order entry; warehousing, pick, pack, and shipping of product; and return handling).

The marketing and merchandising people will prioritize and select the tests that will be included in the initial promotion. Such tests could include

- lists
- space advertising to generate new leads
- product pricing
- product categories and depth of product offering
- offers
- seasonality of mailing
- copy platforms
- promotion format (very expensive to test in catalogs)
- frequency of promotion
- lead generation follow-up for business-to-business prospects

This is the where the "rubber meets the road"—where you determine whether customers will respond and what their average order will be. One regimen followed by Fingerhut Corporation was to develop a short write-up or summary of every test that clearly stated the purpose, cost, previous relevant test history, potential benefit, and breakeven. Going through this process helps you easily differentiate between tests that are "nice to know" and those that will make a significant economic difference. Every testing tip in this chapter will be important if the tests are to be statistically valid and reliable.

Phase 4: Post-Test Analysis

If every test in Phase 3 is properly planned and executed, then every test will have excellent tracking and can be read and analyzed. We recommend that a formal post-test evaluation be done on every test to ascertain what happened, what worked, and how it did compared with the breakeven. Another "W" question that everyone would like to have answered but that can rarely be determined with direct marketing testing is *why*. This is nearly always left to Phase 5. Although most marketers know that post-test analysis may be the most important aspect of testing, many times it is haphazardly done. Proper testing is well planned, carefully tracked, and formally concluded to show what happened and what the implications are for the future. Smart catalogers and direct marketers establish a library of test results for future review.

Phase 5: Post-Test Customer and Noncustomer Research

With new ventures, adding Phase 5 is becoming more and more common. It entails using postmailing customer research that can be done through the mail, by telephone, or even in an in-the-package questionnaire. Interviews are often conducted with people who responded to the mailing as well as with nonresponders. With buyers, the marketer seeks to determine why they purchased, how they felt about the entire transaction, and whether they anticipate buying again. With nonbuyers, the marketer looks at whether they recalled receiving the mailing, whether they read it, why they didn't respond to the mailing, and what would get them to respond in the future. This information, coupled with the actual results from Phase 4, gives the marketer a great deal of information about structuring future mailings.

"How To" Tips for Improving Direct Marketing Testing

Tip 1: Prioritize Your Testing

According to the old adage, test important things that are going to make the most difference in results. Here are our priorities for testing:

1. *Product:* Since merchandising is the foundation of any direct-marketing or catalog program, it has to be ranked first.
2. *Media:* Lists, space ads, package inserts, and so on can provide differences over 100 percent, especially when you consider house lists versus outside names and even list segments within the house file.
3. *Offers:* Sometimes called the proposition, these can make a difference of 30 percent to 50 percent.

4. *Format or package:* Catalog, solo, self-mailer, and multimailer are all format types that can be tested, depending on the breadth and depth of merchandise. There are major differences in cost by format type.
5. *Seasonality or timing:* This can make a 20 percent to 40 percent difference.
6. *Copy platform:* This item is probably more important in solo mailings and can make a 10 percent to 15 percent difference in results.
7. *Cover or wrap:* This can make differences up to 30 percent and 40 percent for catalogers.

Tip 2: Know When to Test and When Not to Test

Great differences exist between consumer, business, and retail; size of the company and its mailing quantity; whether a company is a start-up, in the growth stage of its life cycle, or a mature company; the number of times the marketer reaches the customer list during the year; and so on. The rule of thumb that makes the most sense, regardless of size, is to include at least one test with every mailing. Most companies prefer to test in their best seasons and with their best list segments to improve the readability and reliability of tracking. Under what circumstances shouldn't you test? As you strive to maximize the profit from any mailing, test only those aspects that haven't been tested before. If you are concentrating on customer list mailings, list testing and segmentation will probably pay the largest dividends.

Tip 3: Establish Proper Statistical Controls for Every Test

Ideally, every test should have a control to test against, and each test segment needs to be statistically controlled. Exhibit 16-1 compares a simple test with a more complex test.

Every test has a control against which you can measure it. A control is usually your standard, regularly used promotion or offer. If you are a new mailer, with no test history, pick your favorite—the one that you judge will be the winner—and make that your control.

Tip 4: Ensure That Your Test Is Statistically Valid and Reliable

Validity tests check actual results and tell you whether the numbers make sense (a reality check) and are in a predictable range. Reliability tests tell you whether you can expect the same results again in the future. The law of large numbers says that the more pieces you mail, the closer the response will be to the true response rate.

The biggest pitfall for many smaller direct marketers is this one: establishing tests that are totally invalid and unreliable because of the sample size. As Exhibit

Exhibit 16-1

TEST COMPONENTS

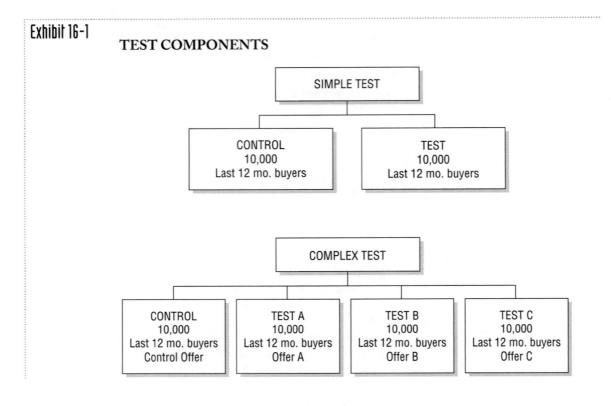

16-2 implies, the greater the percentage response, the fewer pieces that need to be mailed for predictable results.

The Rule of 100

If in doubt about your test size, remember this simple statistical rule: if you have 100 responses to every mailing's control and test side, you can assume that you're at least in the statistical response ballpark. For example:

> If you expect a 1 percent response rate, you need to mail 10,000 to get 100 responses.
> If you expect a 2 percent response rate, you need to mail 5,000 to get 100 responses.
> If you expect a 4 percent response rate, you need to mail 2,500 to get 100 responses.

When you see test mailings drawing 12, 35, or even 50 responses, be leery of the statistical reliability. A common problem of testing is having test panels that are too small.

Exhibit 16-2

PREDICTABLE RESULTS

TEST SIZE	RESPONSE RATE	# RESPONSES	PREDICTED RESPONSE RATE*
1,500	1.00%	15	.50–1.50%
5,000	.85%	43	.60–1.10%
5,000	3.50%	175	3.00–4.00%
6,000	1.00%	60	.75–1.25%
20,000	3.00%	600	3.25–3.75%

*Statistics say that 95 percent of the time this will be the range of responses when you remail.

Source: *Target Marketing*, January 1996.

Tip 5: Don't Test If You Can't Track Results

Proper testing starts by your planning how you will track results. Begin by developing a unique code number (called a sales or source or key code) for each offer or customer segment. This code becomes part of the mailing address of each promotion and is either ink-jetted on the mailing or is part of a Cheshire label applied to the address section. For magazines, the source code is normally included somewhere on the order form or as part of the phone number (e.g., "Extension 400"). Next is to capture each code during the order entry process through the mail or by phone, fax, or even e-mail. This is the heart of testing.

Historically, consumer mailers experienced an average of almost 15 percent unknown source codes when they used Cheshire labels. When ink-jetting came along and lettershops were able to address (with source code) on the order form as well as the mailing section, tracking of orders went up. Unknown source codes went down to 5 percent or 6 percent. Businesses have always had more trouble tracking source codes because of the use of purchase orders and "bill me" practices. The only technique that can be recommended for better tracking is to maintain a tape of the mailing file and, after the mailing, look up each buyer for which there is no code. Many medium and small catalogers, retailers, and business mailers continue to have enormous difficulty in planning and tracking source codes, which are so critical to business decision-making.

In one simple method of handling source codes, each digit of the code means something. The first two digits define the list (BU = buyer, SI = Sharper Image, etc.). The next two digits represent the year of the promotion (e.g., 97 = 1997). The final alpha character relates to the list segmentation (e.g., last-three-month buyers = A; four-to-six-month buyers = B). The code BU97A, for example, represents a buyer in a 1997 promotion who has purchased within the last three months.

Every circulation plan designates each list segment with a unique source or key code for tracking. In the example in Exhibit 16-3, note the differences in the second column from the left, identified by the heading "Source Code."

Tip 6: Nontraditional Testing Can Also Pay Off

Testing is typically thought of in terms of lists, offers, pricing, and media, but a whole realm of creative testing is possible that, although nontraditional, may pay off well in improving response and average order values (AOVs) for your company. Here are some of the nontraditional creative tests that should be considered:

- *Outer envelopes, covers, or wraps.* Differences of 25, 30, and as high as 40 percent have been observed in catalog covers, outer envelopes, and special message wraps when compared with a control. Larger catalog companies and larger solo mailers are constantly testing the outer carrier to obtain higher responses.
- *Formats.* Consistency in creative presentation is ordinarily viewed as a hallmark of a good mailing program. Sometimes, however, a change in format can help reactivate inactive customers or obtain better readability of a mailing piece in a poorer season. A mailer can vary the size or shape or can switch to a different format for a remailing. Some catalogers have found that remailing their catalog on newsprint works, by giving the mailer more of a sale feeling. Another technique is to vary formats between a bound catalog and a multimailer, a format that is half catalog and half multimailer. Fingerhut, American Express, and Horchow have used this alternative multimailer format with good success.
- *Personalization.* As your database sophistication increases, testing the use of personalization in your mailings can pay handsome dividends. You can reference such variables as

    - specific product or product category purchases
    - date of last purchase (recency)
    - demographic information (e.g., being a member of a birthday club)
    - recent move to a new address

People like to see their names in print, but only if the information is correct and the name is properly spelled. The use of personalization allows you to be able to talk one-to-one with your customer and should increase response and AOV.

- *Reply devices or order forms.* It is generally accepted that an order form is mandatory for consumer direct marketing but optional for business-to-business marketing. Sometimes, testing nontraditional order forms or reply devices can pay off. Generally a bound-in order form will increase the response over an on-page order form. With the growing importance of the fax for ordering, we recommend an order form for every business mailer. Call it a "telephone organizer and fax form," and you will be surprised what a difference it will make.

Exhibit 16-3

SOURCE FREQUENCY REPORT

		SOURCE CODE	LIST	QUANTITY MAILED	ORDERS RECEIVED	SALES	AVERAGE ORDER	PERCENT RESPONSE	SALES PER MAILING
1	House	SU931A	1996 subscribers 7/96	13	6	$ 176	$29	46.2%	$13.54
2	Multis	MB915B	3+ time multibuyers	1,280	166	8,456	51	13.0	6.61
3	House	IN913C	1995 inquiries	1,353	173	7,704	45	12.8	5.69
4	House	BU913A	1996 buyers	2,783	334	15,022	45	12.0	5.40
5	House	BU913C	1994 buyers	13,440	1,327	66,678	50	9.9	4.96
6	Multis	MB915A	2-time multibuyers	11,508	890	43,254	49	7.7	3.76
7	House	BU913B	1995 buyers	33,824	2,274	111,681	49	6.7	3.30
8	Contin.	CM916	Rental list O	9,167	536	24,298	45	5.8	2.65
9	House	SU913E	Subscribers GBP	2,000	79	4,962	63	4.0	2.48
10	New test	OC914	Rental list N	3,217	172	7,900	46	5.3	2.46
11	Contin.	AC916A	Rental list M	37,155	1,475	78,633	53	4.0	2.12
12	Contin.	CL916	Rental list L	58,828	2,585	116,919	45	4.4	1.99
13	House	IN913A	1996 inquiries	5,860	306	11,299	37	5.2	1.93
14	New test	HC914	Rental list K	4,404	192	8,120	42	4.4	1.84
15	House	SU913B	1995 subscribers	9,045	372	15,932	43	4.1	1.76
16	Contin.	CS918	Rental list J	5,000	194	8,511	44	3.9	1.70
17	House	BU913D	Buyers preceding 1994	7,228	246	11,824	48	3.4	1.64
18	Contin.	FD916	Rental list I	11,834	497	18,931	38	4.2	1.60
19	New test	HS914	Rental list H	3,949	146	5,689	39	3.7	1.44
20	New test	LA914	Rental list G	4,718	151	6,664	44	3.2	1.41
21	House	IN913E	1995 inquiries	16,091	488	22,099	45	3.0	1.37
22	Contin.	SW916	Rental list F	14,680	461	19,461	42	3.1	1.33
23	Contin.	NF916	Rental list E	20,401	645	26,438	41	3.2	1.30
24	New test	LB914	Rental list D	4,803	153	5,764	38	3.2	1.20
25	New test	TH912	Rental list C	5,000	155	5,736	37	3.1	1.15
26	Contin.	JH916	Rental list B	19,358	467	21,431	46	2.4	1.11
27	House	IN913B	1995 inquiries	2,588	84	2,851	34	3.2	1.10
28	House	SU913C	1994 subscribers	11,752	247	9,570	39	2.1	0.81
29	New test	PP917	Rental list A	5,000	99	3,946	40	2.0	0.79
30	House	SU913D	Subscribers before 1994	11,463	183	6,989	38	1.6	0.61
			Grand total	337,742	15,103	$696,938	$46	4.5%	$ 2.06

- ◆ *Other creative testing* can focus on typography, use of color, type of paper, use of cover stickers (or, as they are called by some printers, "dot whacks"), and so on. Every test needs to be justified and measured, but creative testing can help you understand your customer and improve your results.

Tip 7: Understand When to "Test Back"

If every test has a proper control, the measurement process is quite straightforward. Each test aspect is quantified against the control. Once a test significantly beats the control, it then becomes the control. Smart marketers don't rest on their laurels. They are constantly testing new offers, media, formats, timing, and so on to produce the best results. Smart marketers consider retesting important results to ensure that the results aren't a fluke or affected by seasonality. The greater the magnitude of the test results, the more that perceptive marketers consider using a "test-back" plan. If your name is Publishers Clearing House or Readers' Digest and a new sweepstakes promotion test crushes the control, you switch to the new winner but retest the old control against the new control at the earliest convenience. Sometimes seasonality can impact results; other times the size of the sample has an effect. The more important and financially significant the change, the more important it is to retest the old control.

Tip 8: You're Never Too Small to Test

What do you do if you are a medium-size or small company and have a hard time meeting the minimum requirements for testing volumes? We recommend that at least one test be done every time you mail. It may be one for seasonality to determine the best month to mail. It may be a price or offer test. Start with the important concepts—those that will make a big difference in your business—and make certain that each mailing has at least one test. By combining test sides or looking at sequential tests, most mailers will have a large enough quantity to read and project from the results.

Tip 9: Understand When to Test

Most businesses have distinctive selling seasons. Selling to schools is dramatically different from selling to other types of businesses. The consumer food gift business is quite different from apparel and from sporting goods. Understanding the seasonality of your company and industry segment is critical in testing.

Exhibit 16-4 shows a rough composite of the seasonality of all direct marketing—business, consumer, retail, and so on. Although this chart is helpful, it can also be very misleading because it deals with industry norms and generalizations. Perceptive direct marketers study their specific industry segment and build a seasonality testing curve for themselves. Then and only then can they understand when best to test. We recommend testing your company's very strongest season. By doing it then, you will have higher responses (and therefore higher statistical validity), and you can rely on the information for future mailings.

Tip 10: Retesting Pays Off

A number of successful catalog companies (e.g., Fingerhut, Lillian Vernon) take their testing seriously and will seldom make shifts from a control until the new concept has won in the initial test and a retest. In other words, if the test proves successful a second time, a switch is made to the new control. The more important the decision and the greater the financial impact, the more important a second test is.

Exhibit 16-4

DIRECT-MARKETING SEASONALITY

On a Scale of 1–5 (1 = Worst; 5 = Best), What Are Your Best and Worst Months for Mailing and Responses?

(Mean)

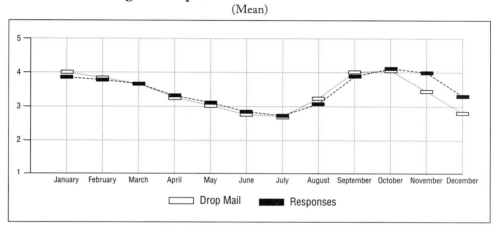

Drop Mail   Responses

Source: The Kleid Company, Inc.

Tip 11: Forecast Tests to Rollout or Full Scale

How many times have you heard mailers complain about test results not holding up from the initial test to full-scale implementation. You get a 2.5 percent response to a new list and then expand the volume of the mailing, and response drops by 20 or 30 percent. This is common. What can be done? You might forecast or project rollout mailings on a more conservative basis. One leading cataloger always subtracts 10 percent for the fact that it's going to a wider, broader segment of the audience. In addition it takes another 10 percent off projected results to be on the conservative side. Consider how you can apply this conservative thinking to your testing to help improve the accuracy of your campaign and annual budgets.

Tip 12: Build a Log of Test History

You have heard the old expression "What goes around comes around." How true this is in direct marketing, especially in testing! Amazingly, companies often hire new people who think every offer, concept, copy platform, or timing needs to be tested. If your company can maintain a central history and summary results of all testing, this can be the starting point for historical research on what has been tested before, to determine whether retesting is worthwhile. Times change and old concepts need to be retested, but a sense of historical results can make the decision-maker a lot smarter going into the mailing.

Tip 13: Budget Some Money for Testing in Every Mailing, Not Just Once a Year

Most marketers like to do their testing in their very best season. Therefore it is imperative to know which months or seasons are the best, in relationship to the others. Gift catalogers' best months are quite naturally late fall, October, November, and even December. They prefer to do their list, offer, and creative testing in this better season, thus maximizing their results. However, we subscribe to the testing strategy that a mailer who tests throughout the year—with every mailing—will spread out the creative effort, will have testing more "front of mind," and will probably use test budget dollars more effectively. Regular testing during the year will help improve overall results.

Tip 14: Build Benchmarks with Sources You Know and Can Trust

Successful direct marketers are hungry for information, especially benchmark data, that can help them determine when to test, where to test, and how to best spend test dollars. One of the best ways is to seek information from "friends in the industry" who are knowledgeable and willing to share confidential information. What are the sources of such benchmark data? This short checklist may be helpful:

◆ Sister companies that report to a common parent company
◆ Noncompeting companies in industries complementary to yours
◆ Consultants
◆ Industry professional associations (e.g., Direct Marketing Association)
◆ Former executives from competing companies

The idea is to better understand key financial ratios (e.g., cost of goods as a percentage of sales or cost per order for fulfillment), list test information, creative test data, and so on. The better you are at finding ways to leverage your business, the smarter you can be in selecting testing that will make a difference.

Tip 15: Track Competitive Mailings

Want to know how, what, and when the competition is mailing? The only foolproof way is to become a customer and carefully track when and what competitors mail. We recommend having several accounts: one a multiple buyer, one a one-time buyer, one that buys and returns the first product. Doing so, you will be able to determine several things:

◆ Timing and number of mailings
◆ Variations of the creative package sent to different buyer segments
◆ Efforts to reactivate inactive buyers
◆ Special offers

The more information you have about what the competition is doing and how it is mailing and testing, the smarter you can become.

Tip 16: Your Telemarketing People Are an Excellent Source of New Test Ideas

The order takers are most often the first line of communication with your customer. They can be a fountain of information about customers' attitudes and "hot buttons." Here are several examples of hot topics:

- New products the customer would like the company to offer
- Shipping and handling expense
- Overnight delivery options
- Loyalty programs customers belong to
- Loyalty programs they might be interested in
- Offer preferences—premium versus discount versus product bonus

We like to suggest that, every week, you give a general research-type or testing question to the telemarketers to ask customers. Every marketer and merchandiser needs to build a kinship with this first line of communication. You will be amazed at what a great source of ideas it can be.

Tip 17: Have an Exit Strategy

When direct marketers undertake major changes in promotion strategy—such as installing a sweepstakes program, starting a reward-based loyalty program, or moving to a discount pricing structure—a key factor is *how to leave the strategy*. It's called having an "exit strategy." Eventually times change, business conditions change, and customers change. What happens when you wish to discontinue using sweepstakes? Or a loyalty program? Do you think American Airlines had an exit strategy when it started its Frequent Flyer Program in 1968? We doubt it. What would happen if Publishers Clearing House were to drop its multimillion-dollar sweepstakes offer with each promotion? Such questions are not always easy to answer, but they reinforce the notion that if you are contemplating a major change in promotional strategy, you must carefully think through the testing process and have an exit strategy.

Summary

Who would have ever thought testing could involve so much thought, tracking, and planning? But it does. Testing, using database information, is key to growth and improved results.

Customer Cloning

*If the past cannot teach the present and the father cannot teach the son,
then history need not have bothered to go on, and the world has wasted a
great deal of time.*

Russell Hoban (born 1925), U.S. author

WHAT IS CUSTOMER CLONING?

Customer cloning is the process of determining what existing customers are like and
then finding prospects who are similar to them. Customer "clones" may live in the
same neighborhood; drive the same type of car; be of a similar age, income, or educa-
tional level; read the same magazines; or buy similar products from other companies.
Cloning implies a research-based approach to both prospects and customers. The
characteristics of different customer types must be described before comparable customers can be found. In other words, before you go looking, you must know what you
are looking for.

The basic assumption underlying cloning is that the best prospects are similar to
the best customers. Prospects you target must be similar to profitable customers, as
opposed to resembling unprofitable customers. Seeking out customers who are likely
to make one small purchase and never buy again makes little sense.

What makes good customers and good prospects involves more than how likely
they are to respond to an offer. One group may be more loyal than another and thus
much more likely to remain customers over time. Another group may spend more or
buy different items. All such aspects must be taken into account before you seek new
customers that are like existing customers.

For example, consider buyers of fine, tailored clothes. They are certainly upscale,
likely to be middle aged or older, and have well-above-average incomes. It is reasonable to assume that people similar to tailored-clothing buyers—their neighbors or perhaps other successful people in similar professions (the customer clones)—are likely to
be good prospects. People who do not resemble the present buyers—those with middle or lower incomes or with blue-collar jobs—are less likely to be good prospects.

In business-to-business marketing, clones are often in the same Standard Industrial Classification (SIC) code as present customers or are in the same areas or have similar numbers of employees. For example, General Motors and Rolls-Royce both manufacture automobiles, but they are hardly clones. Suppose you were selling a small quantity of high-quality wood veneer to Rolls-Royce. GM may not be a prospect for low-volume, high-quality veneers, but perhaps Ferrari would be an excellent prospect.

Most businesses, whether they sell business-to-consumer or business-to-business, get about 80 percent of their profits from selling to about 20 percent of their customers. Cloning the 20 percent makes more sense than cloning the 80 percent. Simply taking a list of customers and adding demographic data is not enough. Finding how old consumers are or where they live or how many employees a business customer has or how many years that customer has been in business is not the important thing. The important thing is to find out if good customers are younger or older than marginal customers or where people live who buy or if business customers are in larger or smaller businesses compared to those who do not buy. The important thing is to find customers similar to those that drive the company's profitability.

STATISTICAL MODELS, MAPS, AND COMMON SENSE

Statistical models used for customer cloning are of two basic types: predictive models and descriptive models.

Predictive models predict either the likelihood or degree of an occurrence, such as a 50 percent chance of rain (likelihood) or one inch of rain (degree). Used in database marketing, such techniques can predict a response rate (likelihood) or an average sale amount (degree). Decision-makers who employ predictive models do not have to understand how they are built (although that doesn't hurt), but must be able to use and interpret them.

Descriptive models describe the world in simple terms that help people make better decisions based on their understandings. To be useful, a descriptive model must give decision-makers worthwhile information they do not already have, or else make the information simpler and easier to comprehend.

Maps, for the most part, are descriptive models. By looking at where customers live in relation to store locations, major roads, rivers, bridges, and competitors' stores, retailers can learn a great deal about their customers. Combining mapping information with demographics and a familiarity with the area being mapped makes for ever greater understanding.

In the case of mapping, when a list of customers or prospects is created, it is defined by geography. The decision-maker can say, "Give me a list of everyone south of the interstate, between Main and High Streets, and north of 75th Street." Mapping software assists in this sort of decision, but it does not make the decision.

Maps can quickly show where customers can or cannot be found. For example, a company making a direct-marketing offer thought most of its responses would be from the West Coast. To confirm that, it could have created a spreadsheet showing the number of customers by state, but that would not have had the impact of a map. Exhibit 17-1 shows what a map looked like that marked the location of each of the 1,600 customers. As you can see, the customers are dispersed all over the United States. If anything, they simply follow population trends. Presenting the data in map form makes understanding it much easier and helps answer such questions as, "If they aren't in California, where are they?"

A company may find that prospects' responses vary based on several variables, such as age, income, and marital status. Sending an offer to people all over the country, using mapping software, will take a long time. Prospects are possible in every city and county in the country.

In a case where prospects have a distinct profile(s), a combination of factors may cause them to be prospects, and a predictive model may be best. For example, when prospects can be successfully selected based on demographics alone (i.e., without response data), a predictive model is a good choice. The predictive model can find prospects in a database who match the characteristics of a likely buyer and can select those most similar to the likely buyer. Normally the model gives each potential buyer

Exhibit 17-1

MAPPING TO FIND CUSTOMERS

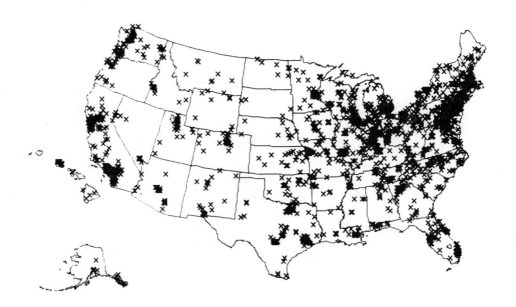

a score or rank based on likelihood of purchase, so the most likely group of buyers can be selected first.

Demographic data, although important, is usually far less crucial than response data. For example, if you are selling symphony tickets, it is one thing to know that someone's neighbor goes to the symphony. It is quite another to know that the prospect enjoys classical music or has recently bought classical CDs. If you are selling mail-order clothing to upper-middle-income, middle-aged men, it is one thing to know a prospect is upper middle income and middle aged. It is quite another to know that prospect recently has bought upscale clothing by mail.

Generally speaking, two things are true about response lists: (1) responses are better than with demographic lists, and (2) demographic choices are limited—you either rent the list or you don't. Most businesses do not allow predictive models to be used to "cherry-pick" from their list. They may offer selections, such as male or female, business or consumer, more recent buyers, amount of purchase, or customers versus information requesters. In a case such as this, decision-makers must determine what to select, based on their understanding and experience, but they cannot use a predictive model.

The one exception to this rule is that most list owners will allow a ZIP code model to be used for list selection—that is, by requesting prospects only in certain ZIP codes that match the profile of ZIP codes that worked for the company in the past.

To clone prospects in media such as magazines, radio, and cable TV, the decision-maker needs to evaluate how many likely prospects are in the audience in relation to the cost of reaching them. For relatively expensive space advertising, such as in a special-interest magazine, the audience needs to be on target. For inexpensive space advertising, such as remnant space in newspapers, this is not so critical.

Many times, such as first-time advertising in magazines, radio, and some rented lists, using a predictive model is impossible. However, when something has worked in the past, such as ads in a certain magazine or renting a certain list, no statistical models may be necessary. Often experience, tracking, and accurate data are all that are needed!

Determining Customer Profiles

The most important thing to keep in mind when profiling customers is that they must be described in such a way that others similar to them can be identified as prospects. Profiling customers based on how much they like the color blue, whether they like puffy clouds or wispy ones, or if they prefer sunrises to sunsets is of no use. Why? Because targeting new customers based on that kind of information is impossible.

Every company should profile customers on the basis of information that is readily obtainable and describe them in common terms. Are they young or old, rich or poor, male or female; do they live in the city or the country; is a company big or small; and do they buy a product like yours now? These are the kinds of questions that must be answered.

Here is an example of a customer profile that will *not* help in finding new, similar customers: "Likes to relax, spends time with family, enjoys eating." That can be anybody! In writing horoscopes, this sort of vagueness works. However, in trying to find more customers like the good customers you already have, it is of little use.

Here is an example of a customer profile that *will* help in finding new customers: "Mail-order buyer, prefers upscale clothing, female, between 45 and 55 years old." This definition is specific enough to give you some idea of what your customers are like and enable you to choose or not choose mail-order lists, magazines, radio stations; to pick the best newspaper section; and to get some idea what your prospects are like. In fact, this description probably profiles one group of buyers, and there may be others—a younger group and an older group, for example.

In any case, a profile is based on understanding, whether that understanding is from experience, a descriptive model, or both. It is usable not only because it can be implemented, (e.g., we really can get lists of upscale, mail-order-buying females), but also because it is understandable. It paints a picture of who customers and prospects are, becoming a foundation for creating strategies and tactics to reach them.

What to Look for in a Look-Alike

The most important thing to look for in look-alikes is whether they have bought a similar product or service from a similar marketing channel before. For example, most men buy shirts, but do they buy dress shirts by mail? Everyone buys food at one time or another, but how many buy food and have it sent as gifts?

The second most important thing to look for is whether prospects match the profiles of good customers. It makes far more sense to clone profitable customers than unprofitable customers. Look for what describes the difference between a very profitable customer and an unprofitable customer; seek out the things that make good customers good and avoid the things that make bad customers bad.

These criteria offer a simple, one-two approach to finding new customers. First, find a group of people buying similar products. This could be a list of men who buy clothes by mail or a list of companies that buy high-grade steel. Then select within that list, if possible, to choose the prospects that best match the profile of your own good customers.

Finding Consumer Clones

How consumer clones are described depends to a great extent on where you are looking for them. Whether you are targeting prospects through response lists, subscription lists, compiled lists, magazine ads, radio, TV, or the Internet affects which descriptive variables can be used in your selection process.

Here is a set of strategies to use for three common types of media (response lists, subscription lists, and compiled lists) to find customer clones. Note how the availability of information about the target audience affects how the various types can be targeted.

Response Lists

A response list is a list of consumers who have either made a purchase or requested information from another company. This type of list, typically rented for one-time use, is the traditional way for mail-order companies to build customer lists. These lists can be very effective, because they contain known buyers or responders.

Huge universes are available for consumer and business-to-business offers. These lists are the most expensive but generally are a good investment because the market being reached is people or companies with known mail-order purchasing characteristics. Examples:

Consumer:	Williams Sonoma, Fingerhut, Spiegel, Wolferman's English Muffins, Horchow, Gooseberry Patch
Business:	Reliable, Viking, Omaha Steaks Business Buyers, National Seminars, Gateway 2000, Paper Direct

Information about the types of consumers on the list, what they bought, and where they bought (in-store, catalog, magazine ad, etc.) is available on rate, or data, cards that describe them. A *data card* will tell how many are available, the rental cost per 1,000 names, the selections available, and the cost for each selection. It will tell when the list was last updated (very important) and what other companies are renting the list on a regular basis.

Targeting customers through these lists initially is a matter of matching up demographic and buying profiles as best as possible. If companies selling similar products have successfully used the list in the past, that is a good indicator. A list that has been used more than once will be listed as a *continuation*, meaning the company used it before and was pleased enough with the results to use the list a second time. After list selection is done and testing has begun, tracking is necessary to determine which lists performed best.

Matching up not only the demographic profile but also the type and method of purchase is important. For example, the list may contain 45- to 55-year-old women; however, if they buy gardening tools and you are selling tennis equipment, it is not likely to be a good match. If it is a list of retail buyers and you are selling by mail, they may not be willing to buy sight unseen. If you are selling a $500 item and the average order of the company renting the list is $25, they may not be willing to spend such a large amount.

The best way to determine which response lists to rent is to work with a good list broker. (If you don't know one already, look under "List Broker" or "Mailing Lists" in the yellow pages.) List brokers can find lists that match the profile of your buyers. They can furnish you with rate cards, which describe each list. A sample data card for a response list is shown in Exhibit 17-2. The description of the list's demographics is fairly cryptic. This is typical for a response list. "Selects" are available, such as all female names, most recent buyers, and purchase level.

Keeping a library of competitors' data cards makes sense if their lists are on the market. You can find out what their customers are like, whether their list is growing or shrinking, and what their sales are likely to be. This is easy research to do. It is free and should be done on a periodic (at least yearly) basis.

Successfully finding customer clones through response lists depends on effective tracking, testing, and experimentation. Done right, it can be a very effective means of finding new customers.

Compiled Lists

Using compiled lists is similar to using response lists, and both are obtained through a list broker. However, unlike those on a response list, consumers on compiled lists have not shown an interest in a particular product. Compiled lists can be bought, as opposed to rented, and reused for up to one year. This makes creating a multiple-follow-up campaign easier.

Compiled lists come from government, censuses, telephone directories, warranty cards, and other publicly available information. They are the least expensive and the most basic type of list. Extensive selections are available for both business and consumer lists. For example, business compiled lists typically can select by any of the following:

◆ Type of business, by SIC code
◆ Geographic location
◆ Size of company by either number of employees or sales
◆ Telephone number
◆ Whether the company is a headquarters or a branch
◆ Name of key company officers (not available in all instances)

Consumer lists can be selected by almost any census demographic and even some lifestyle factors, including these:

◆ Household income
◆ Number of people living in the dwelling
◆ Ages of people
◆ Presence, number, and ages of children

Exhibit 17-2

DATA CARD FOR RESPONSE LIST

HORCHOW COLLECTION

33400

632,957	LAST 24 MONTH BUYERS (THRU 11/90)		$90.00/M
289,292	LAST 12 MONTH BUYERS	ADD	$10.00/M
108,521	LAST 7-12 MONTH BUYERS	ADD	$5.00/M
180,771	LAST 6 MONTH BUYERS	ADD	$15.00/M
106,273	LAST 3 MONTH BUYERS	ADD	$20.00/M
	SUBSCRIPTIONS/FUNDRAISERS		$60.00/M
	PAID CATALOG REQUESTS		$40.00/M

AFFLUENT MAIL ORDER BUYERS WHO HAVE PURCHASED FINE QUALITY GIFTS, JEWELRY, FASHIONS, HOUSEWARES, FURNITURE AND MANY MORE EXCLUSIVE ITEMS FROM THE HORCHOW COLLECTION CATALOGS. MEDIAN AGE 51 MEDIAN INCOME $85,000.

SELECTIONS: STATE, SCF, ZIP $7.50M (ZIP TAPE MUST BE 20 BLK-100 FOR ZIP SELECT) SEX $5/M BUYERS BY AVG SALE $15.00M MULTI-BUYERS $10.00M SINGLE PURCHASE BUYERS $5.00M (DOLLAR SELECT IS ADDITIONAL TO THESE CHARGES) CUMULATIVE $30+ $10.00M, $50+ $15.00M, $75+ $25.00M, $100+ $35.00M

SOURCE: BUYERS 100% DIRECT MAIL CATALOG REQUESTS SPACE ADS AND RESPONSE CARDS

PRODUCT SELECTS $15.00M (INQUIRE FOR COUNTS) WOMEN S & MEN S APPAREL, CHILDREN S ITEMS, JEWELRY, DESK/OFFICE, ELECTRICAL/MECHANICAL, BED/BATH, TABLETOP, COLLECTIBLES, OUTDOOR, TRAVEL, HOME FURNISHINGS, FOOD SERVICE, FOOD, FURNITURE, SHOES/ACCESSORIES, BAR/GLASSWARE
.
WOMEN S APPAREL RETAILING AT $100+ (DOLLAR SELECT IS ADDITIONAL).
*PUBLISHERS ONLY - CAN SELECT CHADS @ $55.00M.
*FUNDRAISERS ONLY - CAN SELECT BY DATE BUYERS FIRST PURCHASED FROM HORCHOW @ $10.00M EXTRA.
.
CANCELLED ORDERS BEFORE MAIL DATE $5/M RUNNING CHARGES PLUS SHIPPING. MINIMUM CHARGE $50. AFTER MAIL DATE FULL CHARGES INCURRED.

SOME MAILERS, CURRENT AND NEW, WILL BE REQUIRED TO SIGN A LIST RENTAL USE AGREEMENT.

12

****
63 46 45 44
49, 55, 61, ,

UNIT-OF-SALE
$100.00 AVERAGE

*******SEX********
66% WOMEN, 10% MEN

****ADDRESSING****
4-UP CHESHIRE
MAGNETIC TAPE**
9-TRACK 1600 BPI
PRES. SENS. $5.00M

*****KEY-CODING***
NO CHARGE
UP TO 7 DIGITS

***MINIMUM-ORDER**
5,000

SAMPLE MAILING
PIECE REQUIRED

******NET-NAME****
85% + $5.00M
RUNNING CHARGE ON
100,000 AND OVER

MAG-TAPE-INSTR
**$20.00 NON-
REFUNDABLE CHARGE

- ◆ Whether a single- or multiple-family dwelling
- ◆ Type, make, and age of automobiles
- ◆ Whether a mail-order buyer
- ◆ Lifestyle preferences such as sports, pets, arts and culture, cigar/pipe smoking

Examples of compiled lists include:

Consumer:	high school or college students, senior citizens, affluent Americans, residents of Missouri, people who bought new automobiles in 1997, Black & Decker warranty cards
Business:	attorneys, accountants, teachers of reading or grade two, company presidents or other executives by name or title, engineers, businesses with fewer than 10 employees.

Compiled lists work well for retail stores that want to reach all likely prospects living near their stores. Prospects can be selected by where they live, age, gender, income, and many other variables. (Exhibit 17-3 shows a data card for a compiled list.) Compiled list information can be used with mapping software to show where potential customers are and to make list selection easier. This is often much better than selecting prospects in, for example, a five-mile radius. Rivers, highways, and other barriers affect where people shop, and mapping will help avoid obvious mistakes.

Compiled lists are the least expensive. However, as with most things, you get what you pay for. Compiled lists do not contain known mail-order buyers, the way response lists do. Remember, it costs just as much for printing and postage to use a compiled list as it does a response list, so don't be penny-wise and pound-foolish.

Subscription Lists

Many magazines cover lifestyle niches that allow advertisers to reach a distinct market nationwide. A magazine may appeal to gardeners, chefs, runners, or any of myriad other hobbies and lifestyles.

Subscription names come from people who subscribe to magazines, newspapers, or newsletters. The lists are somewhat less expensive than response lists but can be highly targeted to consumer or business audiences due to the niche nature of magazines today. Large universes are available, but lists must be tested carefully because they don't always work well, especially for consumer offers. Also, many subscriber lists are not direct-mail sold (they are generated by fund-raisers, organizations, etc.) and are not all paid subscribers. Most industries have a number of so-called controlled-circulation subscriptions, in which the publication is free to people working in the field. Examples:

Consumer:	*Skiing Magazine, Travel & Leisure, Better Homes and Gardens, Martha Stewart, Elle, Rob Report*
Business:	*Boardroom Reports, Wall Street Journal, Datamation, Inc. Magazine, Target Marketing, Catalog Age, Automotive News*

For potential advertisers, magazines provide media kits that describe the demographic and buying patterns of their readers. This helps advertisers decide not only whether to advertise but how to advertise. The information describes who reads the

Exhibit 17-3

DATA CARD FOR COMPILED LIST

LAWYERS AT LAW FIRMS	39178

```
271,496   LAWYERS AT LAW FIRMS            $50.00/M
 63,336   LAW FIRMS - ONE PER            $50.00/M     14

A COMPREHENSIVE COMPILATION OF LAWYERS IN LAW FIRMS,     ****************
97% WITH 2 OR MORE PARTNERS.   MANY SELECTIONS ARE       16
AVAILABLE INCLUDING SIZE OF FIRM, INDIVIDUAL NAME,
SENIOR PARTNER BY NAME, 36 SPECIALTIES, YEAR OF          ****ADDRESSING****
BIRTH AND PHONE NUMBERS.   CALL FOR COUNTS AND OTHER     4-UP CHESHIRE
SELECTIONS.                                             MAGNETIC TAPE*
                                                         9-TRACK 800 BPI
SELECTIONS:    STATE, SCF $3.00M; ZIP $5.00M; SEX        9-TRACK 1600 BPI
               $5.00M; SENIOR PARTNER $5.00M; YEAR OF    PRES. SENS. $7.00M
               BIRTH $5.00M; SPECIALTY $5.00M; PHONE
               NUMBERS $10.00M; NTH NAME N/C; CROSS      *****KEY-CODING***
               SECTION N/C                               NO CHARGE

SOURCE:        COMPILED                                  ***MINIMUM-ORDER**
                                                         $195.00
    SIZE OF FIRMS $5.00M:
    NO. OF LAWYERS       ONE-PER       ALL LAWYERS        **MAG-TAPE-INSTR**
        2-5               53,425         116,847          *$25.00 NON-
        6-14               7,333          61,629          REFUNDABLE CHARGE
       15-29               1,607          32,179          FLOPPY DISK -
       30-49                 516          19,486          PLEASE INQUIRE
       50-99                 320          21,118
      100-199               118          15,645
      200-OVER               17           4,592

    STATE COUNTS ARE FOR LAWYERS-CALL FOR COUNTS OF
    FIRMS.
```

AL:	3,004	AK:	799	AZ:	3,070	AR:	1,605
CA:	25,818	CO:	4,855	CT:	4,005	DE:	778
DC:	9,947	FL:	12,107	GA:	5,888	HI:	1,134
ID:	944	IL:	12,087	IN:	5,060	IA:	3,402
KS:	2,506	KY:	3,608	LA:	5,326	ME:	1,643
MD:	3,261	MA:	9,487	MI:	10,718	MN:	5,301
MS:	1,947	MO:	5,965	MT:	1,000	NE:	1,600
NV:	664	NH:	1,231	NJ:	9,440	NM:	1,512
NY:	30,478	NC:	4,621	ND:	554	OH:	11,512
OK:	3,786	OR:	3,218	PA:	9,190	RI:	1,040
SC:	2,584	SD:	606	TN:	4,196	TX:	17,523
UT:	1,597	VT:	726	VA:	8,032	WA:	5,662
WV:	1,232	WI:	5,185	WY:	462	GU:	0
PR:	0	VI:	0	CN:	0	FO:	0

magazine, their age ranges, other interests, and so on. Exhibit 17-4 shows a data card for a subscription list. However, do not assume that because a certain group of golfers subscribe to *Golf Digest*, they will buy golf equipment by mail. A better strategy may be to have a small direct-response ad in the magazine, offering potential buyers a free catalog, or even to advertise one of your best-selling products.

Exhibit 17-4

DATA CARD FOR SUBSCRIPTION LIST

 az marketing services, inc.   list management • list brokerage • fund raising services • 31 river rd., cos cob, ct. 06807 • (203) 629-8088 or 661-3004

BH&G MAGAZINE   Z 0810
                                                                                        MERCOR

6,697,000 ACTIVE SUBSCRIBERS	$70.00/M	
48,000 CANADIAN SUBSCRIBERS	$90.00/M	
FUNDRAISERS	$60.00/M	

DOLLAR UNIT:
    $16.00 AVERAGE

 90% FEMALE
CAN SELECT

BETTER HOMES & GARDENS MAGAZINE CONTAINS FEATURES
ON FOOD, FAMILY HEALTH, FAMILY TRAVEL, DECORATING
PROJECTS, GARDENING, BUILDING, PETS, CHILDREN AND
MORE. AVERAGE AGE 50; AVERAGE INCOME $44,467.

ADDITIONAL CHARGES:

STATE/SCF	$5.00/M
ZIP	$5.00/M
SEX	$5.00/M
RECENCY	$5.00/M
AGE	$5.00/M
SOURCE	$5.00/M
CHILDREN	$5.00/M
LEN OF RES	$5.00/M
INCOME	$5.00/M
DWELL SIZE	$5.00/M
UNIT SIZE	$5.00/M
PRES SENS	$10.00/M

SOURCE: 90% DIRECT MAIL, 10% SPACE

ADDRESSING: 4-UP CHESHIRE LABELS,
            PRES SENS LABELS, 9 TR 1600 BPI

MINIMUM: 5,000 2 SAMPLES REQUIRED

SPECIAL INTEREST: CRAFTS & HOBBIES, COLLECTIBLES
& SPECIALTY FOODS, GARDENING & FARMING, CULINARY
INTEREST, HEALTH & FITNESS, DO-IT-YOURSELFERS,
RELIGIOUS FUNDRAISER DONORS, POLITICAL FUNDRAISERS
DONORS, HEALTH & INSTITUTIONAL DONORS

70.4% COLLEGE ATTENDEES OR GRADUATES
91.3% HOME OWNERS
59.5% WORKING WOMEN
MEDIAN FAMILY SIZE 3.3
MEDIAN HOME OVER HOUSE VALUE - $105,000

85% NET NAME AND $5.00/M RUNNING CHARGES ON 100,000

AVERAGE AGE: 50

AVERAGE INCOME: $44,467

USAGE:

        CONSUMERS UNION
        MAYO CLINIC
        REIMAN PUBLICATION
        SOUTHERN LIVING
        DOUBLEDAY
        INT'L MASTERS
        LILLIAN VERNON
        FOSTER & GALLAGHER
        DISABLED AMERICAN VETERANS

Co-op Lists

A fourth type of list, a phenomenon of the '90s, is the *co-op list*. Several organizations that emerged in the mid-'90s have put together, in a cooperative venture, a massive database of known mail-order buyers. Many mail-order list owners give the co-op their customer databases with all purchase history. The owners have those lists statistically modeled and can test and mail names from other participants that the model predicts will be successful for their company. List costs are 30 to 40 percent lower than response names being offered by list brokers and managers. Thus far, co-op lists are only available with consumer mail-order names, but segmented business lists might work as well. Examples of co-op lists of mail-order companies include Abacus, Z-24, and SmartBase.

Finding Business-to-Business Clones

Business marketers have many of the same tools at their disposal as consumer marketers do, but they must use those tools in slightly different ways. Here is a set of strategies for using lists and trade publications.

Business Lists

Compiled lists often make more sense in business-to-business than in consumer marketing; fewer response lists are available, and many businesses target all companies of certain types as prospects. Another advantage is that business marketers can create a multiple-contact strategy, which may not be possible with rented lists.

For many businesses, even the best lists are not specific enough to identify who their targets should be. Although selections such as job title are normally available, a company may need to reach several people in the company that are not on any list. Exhibit 17-5 shows a data card for a business-to-business list.

Business marketers often must start with a list of prospects and then call each one to update, verify, and correct the list. In the process, they may add new names, determine who makes which decision (buyer, influencer, decision-maker), and obtain a phone number for each person, as opposed to each company. Only then do they start the "selling" part of the marketing campaign.

Trade Publications

Trade publications are industry-specific magazines. Normally they have a controlled circulation, which means their readers must be employed in the industry they cover. In return for receiving detailed information about the person and job, they give a free subscription. They reserve the right to refuse nonqualifying subscribers.

Exhibit 17-5

DATA CARD FOR BUSINESS-TO-BUSINESS LIST

az marketing
services, inc.   list management • list brokerage • fund raising services • 31 river rd., cos cob, ct. 06807 • (203) 629-8088 or 661-3004

RELIABLE CORPORATION-BUSINESS BUYERS   C6660
                                                                    DMI BLM

   155,522 1ST QTR 1993 BUYERS $85.00/M   DOLLAR UNIT:
    55,583 4TH QTR 1992 BUYERS $80.00/M $100.00 AVERAGE
    38,079 3RD QTR 1992 BUYERS $80.00/M

                                                                    65% FEMALE
THESE ARE MAIL ORDER BUYERS OF OFFICE SUPPLIES   CAN SELECT
SUCH AS PENS, MARKERS, OFFICE EQUIPMENT, COMPUTER
SUPPLIES AND FORMS, BINDERS, OFFICE FURNITURE, EN- ADDITIONAL CHARGES:
VELOPES, STATIONERY, AND A WIDE VARIETY OF OTHER   STATE/SCF $5.00/M
OFFICE SUPPLIES. 94% AT BUSINESS ADDRESS, 92% -   ZIP $5.00/M
4/5-LINE ADDRESS.   SEX $5.00/M
                                                    4-LINE ADDRS $5.00/M
SOURCE: 100% DIRECT MAIL   PRES SENS $5.00/M
                                                    11 DIGIT KEY   N/C

ADDRESSING: 4-UP CHESHIRE LABELS,

*INQUIRE FOR NET DISCOUNT BILLING

*ALL PAYMENTS ARE DUE 30 DAYS AFTER MAIL DATE. NO ADDITIONAL ORDERS
WILL BE PROCESSED IF A MAILER OWES ON ANY INVOICE MORE THAN 45 DAYS
FROM MAIL DATE.

USAGE:

    CASUAL LIVING
    COLORFUL IMAGES
    MUSIC STAND
    PARAGON
    TAPESTRY
    WINTERTHUR
    WIRELESS

Being so specific to a particular audience, trade publications can be very effective in reaching the right prospects. In the process of determining who is qualified to receive their magazine, they also build quite accurate databases. Many companies use a one-two punch, by advertising in the trade publication and then targeting specific individuals through the mail. (This approach usually does not make sense for consumer marketers.)

Trade publication advertising and list rental can also be used to promote other events, such as trade shows. For example, just before a trade show, a company advertising in a trade publication could send invitations to readers to stop by their booth. Business-to-business marketers should consider all the opportunities trade publications offer, such as targeted advertising, list rental, and event tie-ins.

CASE STUDY

FINDING CLONES FOR ADOLPHSON'S: CUSTOMER CLUSTERS (E)

Adolphson's Women's Ready-to-Wear has created a descriptive model of its customers, revealing five distinct groups of buyers to target. The actual list rental and advertising plan Adolphson's will use to target these groups will be discussed in Chapter 18, on customer and prospect communication. Here we'll review the five types of customers Adolphson's has, as well as how the company potentially could target each cluster.

COMMUNITY DOERS

The primary target audience for the store is the *community doers*, the movers and shakers of the city in which they live. They head the business, cultural, and social segments of each city. Their characteristics are:

◆ They are 45 to 60 years of age.

◆ Average household income is $80,000.

◆ Ninety-five percent own their homes and live in single-family dwellings.

◆ They are working, professional women.

◆ Nonworking women are highly involved in the city's society, not-for-profit organizations, and community causes.

◆ They are well educated—mostly college graduates or higher.

◆ Most are married, with some single female heads of household.

◆ Children are either in college or have left the household.

Community doers are Adolphson's largest and most profitable segment of customers. Traditionally, Adolphson's has reached them through newspaper advertising in the fashion or women's sections and has geared its fashions primarily toward this audience.

Adolphson's will find similar catalog prospects primarily by renting upscale lists from companies that offer women's clothing.

YOUNG MOVERS

Young movers are primarily younger, professional women who aspire to be community doers. Because of their working status and the availability of disposable income, they are a strong secondary target for the store. Their characteristics are:

◆ They are 25 to 45 years of age.

◆ Average household income is $50,000.

◆ Fifty-eight percent live in single-family dwellings.

◆ Ninety-five percent are employed in scientific, managerial, or professional positions.

◆ Most are college graduates or have professional advanced degrees.

◆ Thirty-five percent are single.

◆ Married women tend to be married to other professionals.

◆ Children are present in the home in over half of the households.

Young movers are a smaller but growing segment of Adolphson's business. Today's young movers are likely to be the most profitable customers in the future, if Adolphson's cultivates their business. Adolphson's has seen good response to its business-section ads targeted to this cluster.

This group can be reached through rental of upscale-clothing lists, but mainly through lists that cater to a younger audience. Some can be found through compiled business lists of female executives.

OFs (OLD FARTS)

OFs, the third most important cluster of the store's target audiences, have been store customers for 20 or 30 years and are the wealthy pillars of the community. Dressing well is very important to them. Here are their characteristics:

- They are 65 to 90 years of age.
- Average household income is $60,000.
- Seventy percent live in single-family dwellings.
- Most are retired but continue to be active in community associations, events, churches, and so on.
- Sixty percent are married, with no children living at home.
- Forty percent are single (either widowed or nonmarried) women who maintain their own households.
- This group travels, takes cruises, spends months in warmer climates in the winter and belongs to country clubs.

The OFs are fewer in number than other segments but tend to buy more expensive merchandise, often for vacations (resort wear) and special occasions. Adolphson's research shows this group appreciates personal service, they often have their clothing tailored to fit, and most have a salesperson who knows them by name.

Although OFs are a profitable segment for the stores, they are not as likely to be a strong mail-order segment. Lists intended to reach the community doers are also likely to contain OFs. As such, this cluster will not be specifically targeted.

COEDS AND TEENYBOPPERS

The fourth group in terms of importance, but one that has considerable buying power is the group of younger teenage and college women known as *coeds and teenyboppers*. Although few are employed full time, many have part-time jobs and affluent parents to

pay for their clothing. The key characteristics of the group:

- They are 15 to 28 years of age.
- Most are single.
- They live at home or in apartments.
- Forty-nine percent attend college some or all of the year.
- Nineteen percent finished college, are working full time in entry-level positions, and live at home.
- Thirty-two percent are in high school, with over ten percent attending private school.
- They come from upscale households.

Coeds and teenyboppers tend to be the daughters of the community doers and young movers. As such, they are usually found in the same households. Rather than target mail offers to them, Adolphson's will continue to reach them through ads in school newspapers and the teen section of the paper and by hiring local high school– and college-age girls to model at in-store and community fashion shows.

PLAIN JANES

The last group in importance is a group of moderate-income, value-conscious women who usually shop at J C Penney, Sears Roebuck, or other middle-of-the-road fashion retailers for everyday commodity clothing such as underwear, hosiery, and casual wear. Their characteristics:

- They are 40 to 60 years of age.
- Average household income is $35,000.
- Eighty-five percent are married.
- Fifty-five percent own their homes (single-family dwellings).
- Strong evidence exists of farm ownership.
- Fifty-five percent work at moderate-level

positions (e.g., secretaries, computer operators, nursing assistants) and in retail service jobs.

◆ Most families have children at home.

Plain Janes are the smallest cluster, but the one with the largest group of potential suspects. Adolphson's will need to test less-upscale lists to reach this group, relying on selects such as female name, type of product purchased, and age to get the best prospects possible.

Since this group is expected to buy less-expensive merchandise, the average order is likely to be lower. Testing enough lists to find a profitable niche in this segment will require considerable effort. Adolphson's must test both a variety of lists and a variety of selects to maximize response from this segment.

18

Customer and Prospect Communication

In preparing for battle I have always found that plans are useless, but planning is indispensable.

Dwight D. Eisenhower (1890–1969), U.S. general and president

The real power of database marketing lies in being able to send targeted messages to specific groups and obtain consistent, predictable results. Whereas some think the purpose of database marketing is to store and manipulate data, in fact the whole purpose of database marketing is to support communication with customers and prospects.

To take full advantage of a marketing database, tracking and analyzing communication with customers are not enough. Planning how the communication process will be managed, which media will be selected, and how changes can be made based on actual results is imperative.

To best explain how database marketers can use their marketing databases to plan customer communications, we will first review how direct marketers have traditionally managed this process. We will then apply these traditional principles to all types of methods of communicating with customers.

Circulation Planning: A Systematic Approach

This chapter will answer three questions:

1. What is circulation planning?
2. Why is it important to database marketers?
3. How does the database interact with and impact circulation planning?

Circulation is a word most commonly used in businesses that deal with subscriptions. There it refers to the number of issues that a certain magazine or newspaper or newsletter puts out. *Better Homes and Gardens* lists a paid circulation of approximately 8 million. *Sports Illustrated*'s circulation is 3 million. Marketers of magazines or newspapers or newsletters constantly are developing strategies to build, increase, or control their circulation.

In direct marketing, *circulation* has a different meaning. When marketers talk about circulation and circulation planning, they are referring to the number of people reached by a campaign or multiple campaigns for the year. They are talking specifically about three things:

◆ *What is the message* (e.g., a 48-page holiday catalog with three mail drops, a magazine ad)?
◆ *When will it reach customers or prospects* (e.g., drop 1 will be on September 5, drop 2 on October 15, and drop 3 on November 27; a December magazine issue; a telemarketing campaign beginning March 10)?
◆ *To whom will the promotion be targeted* (specifically, which customers, inquiries, prospects, gift recipients, magazines, newspapers, and so on will receive the mailing)?

Sometimes circulation planning is called mail planning. Some companies refer to list planning. But whatever the names are, the tasks are common to every direct marketer, and they are driven by the customer and prospect database.

Simply, circulation planning is the process of determining how a company will reach prospects and customers—that is, acquire new customers and communicate with them over time. Look at Exhibit 18-1 to see how circulation planning fits into the broader scheme of communication.

Circulation planning is all about the two marketing functions highlighted on the chart. Both are fundamental to the success of any direct-marketing function. Building a repeat-buying customer list is one of the significant drivers of every direct response business. We will examine each of these functions—new customer acquisition and customer communication—from a circulation or targeting standpoint.

New Customer Acquisition, or Prospecting Circulation

Database marketers rely on innumerable and often highly innovative ways to build their customer lists. Historically, rented mailing lists have been the source of choice for direct marketers to build their buyer lists. From Chapter 17 you know the three basic types of lists:

1. *Response lists* are buyers of mail-order products. Huge universes are available for consumer and business-to-business offers. These lists are the most expensive but generally are a good investment because the mailer is reaching people or companies with known mail-order purchasing behavior.

Exhibit 18-1

THE DATABASE MARKETING PROCESS

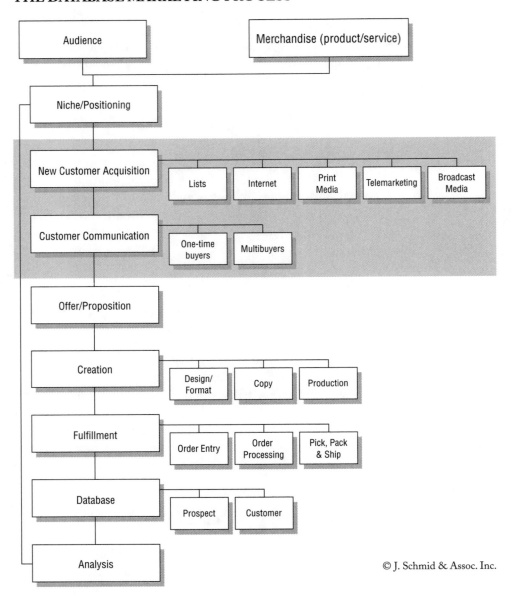

© J. Schmid & Assoc. Inc.

2. *Circulation lists* are subscribers to magazines, newspapers, or newsletters. These lists, somewhat less expensive than response lists, can be highly targeted to consumer or business audiences because of the niche nature of magazines today. Large universes are available, but lists must be tested carefully; they don't always work well, especially for consumer offers.

3. *Compiled lists* come from the government, censuses, telephone directories, warranty cards, and other publicly available information. They are the least expensive and the most basic type of list. Extensive selections are available for both business and consumer.

Prospect Hierarchy

A hierarchy of prospect names must be addressed in building the mailing plan for any season or campaign. Exhibit 18-2 is a typical ranking of the prospect (nonbuyer) names by a database marketer. Normally such rankings will be based on historical results.

Unlike the customer list, a great deal of segmentation of outside lists is not done before mailing. Smart mailers start their list testing with as tight a select as possible

Exhibit 18-2

RANKING PROSPECT-NAME CATEGORIES

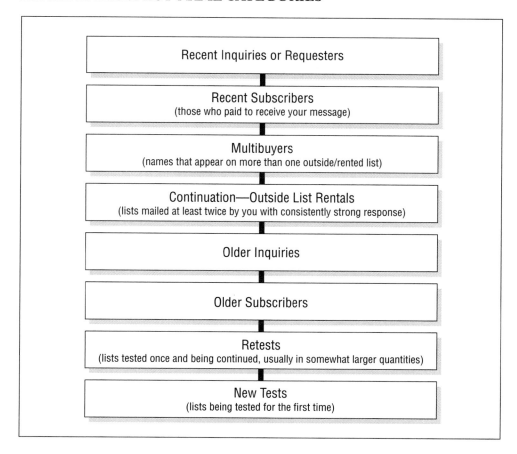

Recent Inquiries or Requesters

Recent Subscribers
(those who paid to receive your message)

Multibuyers
(names that appear on more than one outside/rented list)

Continuation—Outside List Rentals
(lists mailed at least twice by you with consistently strong response)

Older Inquiries

Older Subscribers

Retests
(lists tested once and being continued, usually in somewhat larger quantities)

New Tests
(lists being tested for the first time)

(e.g., last three month hotline mail-order buyers, female, with a $100 last purchase). The rationale is that if the tight select doesn't work, a more general select probably will not pay off.

Postal Code Modeling

One type of database modeling used successfully with the front-end, or new, customer acquisition is geographic or postal code segmentation. By comparing the characteristics of responders to a mailing versus those who did not respond, the marketer can start to identify portions of a rented list that will work better. A sample of postal code modeling (breaking the mailing into deciles) appears in Exhibit 18-3. The sample has been constructed by using a CHAID analysis with more than 100 demographic variables to determine for each company which characteristic is the most reliable in differentiating buyers from nonbuyers.

Developing the Prospect Circulation Plan

Exhibit 18-4 shows the typical layout of a prospect circulation or mailing plan for one drop. After identifying the prospect hierarchy and determining counts by list, the mailer is ready to start constructing a mail plan. Here is a checklist of the things a mailer must remember to do in building a mail plan:

- Give every list a unique source code (sometimes called a key, or media, code).
- Design the source code to reflect some rationale. For example:

VS81 = *Victoria's Secret* list, mailing in 1998, the first mailing of the year

- Note the exact list select for future reference and measurement.
- Record the total list quantity available for the precise select, as well as the quantity actually being mailed.
- Forecast response rate and average order value (AOV) for each list.
- Determine key measurement of any mailing: sales generated per piece mailed or per thousand pieces mailed. This is obtained by multiplying the percentage of response times the AOV. For example:

$$1.5\% \times \$50 = \$.75 \text{ per mailing, or } \$750 \text{ per thousand pieces mailed}$$

- Project the number of orders per list.
- Project gross sales by list and for the mailing.
- Calculate the breakeven to have an idea where the mailing is covering variable expenses and where it is generating a positive contribution to overhead and profit.

We recommend establishing a mail planning chart such as the one in Exhibit 18-5, showing marketing's forecast or projection and then comparing it to actual results.

Exhibit 18-3

GEOGRAPHIC MODELING

	Zips	Mailed	Response	Response Rate	% Sample	Estimated Lift
Group 1	**1,760**	**90,006**	**1,983**	**2.20%**	**10.26**	**17.82**
Segment 7	396	27,563	624	2.26	3.14	21.06
Segment 12	901	21,817	480	2.20	2.49	17.65
Segment 21	463	40,626	879	2.16	4.63	15.70
Group 2	**1,596**	**91,211**	**1,936**	**2.12**	**10.39**	**13.51**
Segment 14	448	33,011	707	2.14	3.76	14.53
Segment 22	1,148	58,200	1,229	2.11	6.63	12.92
Group 3	**1,154**	**78,867**	**1,636**	**2.07**	**8.99**	**10.93**
Segment 16	604	45,201	947	2.10	5.15	12.04
Segment 20	550	33,666	689	2.05	3.84	9.44
Group 4	**1,214**	**87,202**	**1,734**	**1.99**	**9.94**	**6.34**
Segment 11	765	53,762	1,079	2.01	6.13	7.33
Segment 19	449	33,440	655	1.96	3.81	4.75
Group 5	**2,699**	**75,992**	**1,476**	**1.94**	**8.66**	**3.87**
Segment 15	1,998	35,990	701	1.95	4.10	4.16
Segment 8	701	40,002	775	1.94	4.56	3.60
Group 6	**1,999**	**93,004**	**1,789**	**1.92**	**10.60**	**2.86**
Segment 23	1,603	40,221	777	1.93	4.58	3.31
Segment 10	396	52,783	1,012	1.92	6.01	2.53
Group 7	**1,429**	**83,114**	**1,462**	**1.76**	**9.47**	**−5.93**
Segment 18	679	26,999	501	1.86	3.08	−0.77
Segment 13	299	28,003	484	1.73	3.19	−7.57
Segment 6	451	28,112	477	1.70	3.20	−9.26
Group 8	**3,207**	**115,486**	**1,934**	**1.67**	**13.16**	**−10.45**
Segment 17	612	75,611	1,275	1.69	8.61	−9.83
Segment 25	2,595	39,875	659	1.65	4.54	−11.62
Group 9	**4,959**	**87,137**	**1,407**	**1.61**	**9.93**	**−13.65**
Segment 4	662	34,311	561	1.64	3.91	−12.56
Segment 9	3,812	38,014	619	1.63	4.33	−12.92
Segment 5	485	14,812	227	1.53	1.69	−18.05
Group 10	**21,897**	**77,843**	**1,032**	**1.33**	**8.87**	**−29.10**
Segment 3	1,799	10,964	156	1.42	1.25	−23.91
Segment 2	999	9,009	116	1.29	1.03	−31.14
Segment 26	17,001	43,763	507	1.16	4.99	−38.05
Segment 1	1,786	12,907	133	1.03	1.47	−44.90
Segment 24	312	1,200	120	10.00	0.14	434.76
Overall				**2.14**	**100.00**	**0.00**

Exhibit 18-4

FALL/HOLIDAY CIRCULATION PLAN

(Ranked in Alphabetical Order)

MAIL DATE: September 6

List Type/ Name	Source Code	Selection	Quantity Available	Quantity Selected	Postmerge Quantity
Anticipations	AN81	6 mo 50+ MOB		5,000	4,923
Ballard Designs	BD81	6 mo hotline MOB	57,397	5,000	4,752
Bloomingdale's by Mail	BL81	3 mo MOB, Dom/ home furn/tbl gifts	68,688	10,000	9,800
Chadwick's of Boston	CB81	Monthly hotline MOB	636,818	5,000	4,759
Charles Keath	CK81	3 mo hotline MOB	82,000	5,000	4,856
Careertrack Seminars	CT81	Quarterly hotline MOB, female	63,800	5,000	4,632
Exposures	EX81	3 mo hotline MOB	37,828	5,000	4,589
Faith Mountain	FM81	3 mo hotline MOB	41,164	5,000	4,956
Frederick's of Hollywood	FR81	3 mo hotline MOB	180,000	5,000	4,812
Garnet Hill	GH81	6 mo hotline MOB	129,300	5,000	4,723
Grand Finale	GF61	6 mo hotline MOB	15,466	5,000	4,695
Lillian Vernon at Home	LV81	3 mo hotline MOB, $100	27,000	5,000	4,985
Maryland Square	MS81	6 mo hotline MOB	60,000	5,000	4,853
Paragon	PA81	6 mo hotline MOB	422,000	5,000	4,759
Plow & Hearth	PH81	6 mo hotline MOB	84,281	5,000	4,587
Potpourri	PO81	3 mo hotline MOB, $75+	22,000	5,000	4,698
Pottery Barn	PB81	Monthly hotline MOB	163,048	8,000	7,698
Ross-Simons	RO81	3 mo hotline MOB, tabletop and gift	105,495	8,000	7,722
Spiegel	SP81	3 mo MOB, housewares, home furn	96,890	10,000	9,614
Storybook Heirlooms	SH81	6 mo hotline MOB, $50+	93,366	7,500	7,248
Sturbridge Yankee Workshop	SY81	6 mo hotline MOB	45,065	5,000	4,900
Tapestry	TA81	3 mo hotline MOB, $75+	33,845	10,000	9,758
Victoria's Secret	VS81	Monthly hotline MOB, female	540,000	10,000	9,826
W. M. Green	WG81	6 mo hotline MOB	35,944	5,000	4,862
Williams Sonoma	WS81	3 mo hotline MOB, female	104,300	8,000	7,522
Yield House	YH81	6 mo hotline MOB, gifts and access.	106,289	5,000	4,879
Multibuyers	MB81A	2X Multibuyers— Spring 1998			6,754
Multibuyers	MB81B	3+X Multibuyers— Spring 1998			2,701
Total outside lists			**3,251,984**	**161,500**	**164,863**

Merge-Purge of Outside Lists

If you are mailing extensive quantities of outside names, put all the lists through the *merge-purge*, or *dedupe*, process. In this computer application, all names that the marketer owns (sometimes called house names), such as buyers, inquiries, subscribers, and gift recipients, are checked against all outside lists to create a clean, unduplicated list. Typically in this process, all names are put in priority order, and each outside name is compared with names above in the list hierarchy. Any name that matches a house-owned name is marked so that it will not be mailed. Outside names that do not match the house names but do match other rented names are called *multibuyers*; they either are allocated back to the rented lists on a priority basis or are set up as a separate multibuyer list, given a unique source code, and mailed as such.

Since the merge-purge is done by the computer, each list (whether inside or a rental list) must be produced on an electronic file, usually magnetic tape. Complex algorithms are used to produce a zero (or near-zero) duplication of names. Smart marketers find that the detailed statistical reports produced as a by-product of the merge-purge contain a great deal of list intelligence as to how names match against their house names. The merge-purge technique is being used more scientifically in circulation planning to gain knowledge and use the information to enhance the response of outside names.

ADDING ALTERNATIVE MEDIA TO THE PLAN

More and more often, marketers are finding that alternative media (magazines, newspapers, package inserts, trade shows, referral programs, the Internet, radio, television) are performing better in generating new prospect leads or inquiries. As list rentals have declined in performance, alternative media has proven more beneficial for most marketers.

Space advertising is the most commonly used alternative medium. Marketers have three options in space advertising:

1. Sell a product.
2. Generate a lead or inquiry.
3. Both sell a product and generate an inquiry in the same ad.

Most consumer marketers opt for option 3, identifying a winning and popularly priced product that can be directly sold and also generating a lead if the prospect doesn't desire to purchase that item. Examples of each type of ad appear in Exhibit 18-6.

Exhibit 18-5

FALL/HOLIDAY CIRCULATION PLAN: FORECASTS
(Ranked by Estimated Dollars Generated per Mailing)

MAIL DATE: September 6

LIST TYPE/ NAME	SOURCE CODE	SELECTION	QUANTITY AVAILABLE	QUANTITY SELECTED	POSTMERGE QUANTITY	FORECAST % RESPONSE	FORECAST AOV	FORECAST $/MAILING	ORDERS	GROSS SALES
Spiegel	SP81	3 mo MOB, housewares, home furn	96,890	10,000	9,614	3.00%	$115	$3.45	288	$33,168
Multibuyers	MB81B	3+X Multibuyers— Spring 1998			2,701	3.61	95	3.43	98	9,263
Multibuyers	MB81A	2X Multibuyers— Spring 1998			6,754	2.57	89	2.29	174	15,448
Careertrack Seminars	CT81	Quarterly hotline MOB, female	63,800	5,000	4,632	2.00	100	2.00	93	9,264
Ross-Simons	RO81	3 mo hotline MOB, tabletop & gift	105,495	8,000	7,722	1.75	90	1.58	135	12,162
Williams Sonoma	WS81	3 mo hotline MOB, female	104,300	8,000	7,522	2.00	75	1.50	150	11,283
Yield House	YH81	6 mo hotline MOB, gifts & access.	106,289	5,000	4,879	1.25	99	1.24	61	6,038
Sturbridge Yankee Workshop	SY81	6 mo hotline MOB	45,065	5,000	4,900	1.25	89	1.11	61	5,451
Pottery Barn	PB81	Monthly hotline MOB	163,048	8,000	7,698	1.25	85	1.06	96	8,179
Chadwick's of Boston	CB81	Monthly hotline MOB	636,818	5,000	4,759	1.50	68	1.02	71	4,854
Garnet Hill	GH81	6 mo hotline MOB	129,300	5,000	4,723	1.25	80	1.00	59	4,723
Victoria's Secret	VS81	Monthly hotline MOB, female	540,000	10,000	9,826	1.25	75	0.94	123	9,212

(continued on next page)

FALL/HOLIDAY CIRCULATION PLAN: FORECASTS (continued)
(Ranked by Estimated Dollars Generated per Mailing)

List Type/Name	Source Code	Selection	Quantity Available	Quantity Selected	Postmerge Quantity	Forecast % Response	Forecast AOV	Forecast $/Mailing	Orders	Gross Sales
Lillian Vernon at Home	LV81	3 mo hotline MOB, $100	27,000	5,000	4,985	1.25	$75	0.94	62	$4,673
Ballard Designs	BD81	6 mo hotline MOB	57,397	5,000	4,752	1.25	72	0.90	59	4,277
Exposures	EX81	3 mo hotline MOB	37,828	5,000	4,589	1.25	68	0.85	57	3,901
Paragon	PA81	6 mo hotline MOB	422,000	5,000	4,759	1.25	65	0.81	59	3,867
Storybook Heirlooms	SH81	6 mo hotline MOB, $50+	93,366	7,500	7,248	1.00	80	0.80	72	5,798
Charles Keath	CK81	3 mo hotline MOB	82,000	5,000	4,856	1.00	70	0.70	49	3,399
W. M. Green	WG81	6 mo hotline MOB	35,944	5,000	4,862	1.00	68	0.68	49	3,306
Bloomingdale's by Mail	BL81	3 mo MOB, dom/home furn/tbl gifts	68,688	10,000	9,800	0.75	90	0.68	74	6,615
Grand Finale	GF61	6 mo hotline MOB	15,466	5,000	4,695	0.70	95	0.67	33	3,122
Frederick's of Hollywood	FR81	3 mo hotline MOB	180,000	5,000	4,812	0.90	70	0.63	43	3,032
Tapestry	TA81	3 mo hotline MOB, $75+	33,845	10,000	9,758	0.90	68	0.61	88	5,972
Potpourri	PO81	3 mo hotline MOB, $75+	22,000	5,000	4,698	1.00	50	0.50	47	2,349
Plow & Hearth	PH81	6 mo hotline MOB	84,281	5,000	4,587	0.50	90	0.45	23	2,064
Maryland Square	MS81	6 mo hotline MOB	60,000	5,000	4,853	0.80	50	0.40	39	1,941
Anticipations	AN81	6 mo 50+ MOB		5,000	4,923	0.60	65	0.39	30	1,920
Faith Mountain	FM81	3 mo hotline MOB	41,164	5,000	4,956	0.50	60	0.30	25	1,487
Total outside lists			3,251,984	161,500	164,863	1.35%	$84	$1.13	2,218	$186,769

Exhibit 18-6

SPACE ADVERTISING OPTIONS

Long-Term Use of Space in a Circulation Plan

Exhibit 18-7 shows the longer-term view (five-year plan) of how space advertising (or any other alternative medium) fits into the circulation effort for a marketer. The concept is applicable for either consumer or business marketers.

One of two things occurs when a person responds to your space ad:

1. The person or company becomes a buyer and is added to your company's customer list with all the recency, frequency, monetary, and product (RFMP) information added to the database.
2. The person or company requests information about your company and is added to the prospect or inquiry file with all key information such as name, address, telephone number, date of inquiry, and source code identifying the publication or medium.

Business-to-Business Contact Strategy

Business marketing differs greatly from its consumer counterpart. Although some similarities exist in media used (e.g., list rentals and business publications), a great number of media are unique to those marketing to other businesses. The media described below are used almost exclusively by business marketers.

- *Sales representatives.* One role of every salesperson who has a territory is to identify new prospects. Whether through a local association, referral, or discovering a new business by driving past it, the job of salespersons is to be aware of every potential customer in their territory.
- *Trade shows.* Almost every industrial segment has an annual convention or trade show where people can show and sell their wares. Generating leads from a trade show is an excellent method of building a company's prospect database.
- *Card decks.* A phenomenon of the '80s and '90s is a mailer called a card deck: a series of 3″ × 5″ cards riding together in a plastic envelope that contain lead generation offers. Cards may offer a free catalog, free information, a product for sale, or a myriad of offers to entice the person opening the deck to respond. Card decks are typically offered by publishers to enhance their revenues and provide a service to companies in their industry.

Whatever media are used to generate an inquiry, business marketers are much more aggressive in their follow-up contact communication with prospects. Today they may follow up on a business lead via one or all of the following:

- Direct mail
- Telephone or fax
- Sales representative or agent personal call

Exhibit 18-7

LONG-TERM SPACE PLAN

(at $5 per Thousand Circulation)

	1997 QUANTITY	1998 QUANTITY	1999 QUANTITY	2000 QUANTITY	2001 QUANTITY
Circulation: first half	2,000,000	5,000,000	10,000,000	10,000,000	10,000,000
Total cost of ads	$10,000	$25,000	$50,000	$50,000	$50,000
Response rate for inquiries	0.50%	0.50%	0.50%	0.50%	0.50%
Number of inquiries—catalog	10,000	25,000	50,000	50,000	50,000
Conversion rate per mailing	5.00%	5.00%	5.00%	5.00%	5.00%
Number of mailings per inquiry	2	2	2	2	2
Total number of orders from inquiries	1,000	2,500	5,000	5,000	5,000
Inquiries from previous season	0	10,000	37,500	50,000	50,000
Conversion rate	0.00%	4.00%	4.00%	4.00%	4.00%
Number of mailings per inquiry	0	2	2	2	2
Orders from previous-season inquiries	0	800	3,000	4,000	4,000
Response rate for orders—direct	0.015%	0.015%	0.015%	0.015%	0.015%
Total number of orders—direct	300	750	1,500	1,500	1,500
Total new buyers—first half	1,300	4,050	9,500	10,500	10,500
Circulation: second half	2,000,000	7,500,000	10,000,000	10,000,000	10,000,000
Total cost of ads	$10,000	$37,500	$50,000	$50,000	$50,000
Response rate for inquiries	0.50%	0.50%	0.50%	0.50%	0.50%
Number of inquiries—catalog	10,000	37,500	50,000	50,000	50,000
Conversion rate per mailing	5.00%	5.00%	5.00%	5.00%	5.00%
Number of mailings per inquiry	2	3	3	3	3
Total number of orders from inquiries	1,000	5,625	7,500	7,500	7,500
Inquiries from previous season	10,000	25,000	50,000	50,000	50,000
Conversion rate	4.00%	4.00%	4.00%	4.00%	4.00%
Number of mailings per inquiry	2	2	2	2	2
Orders from previous-season inquiries	800	2,000	4,000	4,000	4,000
Response rate for orders—direct	0.015%	0.015%	0.015%	0.015%	0.015%
Total number of orders—direct	300	1,125	1,500	1,500	1,500
Total new buyers—second half	2,100	8,750	13,000	13,000	13,000
New buyers—space ads	**3,400**	**12,800**	**22,500**	**23,500**	**23,500**
New inquiries—space ads	**20,000**	**62,500**	**100,000**	**100,000**	**100,000**

The larger the potential, the more personalized the contact and communication. Most business marketers are using the mail and phone to help qualify leads and improve the efficiency of their sales force.

Developing a Customer, or House, List Circulation Plan

A leading direct marketing consultant was asked to name the biggest pitfall or problem in working with the house list. The answer was instantaneous: "Not mailing the customer list often enough." If the buyer file is where the profits of the business come from to sustain and build the business and pay the shareholders, then using it to its fullest makes good sense. As a generality, most database marketers underutilize their customer names. That is not to say every name should be mailed every time, but the business will almost certainly increase both sales and profits by selectively mailing better customers more often. And that's where the database comes in.

The customer list is a company's most valuable asset. It is far more valuable than inventory, the office building, the distribution center, computers—maybe even more important than the mailer's people (staff). Some companies feel so strongly about the value of this asset that they are starting to carry it on their balance sheet, just as they do other assets. After all, if a mailer were to liquidate the company, the one asset that can be sold for full value is the buyer list. The better the file, the higher the value.

How does a company put a value on its customer list? An accountant might agree with the following three methods.

Cost Replacement Method of Appraising List

With the cost replacement method, the company determines the average cost to acquire a customer and multiplies it times the number of customers. For example, if a business catalog company has 100,000 buyers and it spends, on average, $20 to acquire each new buyer, the calculation would look like this:

$$100,000 \times \$20 = \$2,000,000$$

The only necessity for this calculation is knowing what it costs to obtain a customer.

Future Value Method of Appraising List

In focusing on future value, the company looks to the future for the earning potential of existing buyers. Lifetime value (discussed in Chapter 12) comes into play. The future name value of one's buyers is determined and multiplied by the number of buyers. For example, if a retailer has 50,000 recent buyers (last 12 months) and 25,000 13- to 24-month buyers, and 25,000 buyers "older" than 24 months and they have a respective future sales value of $250, $100, and $50, respectively, over the next three years, the value will be

$$
\begin{array}{rl}
50,000 \times \$250 & = \$12,500,000 \\
25,000 \times \$100 & = 2,500,000 \\
25,000 \times \$50 & = \underline{1,250,000} \\
\text{Total future value} & = \$16,250,000
\end{array}
$$

This method produces quite a different list value from replacement cost. It also assumes that you know the future value of your buyers. Is the database important to knowing this information? Absolutely!

Name Rental Method of Appraising List

A company that has its names on the rental market can also determine what the value of these names is from a future rental perspective. A good rule of thumb is that a solid, well-sold list will produce $1.00 to $1.50 rental per name per year. But since the rental of names is generally limited to recent or last-12-month buyers, older buyer names have a restricted value, if any. Suppose the company from the previous example has 50,000 recent buyers. The calculation becomes

$$
\begin{array}{rl}
\text{Year 1: } 50,000 \times \$1.50 & = \$75,000 \\
\text{Year 2: } 50,000 \times \$1.50 & = 75,000 \\
\text{Year 3: } 50,000 \times \$1.50 & = \underline{75,000} \\
\text{Name rental value over three years} & = \$225,000
\end{array}
$$

This calculation also presumes that the company maintains the recency (last 12 months) for the buyers. Again the database is critical in maintaining and updating names for rental purposes.

The House List Inventory

Before a company can start producing a circulation plan for a season, it must know how many names are available by segment. A "house list inventory," or detailed listing of the number of names by recency, frequency, and monetary, is critical. Counts of new-to-file buyers and even nonbuying names (inquiries, subscribers, etc.) that the company owns are important.

Many companies will develop a report similar to the one shown in Exhibit 18-8 and produce it weekly, monthly, or on-demand. Note that the spreadsheet shows at a glance the number of people by cell and compares it to other benchmarks of one month ago and one year ago. From this chart, one can start to determine the quantity of mailings, how deep to consider mailing, and how many times key segments of the house list may be mailed.

Exhibit 18-8

HOUSE LIST INVENTORY

(Month Ending 01/31/97)

Total Buyer Segments in 000s

| RECENCY | FREQUENCY | | | | MONETARY | | | | | | | RECENCY |
	1 TIME	%	2+ TIME	%	<$50	%	$50–$100	%	>$100	%		TOTAL
New this month	8.5	68	4.0	32	3.0	24	6.5	52	3.0	24		12.5
2–3 months	15.0	63	9.0	38	6.0	25	12.0	50	6.0	25		24.0
4–6 months	48.0	71	20.0	29	19.0	28	35.5	52	13.5	20		68.0
7–12 months	50.0	69	22.0	31	20.0	28	35.0	49	17.0	24		72.0
13–24 months	90.0	69	40.0	31	35.0	27	75.0	58	20.0	15		130.0
25-36 months	85.0	74	30.0	26	30.0	26	65.0	57	20.0	17		115.0
> 36 months	60.0	71	25.0	29	25.0	29	40.0	47	20.0	24		85.0
Subtotals	356.5	70	150.0	30	138.0	27	269.0	53	99.5	20		
							Total Buyers					**506.5**

Change in Buyer Segments

RECENCY	1/31/97	12/31/96	% 1-MONTH CHANGE	1/31/96	% 12-MONTH CHANGE
New this month	12.5	11.5	9%	10	25%
2–3 months	24.0	23	4	20	20
4–6 months	68.0	65	5	35	94
7–12 months	72.0	70	3	65	11
13–24 months	130.0	128	2	115	13
25–36 months	115.0	112	3	55	109
> 36 months+	85.0	81	5	30	183

MONETARY	1/31/97	12/31/96	% 1-MONTH CHANGE	1/31/96	% 12-MONTH CHANGE
< $50	138	135	2%	90	53%
$50–100	269	262	3	180	49
> $100	99.5	97.5	2	60	66

Establishing the Mailing and Promotional Strategy for a Season

The customer list marketer's main challenge is to determine how to maximize the number of mailings and sales while optimizing the profitability. The strategy for any mailing should come from the strategy established for the season, which in turn comes from the annual marketing plan and budget. Here's a simple schematic that might help:

Annual marketing plan and budget

↓

Spring season circulation plan

↓

Mail drop 1—Spring

A marketing plan, or "brief," that formalizes all aspects of the mailing plan is commonly produced by the marketing department. The elements of the *marketing brief* typically include the following:

- Number of mail drops
- Quantity to be mailed for each mail drop
- Exact date of each mail drop and expected in-home (or in-office) date
- Objective of the mailing (e.g., new name acquisition, customer/house list mailing)
- Specifications of the mailing (exact size and components)
- Break-even analysis showing three levels:

  - Nonbuyers or prospects (if they are being mailed at the same time): usually at 0 percent (covering only variable costs)
  - Older or inactive buyers: usually measured to cover variable costs and overhead (general and administrative)
  - Best customers: covering variable costs, overhead, and full profit goal

- A detailed profit and loss projection or forecast

Once the marketing brief has been prepared and communicated to all departments, the mailing plan details are ready to be produced. Exhibit 18-9 shows a typical customer mailing plan, which will be discussed in more detail in Chapter 19.

Customer List Strategies

To produce better results, successful direct marketers today are employing a number of key strategies:

1. *Build a special communication plan for new, first-time buyers.* Some mailers don't consider a person or company a "real buyer" until a second purchase has been made. Logically, if the second purchase is that important, special efforts should be made to

Exhibit 18-9

ADOLPHSON'S WOMEN'S READY-TO-WEAR:

Customer List Circulation Plan, Spring 1998

MAIL DATE: January 2; IN-HOME: January 12

Type List	Source Code	List	Selection	Special Message	Quantity Available	Quantity Mailed
House	BU81A	Last 6 month buyers	Credit card buyers—all		60,000	60,000
House	BU81B	Last 6 month buyers	Non–credit card buyers—all		10,000	10,000
House	BU81C	Last 7–12 month buyers	Credit card buyers—all		20,000	20,000
House	BU81D	Last 7–12 month buyers	Non–credit card buyers—all		5,000	5,000
House	BU81E	Last 13–24 month buyers	Credit card buyers—all	We miss you	50,000	50,000
House	BU81F	Last 13–24 month buyers	Non–credit card buyers—all	We miss you	7,500	7,500
House	BU81G	Last 25–36 month buyers	Credit card buyers—all	We miss you	40,000	40,000
House	BU81H	Last 25–36 month buyers	Non–credit card buyers—all	We miss you	5,000	5,000
House	BU81I	Buyers older than 36 mo.	Credit card buyers—all	We miss you	100,000	100,000
House	BU81J	Buyers older than 36 mo.	Non–credit card buyers—all	We miss you	52,500	52,500
House	IN81A	Last 12 month inquiries	All		20,000	20,000
House	IN81B	Last 13–24 month inquiries	All	We miss you	15,000	15,000
House	IN81C	Inquiries older than 24 mo.	All	Last chance	30,000	30,000
Total house					**415,000**	**415,000**

persuade one-time buyers to buy again. Special communications help, and it pays to acknowledge that these are one-time buyers and that you want them as regular customers. Incentives and special offers should be tested to determine if they can be helpful (and pay for themselves).

2. *Reactivate inactive buyers.* Once a company builds a relationship with customers, it generally finds attempting to reactivate those customers far more productive than acquiring new ones. Building on some level of past loyalty in a timely manner is critical. For example, the longer the delay in attempting to reactivate customers, the poorer the response. Many mailers use 12 months as the cutoff between active and inactive customers. If a company has not heard from customers in 12 months, they may be gone. Inactive customers have been shown to respond to special offers and special messages such as these:

- We miss you.
- Don't let this be your last mailing.
- Last chance to respond.

3. *Build special perks or special messages for the best buyers.* Just the opposite of reactivation, "perk building" is based on the 80/20 rule: 20 percent of a company's buyers will produce 80 percent of the revenue and profits. If this tenet is even half right, it pays to consider special praise, incentives, and even loyalty programs to encourage top customers to respond and stay active.

For example, one food catalog mailer identifies from its database those buyers from the past year who purchased over five times and spent over $200 dollars. Just before the prime holiday mailing season, the company sends each buyer a special food gift with nothing but a "Thanks for being such a good customer." Within 10 days, a holiday catalog arrives with a personalized gift recipient list. Can you guess how good the response is? Phenomenal!

Customer loyalty programs, discussed in Chapter 2, are a way of building a special reward system for that top 20 percent of a company's customers. But be aware of the pitfalls.

Chapter 19 will take the circulation planning tasks a step further and show you a case in which prospecting and customer mailings start to come together.

Turning a Communication Plan into a Financial Plan

For the happiest life, days should be rigorously planned, and nights left open to chance.

Mignon McLaughlin, U.S. author and editor

As discussed in Chapter 18, the circulation plan is a process of determining who will receive the company's messages; when the messages will be sent, in what formats, through what media; and what products or services will be offered.

Successful database marketers feel that the circulation plan is *the* major factor in determining the sales and profits of a database-driven marketing company. However, most companies do a very mediocre job of planning their annual and individual promotion campaigns. For large consumer, business, retail, and even fundraising mailers, this discussion will be quite basic, even redundant, to their everyday tasks in planning and executing their mail plans. Smaller mailers, though, should consider carefully the process described in this chapter.

We will again focus on the two types of circulation plans—prospect and house—and then look at how the two types of databases can be integrated into a single campaign. For this example, we will use a campaign that reaches customers and prospects primarily through direct mail.

The Prospect Circulation Plan

Step 1: Talk to a List Broker

If this is your company's first prospect mailing effort, start by talking to a list broker, a person who has access to every kind of mailing list. Brokers exist to facilitate the list-buying process—that is, to give the mailer recommendations (often called a "list reco"). Good list brokers ask a million questions about the product, offer, target audience(s), mailing quantity, and the competition. The more information they have, the better their advice. They will supply detailed list recommendations and a data card for each list. Further, they will tell you what companies have "continued" (tested and then rolled out) on each list and what specific selects they recommend. The more knowledgeable that brokers are about an industry, the better they can serve the mailer. Brokers can also recommend minimum quantities to mail for statistical signif-icance. Brokers can help with your list planning, especially outside rental lists, but are not a substitute for an internal circulation planner.

Segmentation of Outside Lists

Preparing an RFM segmentation on outside lists is not possible. However, it is possible to make a great number of highly targeted selections on most outside lists to help pinpoint the mailing. Here are some of the types of segmentation available on outside lists.

- Male versus female
- Recency of last purchase: last 3 months, 6 months, 12 months
- Mail-order buyer versus subscriber versus compiled name
- Dollar level of purchase (This one can be a bit tricky. In specifying a dollar level, be certain to understand whether this means cumulative [lifetime] dollars or last purchase or average purchase. Each measurement is quite different.)
- Geography: state, ZIP code, or SCF (sectional center facility, the first three digits of the ZIP code)
- Product category purchased
- Size of company (by number of employees or dollar amount of sales)
- Name or position within a company
- Buyer or specifier of product

The important thing to remember is always to be as specific as possible. Shoot rifle bullets, not cannonballs.

Step 2: Consider Alternative Media for Prospecting

Without a doubt, a company planning prospect strategy should not just consider list rental. As discussed in other chapters, a plethora of other media, including this checklist, can be used to build one's customer list:

- Space ads (to sell a product or generate an inquiry)
- Sunday newspaper supplements or freestanding inserts (commonly called FSIs)
- Sunday newspaper magazines such as *Parade* or *USA Weekend*
- Television
- Radio
- Customer referrals

- Package inserts
- Trade shows
- Card decks
- Catalog of catalogs
- Credit card bill ride-alongs
- Airline magazines or ticket inserts
- Doctors' or dentists' offices
- Public relations
- The Internet

And the list goes on! Every industry has unique ways to find prospective customers. Usually the more innovative you can be in finding new customers, the better will be their long-term value.

Step 3: Preparing the Break-Even Analysis

Before actual preparation of the mailing plan, a marketer must know the variable breakeven of the mailing. The breakeven really works a profit and loss statement backward, solving for two important ingredients: (1) what percentage of response the mailing needs to break even and (2) how many sales per piece mailed (or prospect reached) are needed to break even. The latter measurement, sales per piece mailed (sometimes expressed as sales per 1,000 pieces mailed), is the *critical measurement* of a mailing's success and will determine whether a list is or is not considered for mailing and remailing.

Exhibit 19-1 shows the vital calculation for determining the variable breakeven for the prospect portion of the mailing. You are interested in looking at the breakeven at the 0 percent, or variable, level, which covers all variable costs but no overhead or profit contribution. (Variable costs in this case include every cost directly applicable to the mailing but not general and administrative costs such as utilities, building, and management salaries.)

In example A, with a $50 gross order, the mailer first subtracts the estimated returns (5 percent) and cancels (1 percent) to get to net sales. From net sales, cost of goods (45 percent) and fulfillment ($6 per order) are subtracted to give contribution before promotion. After estimating what the variable in-the-mail cost per piece of the promotion will be (including printing, lettershop, list rental, and postage),[1] you divide the promotion cost by the contribution to profit before promotion and overhead to arrive at the answer in decimal format (.0252). By changing that decimal to a percentage (2.52 percent), part of the break-even answer is completed.

---

[1] Some companies will add fixed creative costs (layout, copy, photography, computer production, and color separation) to this calculation.

Exhibit 19-1

BREAK-EVEN RESPONSE RATE ANALYSIS, BY ORDER

Prospect Mailing Example

		A	B
Average unit price		$33.33	$66.67
Average units per order		1.5	1.5
Average per order		$50.00	$100.00
Cancellations	1%	(.50)	(1.00)
Returns	5%	(2.50)	(5.00)
Net sales		$47.00	$94.00
Cost of goods			
Adjustment for salvaged returns and cancellations	45%	(21.15)	(42.30)
Markdowns			
Shipping	$6 per order for fulfillment	(6.00)	(6.00)
Order entry/processing			
Shipping/handling income			
Contribution before promotion			
Overhead and profit contribution at 0% of net sales		$19.85	$45.70
Cost per promotional piece		$.50	$1.00

Conclusion:
Promotion cost:
Gross margin × 100 = Break-even
    response rate (%)
Overhead and profit contribution
    at 0% of net sales

	A	B
Percentage	2.52%	1.09%
$ per mailing*	$1.18	$1.03

*Dollars per mailing = Percentage response × Net sales.

The more important part is determining the *sales per mailing*, or *sales per 1,000 pieces mailed.* This final calculation is done by multiplying the percentage response (.0252) times net sales ($47) to give you a 0 percent, or variable, breakeven for the mailing.

$$.0252 \times \$47 = \$1.18 \text{ per piece mailed}$$

The second observation (B), showing the higher average order value ($100), presents quite a contrast. Following the same procedures as above, you arrive at a contribution before promotion of $45.70, better than double the lower average order. The calculation is the same: divide the promotion cost by the contribution before promotion to arrive at the answer in decimal format (.0109), or 1.09 percent. Similarly, to determine the *sales per mailing* or *sales per 1,000 pieces mailed*, the final calculation is done by multiplying the percentage response (.0109) times net sales ($94) to give you a 0 percent, or variable, breakeven for the mailing.

$$.0109 \times \$94 = \$1.03 \text{ per piece mailed}$$

The good thing about the breakeven is that it is a statistical observation. That is, one can prepare as many "what ifs" as desired.

Step 4: Organizing the Mailing Plan

You have lists selected with the list broker's help, and the breakeven has been prepared. Now the circulation planner is ready to prepare a spreadsheet of the actual mail plan. The worksheet shown in Exhibit 19-2 covers the important information.

Looking at the headings of the table, you will quickly discover how the spreadsheet is organized:

List Type/Name	Rental lists are put in alphabetical order to help assign a source code. When you are testing a great number of lists, lists can be categorized by type and separated from other categories.
Source Code	Each rental list is assigned a unique source code for tracking purposes. These are sometimes called sales codes, list codes, or key codes. No two lists should have the same source code identifier. It makes sense to plan ahead on source codes and to have some logic for the numbers and/or letters assigned. The coding system used in Exhibit 19-2 is very simple and straightforward.
	• AB = a two-digit alphabetical identifier of the list. If two digits aren't enough, use three.
	• 8 = the year of the mailing, 1998
	• A = the sequence of the mail drop during the year. A is the first, B is the second, and so on.
	Be careful not to use more digits than your mailer can accommodate, or they will be cut off and the source code will be lost.
Selection	This column contains the exact selections that are requested from the list owner through the list broker.
Quantity Available	The total number of names available for the specific list select is entered in this column.

Exhibit 19-2

FALL/HOLIDAY CIRCULATION PLAN

(Ranked in Alphabetical Order)

MAIL DATE: September 6

List Type/ Name	Source Code	Selection	Quantity Available	Quantity Selected	Postmerge Quantity
Anticipations	AN81	6 mo 50+ MOB		5,000	4,923
Ballard Designs	BD81	6 mo hotline MOB	57,397	5,000	4,752
Bloomingdale's by Mail	BL81	3 mo MOB, Dom/ home furn/tbl gifts	68,688	10,000	9,800
Chadwick's of Boston	CB81	Monthly hotline MOB	636,818	5,000	4,759
Charles Keath	CK81	3 mo hotline MOB	82,000	5,000	4,856
Careertrack Seminars	CT81	Quarterly hotline MOB, female	63,800	5,000	4,632
Exposures	EX81	3 mo hotline MOB	37,828	5,000	4,589
Faith Mountain	FM81	3 mo hotline MOB	41,164	5,000	4,956
Frederick's of Hollywood	FR81	3 mo hotline MOB	180,000	5,000	4,812
Garnet Hill	GH81	6 mo hotline MOB	129,300	5,000	4,723
Grand Finale	GF61	6 mo hotline MOB	15,466	5,000	4,695
Lillian Vernon at Home	LV81	3 mo hotline MOB, $100	27,000	5,000	4,985
Maryland Square	MS81	6 mo hotline MOB	60,000	5,000	4,853
Paragon	PA81	6 mo hotline MOB	422,000	5,000	4,759
Plow & Hearth	PH81	6 mo hotline MOB	84,281	5,000	4,587
Potpourri	PO81	3 mo hotline MOB, $75+	22,000	5,000	4,698
Pottery Barn	PB81	Monthly hotline MOB	163,048	8,000	7,698
Ross-Simons	RO81	3 mo hotline MOB, tabletop and gift	105,495	8,000	7,722
Spiegel	SP81	3 mo MOB, housewares, home furn	96,890	10,000	9,614
Storybook Heirlooms	SH81	6 mo hotline MOB, $50+	93,366	7,500	7,248
Sturbridge Yankee Workshop	SY	6 mo hotline MOB	45,065	5,000	4,900
Tapestry	TA81	3 mo hotline MOB, $75+	33,845	10,000	9,758
Victoria's Secret	VS81	Monthly hotline MOB, female	540,000	10,000	9,826
W. M. Green	WG81	6 mo hotline MOB	35,944	5,000	4,862
Williams Sonoma	WS81	3 mo hotline MOB, female	104,300	8,000	7,522
Yield House	YH81	6 mo hotline MOB, gifts and access.	106,289	5,000	4,879
Multibuyers	MB81A	2X Multibuyers— Spring 1998			6,754
Multibuyers	MB81B	3+X Multibuyers— Spring 1998			2,701
Total outside lists			**3,251,984**	**161,500**	**164,863**

| Quantity Selected | The actual number of names being rented is given. |
| Postmerge Quantity | This is the quantity of unduplicated names actually being mailed, after the merge-purge. |

Most marketers don't go any further than this. That's a mistake. The proper technique is to select the lists, complete the merge-purge, and then *forecast* how they will respond. Will you be wrong the first time you attempt to forecast new lists, never before mailed? Count on it. But the second time, you will get smarter. And the third time, as you start reusing lists (sometimes called a rollout or full scale), you will be amazed at how accurate forecasting will become. Therefore, we recommend completing the rest of the spreadsheet (see Exhibit 19-3).

Forecast % Response	This is your best guess as to what percentage of the total will respond.
Forecast AOV	Again, you make your best estimate of the average order from each list.
Forecast $ per Mailing	This number can be calculated two ways: 1. Total sales ÷ Quantity mailed 2. Percentage response × Average order value It is the most important measurement of a mailing and should be compared with the break-even analysis discussed above.
Orders	You calculate this number: quantity mailed × percentage response.
Gross Sales	This, your estimated gross sales (before returns and cancellations), is calculated: orders received × average order value.

Sales per mailing is so important that you have sorted and ranked the lists from highest to lowest, based on their forecast, by this factor. Now you can draw a line indicating where the lists are attaining the 0 percent, or variable, breakeven. Mailers will often mail below their breakeven, but it is essential that they know precisely what it costs to get a customer and what they can afford.

Outside rental lists being merge-purged are generally put in priority order with the best list ranked first and the worst list ranked last. In this manner, names are always compared with higher-ranked lists. When a company is mailing for the first time, any guess at priority is OK. After the first mailing, you will have a much better idea which lists are performing best, average, or poorly. Lower-responding lists are typically eliminated, but new list tests are always added and normally put at the bottom of the list priority order.

That's pretty much what a mailing or prospect or circulation plan is all about. If there are multiple drops of prospect lists, each mail drop and each list in the mailing is given a unique source code for tracking.

Exhibit 19-3

FALL/HOLIDAY CIRCULATION PLAN: FORECASTS
(Ranked by Estimated Dollars Generated per Mailing)

MAIL DATE: September 6

List Type/ Name	Source Code	Selection	Quantity Available	Quantity Selected	Postmerge Quantity	Forecast % Response	Forecast AOV	Forecast $/Mailing	Orders	Gross Sales
Spiegel	SP81	3 mo MOB, housewares, home furn	96,890	10,000	9,614	3.00%	$115	$3.45	288	$33,168
Multibuyers	MB81B	3+X Multibuyers—Spring 1998			2,701	3.61	95	3.43	98	9,263
Multibuyers	MB81A	2X Multibuyers—Spring 1998			6,754	2.57	89	2.29	174	15,448
Careertrack Seminars	CT81	Quarterly hotline MOB, female	63,800	5,000	4,632	2.00	100	2.00	93	9,264
Ross-Simons	RO81	3 mo hotline MOB, tabletop & gift	105,495	8,000	7,722	1.75	90	1.58	135	12,162
Williams Sonoma	WS81	3 mo hotline MOB, female	104,300	8,000	7,522	2.00	75	1.50	150	11,283
Yield House	YH81	6 mo hotline MOB, gifts & access.	106,289	5,000	4,879	1.25	99	1.24	61	6,038
Sturbridge Yankee Workshop	SY81	6 mo hotline MOB	45,065	5,000	4,900	1.25	89	1.11	61	5,451
Pottery Barn	PB81	Monthly hotline MOB	163,048	8,000	7,698	1.25	85	1.06	96	8,179
Chadwick's of Boston	CB81	Monthly hotline MOB	636,818	5,000	4,759	1.50	68	1.02	71	4,854
Garnet Hill	GH81	6 mo hotline MOB	129,300	5,000	4,723	1.25	80	1.00	59	4,723
Victoria's Secret	VS81	Monthly hotline MOB, female	540,000	10,000	9,826	1.25	75	0.94	123	9,212

(continued on next page)

FALL/HOLIDAY CIRCULATION PLAN: FORECASTS (continued)
(Ranked by Estimated Dollars Generated per Mailing)

List Type/ Name	Source Code	Selection	Quantity Available	Quantity Selected	Postmerge Quantity	Forecast % Response	Forecast AOV	Forecast $/Mailing	Orders	Gross Sales
Lillian Vernon at Home	LV81	3 mo hotline MOB, $100	27,000	5,000	4,985	1.25	$75	0.94	62	$4,673
Ballard Designs	BD81	6 mo hotline MOB	57,397	5,000	4,752	1.25	72	0.90	59	4,277
Exposures	EX81	3 mo hotline MOB	37,828	5,000	4,589	1.25	68	0.85	57	3,901
Paragon	PA81	6 mo hotline MOB	422,000	5,000	4,759	1.25	65	0.81	59	3,867
Storybook Heirlooms	SH81	6 mo hotline MOB, $50+	93,366	7,500	7,248	1.00	80	0.80	72	5,798
Charles Keath	CK81	3 mo hotline MOB	82,000	5,000	4,856	1.00	70	0.70	49	3,399
W. M. Green	WG81	6 mo hotline MOB	35,944	5,000	4,862	1.00	68	0.68	49	3,306
Bloomingdale's by Mail	BL81	3 mo MOB, dom/ home furn/tbl gifts	68,688	10,000	9,800	0.75	90	0.68	74	6,615
Grand Finale	GF61	6 mo hotline MOB	15,466	5,000	4,695	0.70	95	0.67	33	3,122
Frederick's of Hollywood	FR81	3 mo hotline MOB	180,000	5,000	4,812	0.90	70	0.63	43	3,032
Tapestry	TA81	3 mo hotline MOB, $75+	33,845	10,000	9,758	0.90	68	0.61	88	5,972
Potpourri	PO81	3 mo hotline MOB, $75+	22,000	5,000	4,698	1.00	50	0.50	47	2,349
Plow & Hearth	PH81	6 mo hotline MOB	84,281	5,000	4,587	0.50	90	0.45	23	2,064
Maryland Square	MS81	6 mo hotline MOB	60,000	5,000	4,853	0.80	50	0.40	39	1,941
Anticipations	AN81	6 mo 50+ MOB		5,000	4,923	0.60	65	0.39	30	1,920
Faith Mountain	FM81	3 mo hotline MOB	41,164	5,000	4,956	0.50	60	0.30	25	1,487
Total outside lists			3,251,984	161,500	164,863	1.35%	$84	$1.13	2,218	$186,769

New Names: Cost Versus Quality

A food-by-mail company is considering a number of rental lists for testing a new food mailer. The *list cost per thousand* ($/M) varies from a low of $80 for some response names to a high of $120 for highly targeted response lists with quite detailed selections.

If everything (expected percentage response, average order value, and sales per piece mailed) is equal, it would make sense to choose lists by their cost—always saving money by choosing the least expensive. The company would save by keeping down the cost per promotion in the mail. But everything is never equal. Other factors must be considered.

The second measurement the mailer must consider is the *cost to acquire a new name or new customer*. The formula below shows how to determine the cost per customer on rented names. The formula is quite simple:

> Total mailings × Percentage of response =
>   Total orders or new buyers × Average order value = Gross sales
> Gross sales × Margin percentage before advertising = Gross margin
> Gross margin − Advertising cost, including list rental =
>   Profit contribution or loss
> Profit or loss ÷ New buyers = Cost per name

In Exhibit 19-4, three examples are shown with dramatically different costs per name, depending on response and average order value. Parallel examples are shown for measuring the cost of a new name from space advertising.

Is measuring cost per name the final or ultimate criterion a company should use in determining which lists or space ads to use in the future? The answer is a definite no! The ultimate test of a list or space ad, or of any other media used for new customer acquisition, is the value of these names over time. Chapter 12 dealt extensively with that measurement, *lifetime value*. The better a name performs over time (i.e., rebuys and spends more dollars), the greater the value to your company. Quality of names, not quantity of names, counts in measuring success and profitability.

Customer and House List Circulation Plan

If you have followed the logic of the prospect circulation plan, then applying the same process to the customer and other house-owned names will be quite simple. But first, review several almost obvious tenets about the customer, or house, file.

The Importance of Building the House File

One of the drivers of success of any database marketing–driven company is the number of customers or prospect names that the company owns and can regularly communicate with or promote. Why is this important? Consider these reasons:

Exhibit 19-4

MEASURING THE COST OF ACQUIRING A CUSTOMER

A. One-Step Direct Sale: List Rental

	VARIABLE COSTS	CALCULATION		
		EXAMPLE A	EXAMPLE B	EXAMPLE C
Total mailings		1,000,000	1,000,000	1,000,000
Response rate		2.00%	1.00%	2.00%
Total responses—new buyers		20,000	10,000	20,000
Average order value		$50	$50	$100
Gross sales		$1,000,000	$500,000	$2,000,000
Margin before advertising*	35%	$350,000	$175,000	$700,000
Advertising cost, including list rental	$0.60	$600,000	$600,000	$600,000
Profit contribution (loss)		($250,000)	($425,000)	$100,000
Cost per name—profit (loss)		($12.50)	($42.50)	$5.00

B. One-Step Direct Sale: Space Ad

	VARIABLE COSTS	CALCULATION		
		EXAMPLE A	EXAMPLE B	EXAMPLE C
Total circulation		1,000,000	1,000,000	1,000,000
Response rate		0.10%	0.05%	0.05%
Total responses—new buyers		1,000	500	500
Average order value		$19.95	$19.95	$39.95
Gross sales		$19,950	$9,975	$19,975
Margin before advertising*	35%	$6,983.50	$3,491	$6,991
Advertising cost— space ad, per 1,000	$10.00	$10,000	$10,000	$10,000
Profit contribution (loss)			($6,509)	($3,009)
Cost per name—profit (loss)		($3.02)	($13.02)	($6.02)

*Sales – Cost of goods and fulfillment.

◆ These are names that you own and don't have to rent or spend money to prospect. Your savings can be 10 to 12 cents per name.

◆ Once a customer buys from your company, you can start building an affinity relationship—something that you will never have with rental names or prospects from other media.

- Customers will outperform noncustomers by a factor of 2 or 4 or even as high as 10. The higher a customer is on the recency-frequency-monetary (RFM) hierarchy, the greater the difference in sales per piece mailed.
- When a company builds the house file and captures the relevant purchase and demographic history on its database, it can model, test, and statistically manipulate the names for maximum effectiveness and profitability.

Therefore, the house file (customers, prospects, inquiries, gift recipients, etc.) is really the starting place for circulation planning. When times are tough, smart companies will limit their prospecting and concentrate on their house list promotions. And even for these house names, they will use tighter selection criteria.

Now, on to the steps in preparing a customer communication plan.

Steps in Plan Preparation

Step 1: Prepare the Annual Mailing Plan

Developing the annual mailing or communication strategy for the year (number of customer and other list mailings) is the starting point. As mentioned in Chapter 18, most companies tend to undercommunicate with their own customers. The challenge is to build a communication plan that maximizes the company's sales yet doesn't make customers feel they are being inundated with mailings.

Step 2: Review the Current Customer and House List Inventory

The rationale for the house list and buyer inventory, as mentioned earlier, now starts to make more sense. As mailers contemplate the next mailing of the house names, the first question that arises is how many names do they have by recency, frequency, and monetary for buyers and by recency for nonbuyers. Assume that your list inventory gives you the counts shown in Exhibit 19-5.

Step 3: Preparing the Break-Even Analysis

Earlier in this chapter, we looked at the prospect breakeven, or a variable breakeven at 0 percent profit. With the customer and house-owned names, the breakeven goes to two additional levels:

1. *A breakeven covering all fixed costs.* For example, if the company's fixed costs (general and administrative, or G&A, costs) are 7 percent, then that figure is used for this breakeven. If fixed costs are 10 percent, then that number is the break-even goal. This is typically the break-even goal for nonbuyer house names or customers who haven't purchased for a year or two.
2. *A breakeven covering all fixed costs* and *the profit contribution for the company.* Remember the role of the "back-end," or customer, list: to generate the profits to sustain future growth, pay all fixed costs, and pay a satisfactory return to the own-

Exhibit 19-5

COUNTING THE HOUSE NAMES

Buyers

	CREDIT CARD HOLDERS	OTHER BUYERS	TOTAL
Last 6 month buyers	60,000	10,000	70,000
Last 7–12 month buyers	20,000	5,000	25,000
Last 13–24 month buyers	50,000	7,500	57,500
Last 25–36 month buyers	40,000	5,000	45,000
Older than 36 month buyers	100,000	52,500	152,500
Total buyers (by recency only)	270,000	80,000	350,000

Nonbuyers

Inquiry names—last 12 months	20,000		
Inquiry names—last 13–24 months	15,000		
Inquiry names—older than 24 months	30,000		
Total nonbuyer house names	65,000		

ers of the business. Assume for this case that the profit goal is a 10 percent pretax profit. The second customer breakeven is therefore pegged at 10 percent plus the fixed-cost breakeven (7 percent + 10 percent = 17 percent customer breakeven goal). The fully loaded breakeven (17 percent) is the goal for the recent buyers, the last 24 month actives.

The breakeven in Exhibit 19-6 shows the calculation, which is similar to that for the prospect breakeven. The only tricky part is the need to reduce contribution before promotion by 17 percent of net sales (17 percent × $47 = $7.99 for the $50 example; 17 percent × $94 = $15.98 for the $100 example). This breakeven presents a fully loaded breakeven covering all overhead (G&A) and the profit goal. In the example, they are figured at 7 percent overhead and 10 percent for profit goal.

Step 4: Organizing the Mailing Plan

The next step is to prepare a detailed spreadsheet similar to the prospects spreadsheet shown in Exhibit 19-3. Exhibit 19-7 (see the case study at the end of this chapter) shows the detailed layout of the customer and house list mailing plan. Every column is similar to one in the prospect list, except that a "Special Message"column has been added to reflect special reactivation messages that might be added to an envelope, used as a wraparound for a catalog, or affixed in-line at the printer through a "dot whack" (a cover sticker added to selected lists in the binding or insertion phase of the mailing).

Exhibit 19-6

BREAK-EVEN ANALYSIS FOR HOUSE/CUSTOMER LIST

		A	B
Average unit price		$33.33	$66.67
Average units per order		1.5	1.5
Average per order		$50	$100
Cancellations	1%	(.50)	(1.00)
Returns	5%	(2.50)	(5.00)
Net sales		$47.00	$94.00
Cost of goods			
Adjustment for salvaged returns and cancellations	45%	(21.15)	(42.30)
Markdowns			
Shipping			
Order entry/processing	$6 per order for fulfillment	(6.00)	(6.00)
Shipping/handling income			
Contribution before promotion		$19.85	$45.70
Overhead and profit contribution at 0% of net sales		(7.99)	(15.98)
Overhead and profit contribution at 17% of net sales		11.86	29.72
Cost per promotional piece		$.50	$.50

Conclusions

Promotion cost:

Gross margin × 100 = Break-even response rate (%)

Overhead and profit contribution at 17% of net sales

	A	B
Percentage	4.22%	1.68%
$ per mailing*	$1.98	$1.58

*Dollars per mailing = Percentage response × Net sales.

Exhibit 19-7

ADOLPHSON'S CUSTOMER LIST CIRCULATION PLAN, SPRING 1998

Summary

Mail Date	Description of Mailing	In-Home Date	Quantity
January 15	House list—drop #1	January 25	415,000
March 15	House list—drop #2	March 25	232,500
May 15	House list—drop #3	May 25	172,500
Total Spring 1998 mailings			**820,000**

FIRST MAIL DATE: January 2

Type List	Source Code	List	Selection	Special Message	Quantity Available	Quantity Mailed
House	BU81A	Last 6 month buyers	Credit card buyers—all		60,000	60,000
House	BU81B	Last 6 month buyers	Non–credit card buyers—all		10,000	10,000
House	BU81C	Last 7–12 month buyers	Credit card buyers—all		20,000	20,000
House	BU81D	Last 7–12 month buyers	Non–credit card buyers—all		5,000	5,000
House	BU81E	Last 13–24 month buyers	Credit card buyers—all	We miss you	50,000	50,000
House	BU81F	Last 13–24 month buyers	Non–credit card buyers—all	We miss you	7,500	7,500
House	BU81G	Last 25–36 month buyers	Credit card buyers—all	We miss you	40,000	40,000
House	BU81H	Last 25–36 month buyers	Non–credit card buyers—all	We miss you	5,000	5,000
House	BU81I	Buyers older than 36 mo.	Credit card buyers—all	We miss you	100,000	100,000
House	BU81J	Buyers older than 36 mo.	Non–credit card buyers	We miss you	52,500	52,500
House	IN81A	Last 12 month inquiries	All		20,000	20,000
House	IN81B	Last 13–24 month inquiries	All	We miss you	15,000	15,000
House	IN81C	Inquiries older than 24 mo.	All	Last chance	30,000	30,000
Total house					**415,000**	**415,000**

SECOND MAIL DATE: March 15

Type List	Source Code	List	Selection	Special Message	Quantity Available	Quantity Mailed
House	BU81A	Last 6 month buyers	Credit card buyers—all		60,000	60,000
House	BU81B	Last 6 month buyers	Non–credit card buyers—all		10,000	10,000
House	BU81C	Last 7–12 month buyers	Credit card buyers—all		20,000	20,000
House	BU81D	Last 7–12 month buyers	Non–credit card buyers—all		5,000	5,000

(continued)

Exhibit 19-7 (continued)

Type List	Source Code	List	Selection	Special Message	Quantity Available	Quantity Mailed
House	BU81E	Last 13–24 month buyers	Credit card buyers—all	We want you back	50,000	50,000
House	BU81F	Last 13–24 month buyers	Non–credit card buyers—all	We want you back	7,500	7,500
House	BU81G	Last 25–36 month buyers	Credit card buyers—all	We want you back	40,000	40,000
House	BU81H	Last 25–36 month buyers	Non–credit card buyers—all	We want you back	5,000	5,000
House	BU81I	Buyers older than 36 mo.	Credit card buyers—all		100,000	0
House	BU81J	Buyers older than 36 mo.	Non–credit card buyers		52,500	0
House	IN81A	Last 12 month inquiries	All		20,000	20,000
House	IN81B	Last 13–24 month inquiries	All	Last chance	15,000	15,000
House	IN81C	Inquiries older than 24 mo.	All		30,000	0
Total house					**415,000**	**232,500**

THIRD MAIL DATE: May 15

Type List	Source Code	List	Selection	Special Message	Quantity Available	Quantity Mailed
House	BU81A	Last 6 month buyers	Credit card buyers—all		60,000	60,000
House	BU81B	Last 6 month buyers	Non–credit card buyers—all		10,000	10,000
House	BU81C	Last 7–12 month buyers	Credit card buyers—all		20,000	20,000
House	BU81D	Last 7–12 month buyers	Non–credit card buyers—all		5,000	5,000
House	BU81E	Last 13–24 month buyers	Credit card buyers—all	Don't let this be	50,000	50,000
House	BU81F	Last 13–24 month buyers	Non–credit card buyers—all	your last mailing	7,500	7,500
House	BU81G	Last 25–36 month buyers	Credit card buyers—all		40,000	0
House	BU81H	Last 25–36 month buyers	Non–credit card buyers—all		5,000	0
House	BU81I	Buyers older than 36 mo.	Credit card buyers—all		100,000	0
House	BU81J	Buyers older than 36 mo.	Non–credit card buyers		52,500	0
House	IN81A	Last 12 month inquiries	All		20,000	20,000
House	IN81B	Last 13–24 month inquiries	All		15,000	0
House	IN81C	Inquiries older than 24 mo.	All		30,000	0
Total house					**415,000**	**172,500**

Step 5: Forecasting Each Mailing

One difference smart circulation planning can make to long-term profitability is to actually forecast the entire results of the mailing. This is done by individual list segment, much as we saw in the prospect mailing. For each mail drop, you make a number of forecasts: response percentage, average order value (AOV), orders received, total gross sales, and sales per mailing.

As indicated earlier in the chapter, sales per piece mailed is the key indicator of success, especially when related to the breakeven. For the breakeven shown in Exhibit 19-6, two observations are presented: one with a $50 order and one with a $100 order. The full break-even goals (covering overhead and profit contribution) are $1.98 and $1.58, respectively. In the case study, a detailed forecast has been prepared for each list segment in the first mail drop (January 2) (see Exhibit 19-8).

Step 6: Preparing a Financial Forecast for Each Mail Drop

From the final circulation or mail plan forecast comes the last step: the development of a profit-and-loss projection for each mail drop and for the season. The P&L format we suggest is representative of the type of detail that most marketers would like to see. Some of your numbers are going to be hard information—very specific to the mailing, such as cost per promotion in the mail or cost of goods. Other data will come from historical information (returns, cancels, cost to fulfill an order, etc.).

Costs throughout a P&L are broken into two types, fixed and variable. *Fixed costs* are allocated; they are not charged per order or per thousand. The creative cost of designing and writing the mailing or color separations are examples of fixed costs. *Variable costs* vary with the number of pieces mailed or orders received. Printing, postage, fulfillment, and cost of goods are examples of variable costs.

Refer to Exhibit 19-9 in the case study that follows. Notice the detail that goes into cost of goods, fulfillment, and advertising. Most marketers are judged by the contribution to overhead and profit line on the P&L. They seldom can impact or control the overhead (general and administrative) costs allocated to a campaign. Similarly, list rental income is not part of the controllable portion of a mailing's P&L.

Exhibit 19-8   ADOLPHSON'S FORECAST FOR FIRST MAIL DATE

Spring 1998 Circulation Plan:

Source Code	List	Selection	Quantity Available	Quantity Mailed	Percentage Response	Average Order Value	Orders	Sales	Dollars per Mailing
BU81A	Last 6 months buyers	Credit card buyers—all	60,000	60,000	12.5%	$150	7,500	$1,125,000	$18.75
BU81B	Last 6 month buyers	Non–credit card buyers—all	10,000	10,000	6.0	100	600	60,000	6.00
BU81C	Last 7–12 month buyers	Credit card buyers—all	20,000	20,000	10.0	120	2,000	240,000	12.00
BU81D	Last 7–12 month buyers	Non–credit card buyers—all	5,000	5,000	5.0	92	250	23,000	4.60
BU81E	Last 13–24 month buyers	Credit card buyers—all	50,000	50,000	6.0	84	3,000	252,000	5.04
BU81F	Last 13–24 month buyers	Non–credit card buyers—all	7,500	7,500	4.6	61	345	21,045	2.81
BU81G	Last 25–36 month buyers	Credit card buyers—all	40,000	40,000	4.1	78	1,640	127,920	3.20
BU81H	Last 25–36 month buyers	Non–credit card buyers—all	5,000	5,000	2.0	55	100	5,500	1.10
BU81I	Buyers older than 36 mo.	Credit card buyers—all	100,000	100,000	2.1	59	2,100	123,900	1.24
BU81J	Buyers older than 36 mo.	Non–credit card buyers—all	52,500	52,500	1.6	48	840	40,320	0.77
IN81A	Last 12 month inquiries	All	20,000	20,000	3.0	68	600	40,800	2.04
IN81B	Last 13–24 month inquiries	All	15,000	15,000	1.5	49	225	11,025	0.74
IN81C	Inquiries older than 24 mo.	All	30,000	30,000	1.0	45	300	13,500	0.45
Total house			**415,000**	**415,000**	**4.7%**	**$107**	**19,500**	**$2,084,010**	**$5.02**

ADOLPHSON'S SPRING CIRCULATION PLAN (F)

The charts in Exhibit 19-7 show a model mailing strategy Adolphson's might employ for a spring season. Three mailings are planned: January 15, March 15, and May 15. Each mailing is anticipated to take a maximum of 10 days to reach targeted customers, using bulk rate (standard class) mail.

Adolphson's has prepared a detailed forecast for each list segment in the first mail drop, on January 2 (see Exhibit 19-8). The mailing does very well, responding overall at 4.7 percent, with an average order value of $107 or sales per mailing of $5.02. However, several lists are well below the break-even goal for house and customer lists:

- Last 25–36 month non–credit card buyers
- Credit card buyers older than 36 months
- 13–24 month inquiries
- Inquiries older than 24 months

Each list is forecast to be below the break-even goal but may be justified in mailing once to attempt to activate it. Mailing two or three times would not be justified.

Adolphson's followed up its forecast with a profit-and-loss (P&L) projection for the first spring mailing. In examining the P&L (Exhibit 19-9), you can see how fixed and variable costs begin to come together. The projection is in two basic columns showing the financial plan for the mail drop and the actual results. Once the mailing has been made and results are in, the actual numbers can be entered in the right-hand columns, and a comparison of plan to actual can be made.

This is a marvelous learning exercise! Surely your first forecast will be wrong, but each time you plan and project a new mailing, you will improve on your skills. Each mail drop rolls up into a season (in the Adolphson's case there were three spring mail drops). Ultimately, the seasons roll up into the marketing or circulation budget and sales plan for the year.

Exhibit 19-9

ADOLPHSON'S PROFIT-AND-LOSS PROJECTION: SPRING 1998 MAILING, DROP 1

Assumptions:

Mailing	415,000
Response percent	4.70%
Average order value	$107.00
Orders	19,505

	PLAN		ACTUAL	
	$	%	$	%
Gross sales	$2,084,010		$	%
Cancellations	41,680	2.0%		
Returns	229,241	11.0		
Net sales	1,813,089	100.0		
Cost of merchandise	906,544	50.0		
Markdowns	0			
Shrinkage/miscellaneous	0			
+ Co-op advertising discounts	4,500			
Total cost of goods	902,044	49.8		
Gross margin	**911,044**	**50.2**		
Order entry/telephone ($3 per order)	58,515	3.2		
Warehousing/pick/pack ($3 per order)	58,515	3.2		
Computer/systems ($2.50 per order)	48,763	2.7		
Shipping expense ($5 per order)	97,525	5.4		
Bank card charges (2.0%)	41,741	2.3		
Customer service	5,000	0.3		
+ Shipping and handling income ($5 per order)	97,525	5.4		
Total fulfillment	212,533	11.7		
Catalog creative	60,000	3.3		
Color separations	24,500	1.4		
Printing and mailing	166,000	9.2		
Lists/list preparation	7,800	0.4		
Postage	91,300	5.0		
Other promotion/advertising	0	0.0		
Total advertising	349,600	19.3		
Contribution to overhead and profit	**348,911**	**19.2**		
General and administrative salaries	0	0.0		
Fringes	0	0.0		
Utilities + rent	0	0.0		
Other G&A	0	0.0		
Total General & Administrative	162,271	9.0		
List rental income	0	0.0		
Total miscellaneous income	0	0.0		
Pretax profit/loss	186,640	10.3%	$	%

Managing a Marketing Database: Day-to-Day Issues

An ounce of action is worth a ton of theory.

Friedrich Engels (1820–95), German social philosopher

The day-to-day issues that businesses encounter when they employ marketing databases often seem mundane but are nevertheless critical. Different types of businesses have unique challenges that must be overcome, or any database marketing effort will not succeed.

Consumer catalog businesses, consumer retailers, business-to-business catalogers, and businesses that sell through reps may each need to follow different sets of rules in maintaining, correcting, and updating a marketing database. Here are some hints to take the "surprise" out of some typical issues.

Small Company or Professional (Client) Marketing Databases

Small marketing databases are those that can be updated and maintained manually. A car salesperson, an attorney, or an insurance salesperson, for example, should know and regularly contact each customer personally.

The purpose of the database is to organize information for users and allow access in any manner they choose. For example, if a salesperson keeps customers in a database, as opposed to 3″ × 5″ cards, they can be accessed in several ways, such as

- most recent purchasers
- most frequent purchasers
- all purchasers of a particular item or service
- all purchasers from a certain time period (such as last July)
- recent prospects

A salesperson who stores customer data on cards or in a notebook can only store them in one sort order, such as alphabetically or by last contact date. The computer will not relieve the work of adding names, deleting names, or making address changes but will help remind the salesperson whom to call, when to call, and so on.

CONSUMER DIRECT MARKETING

From a database perspective, consumer catalog marketers have the easiest job of maintaining a database. Customers must give their name and address to make a purchase, and the address must be correct for them to receive what they bought. Unlike retail, no transactions are made by "unknown" cash buyers.

Consumer catalogers normally "household" their customers, which means they count a household (a unique address) as if it were one person. For example, if a wife buys from Adolphson's catalog and then her husband calls and places a second order, the wife's customer number will be used for the second transaction. Since Adolphson's plans to send only one catalog per address (which is common for consumer catalogs), this simplification does not affect the output of the database.

Consumer catalogs do, however, have several unique challenges. One is dealing with post office (PO) box addresses and delivery addresses. Only the post office will deliver to a PO box, but UPS requires a physical address. If a customer lives at RR 4, Dubois, Wyoming, that is where the package must be sent; however, the post office may not deliver there. The "postal" address could be PO Box 429, Dubois, Wyoming.

If only the physical address (RR 4 in this case) is recorded, the package will arrive, but no catalogs will reach the customer by mail. Particularly if the catalogs are sent bulk mail (third class), the post office will discard rather than deliver them. To avoid this, a cataloger must record both addresses, mail catalogs to the PO box address, and deliver packages to the physical address.

The same sort of problem can arise when the buyer's address and the ship-to address are not the same. This can happen when a buyer's mailing address is a post-office box, but usually it occurs when buyers order gifts and the cataloger sends the gift directly to the recipient, or when buyers wish to receive delivery at their office (a growing trend).

In the case of gift givers, the recipients at the physical ship-to addresses are not the buyers, but they do become part of the house file. The cataloger needs to track whether they are gift recipients or whether the buyer has more than one address.

Gift recipients should be entered into the customer table and marked as gift recipients. Gift givers should be marked as well, and gift givers should be tied to their recipients. This can be done by giving each recipient a customer ID and storing that ID in a gift recipient field of the invoice table. This makes it possible to track who gave what to whom, and when.

Business-to-Business Direct Marketing

Business-to-business (B-to-B) databases have all the same challenges as consumer databases and then some. Multiple ship-to addresses, PO box and delivery addresses, and even gift giving (food by mail is mainly done business to business) are all challenges for business-to-business marketers.

The main challenge such marketers face is dealing with multiple names at each address. They may have (or need) a name for each of several titles and buying roles. Because businesses change employees faster than they change addresses, keeping names and titles up-to-date is much more of a challenge than keeping addresses up-to-date.

To cope with this challenge, many businesses are forced to call, write, or visit every prospect and customer in their database to keep the information current. For better customers and higher-potential prospects, this makes the most sense. Otherwise, names, titles, and addresses can be updated periodically through outside lists. These lists may be compiled lists or ones from trade publications.

A business-to-business database with multiple names at each address requires a different structure than a consumer database does. The B-to-B customer table gives each company it sells to a unique company ID. An additional table, a contacts table, lists the people at each company. Each has a unique ID plus a company ID that matches the employer in the customer table.

Although maintaining a business-to-business database can take a large amount of time and effort, the payoff in improved marketing effectiveness and in reduced waste mail can be tremendous.

Retail Databases

In making a database work, retailers face three main challenges:

1. Many cash transactions cannot be tracked.
2. There can be a huge amount of data per customer (e.g., a grocery store, where customers buy many items).
3. The data may not be of enough value to justify the cost.

If a retailer cannot track a large percentage of the transactions back to particular customers, telling how much, or what, each customer really buys is not possible. Is the captured amount all they bought or just half? Do they always pay by check, or do they occasionally run through the express lane and pay cash? Such inaccuracy will reduce the value and credibility of the database.

Capturing huge amounts of data can cost huge amounts of money. To track and store data on a $100 item costs just as much as tracking a $1 item, but it costs much less as a percent of sales. The information a grocery store captures, for example, is large amounts of small purchases, with thousands of possible items.

Data is worth capturing if it will improve marketing effectiveness by more than it costs to gather and store. If the data can be used to improve loyalty (*loyalty* being defined as becoming more profitable), that is good. If it is only being used to send discounts to frequent customers, however, it is probably not increasing profits. In all likelihood, customers who were loyal and profitable before will be given discounts and be less profitable. In that case the database actually drives profits down!

Managing Lead Generation

Many businesses generate prospects through magazine or newspaper ads, trade shows, card decks, and other means. The prospects become customers in a two-step process. To measure two-step offers, it is important to track the cost of obtaining the lead, the cost of following up the lead, and the value of the resulting sale (see Exhibit 20-1).

A common problem with advertising that generates sales *and* leads is that marketers often measure them improperly and underrate their value. The marketer may look only at initial sales or only at sales from the first follow-up with prospects.

No follow-up contact means no follow-up sales. As catalogers become more advanced with their marketing, they find out success really does come from hard work and salesmanship. Exhibit 20-1 illustrates this clearly. The example ad both offers a $19.95 item for direct sale and generates information requests. What is offered should be an easy-to-ship, low-priced, featured item specifically chosen for the one-step magazine ad. Consequently the average order, profit margin, and fulfillment cost will all be lower than for the average follow-up order. This is typical of what happens when catalogers feature one-step sale items in magazine ads.

Based on initial sales alone, the ad loses money. With only one or two follow-ups, it still loses money. Only by the fifth contact with each prospect do responses from the ad show a profit. Combining the one-step and the two-step responses to this ad shows it to be successful—an example of results from a good dual-purpose ad.

Judged by initial sales and first contact with prospects alone, the ad might seem to be a loser. If prospects had been followed up only once, it would be more appropriate to say, "We have met the enemy and it is us!" As long as recontacting prospects is profitable, they should be recontacted and the results measured by management.

The opposite mistake is possible. Sending out information, keeping people in a database, and calling long-distance are not free. Neither is employees' time. Only after considering all the costs of following up and making a sale can you effectively judge advertising.

Exhibit 20-1

ADVERTISING EXAMPLE

Two-Step Ad Worksheet—Do Not Enter Data Where Numbers Are Shown in Italics

Cost of space ad	$10,000.00	
Average one-step order	$19.95	
Average one-step cost of goods sold (%)	70.00%	
Average one-step fulfillment	$2.00	(loss after shipping and handling charge)
Contribution per order	*$3.99*	
Number of orders	800	
List rental value per name	$0.00	
Ad cost after sales	*$6,812.00*	(does not reflect lifetime value of new buyers)
Catalog requesters	2,000	
Entry cost of names	$1.00	(inbound 800#, data entry, etc.)
Cost per catalog request	*$4.41*	

Follow-up of catalog requests:

Average follow-up order	$75.00	
Average cost of goods sold (%)	50.00%	
Fullfilment cost per order	$5.00	(loss after shipping and handling charge)
Margin per sale	*$32.50*	

Response rates:		**Cost of each contact:**	
Initial request catalog	6.50%	Initial request catalog	$0.50
1st follow-up	5.50	1st follow-up	0.50
2nd follow-up	4.25	2nd follow-up	0.50
3rd follow-up	3.10	3rd follow-up	0.50
4th follow-up	2.00	4th follow-up	0.50
5th follow-up	0.00	5th follow-up	0.00
6th follow-up	0.00	6th follow-up	0.00
7th follow-up	0.00	7th follow-up	0.00
8th follow-up	0.00	8th follow-up	0.00
9th follow-up	0.00	9th follow-up	0.00

Contribution per contact:	
Initial request catalog	*$1.61*
1st follow-up	*1.29*
2nd follow-up	*0.88*
3rd follow-up	*0.51*
4th follow-up	*0.15*
5th follow-up	*0.00*
6th follow-up	*0.00*
7th follow-up	*0.00*
8th follow-up	*0.00*
9th follow-up	*0.00*

Value per request name	*$4.44*
Rental value per request	*$0.00*

Total value per request name	*$4.44*	
Total two-step sales	*427*	
Gain/(loss) on customer names	*$0.15*	(does not reflect lifetime value—initial sale only)

Supporting Reps or Dealers with a Marketing Database

The key challenge in gathering information through reps and dealers is getting the information at all. Many businesses expect that if they demand the information, they will get it. (This rarely happens.) It has to be worth the rep or dealer's time and not be a threat (they don't want to be cut out of future sales) before they will provide information beyond what they absolutely have to.

The structure of the database will depend on how customers are tracked. If dealers buy and inventory the product, it may not be possible to gather data on end-user consumers. If reps or dealers make the sale and the product is shipped directly to the consumer, then consumer data can be tracked. The rep is then basically the same as a salesperson in terms of database design.

Working with Business and Consumer Mailing Lists

Combining lists from different sources into a single, nonduplicated list is called a merge-purge. Two or more lists are merged together, and duplicate names are purged. Several software packages on the market perform this operation relatively quickly. To have high accuracy, however, the lists must all be in the same format, with the same fields, and addresses must be standardized. Often this is easier said than done.

Consumer addresses are sometimes referred to as three-line addresses because they have three lines, like this:

1. Name
2. Street address
3. City, state, ZIP

Business addresses are sometimes referred to as four-line addresses because they have four lines, like this:

1. Name
2. Company
3. Street address
4. City, state, ZIP

However, having four lines does not always mean an address is a business address. For example, a consumer address could look like this:

1. Name
2. Apartment number
3. Street address
4. City, state, ZIP

An address could have five lines and look like this:

1. Name
2. Company
3. Suite or office number
4. Street address
5. City, state, ZIP

or

1. Name
2. Title
3. Company
4. Street address
5. City, state, ZIP

If names and addresses are stored in a table with a company address line or two address lines, data may get into the wrong field. It is not uncommon to find the company name in the second address line, or an "Attn: Shipping" in the company field. This is a particular problem when there are not enough fields to properly enter the name, title, company name, secondary address, and primary address.

Before you attempt to remove duplicates, data must be in the correct field. Normally, this is an ongoing process. Although corrections can be done with software packages, making sure data is entered properly will avoid such problems later.

National Change of Address (NCOA) can be used periodically to update addresses of customers and prospects who may have moved. This sort of update is particularly useful when done prior to a merge-purge, as it will improve the odds of finding duplicates.

Fixing Broken Databases

Keeping names and addresses clean and up-to-date goes a long way toward preventing problems in the future. At times, however, databases produce incorrect information and must be fixed. Here are some common problems and solutions.

Missing Data
Failing to enter source codes with orders is the most common mistake. This makes tracking which list buyers are coming from impossible. In this case, comparing the list that was mailed and the list of buyers without source codes is often possible. This is done the same way as a merge-purge: the buyers who match an outside list are assigned the source code for that list.

Duplicate Customer Numbers
Customer numbers get duplicated when customer data is entered incorrectly and/or the old customer record is not used with a new order. In this case, matches are found

as in a merge-purge, and either the most recent or the most complete customer record is retained. The customer ID of the invoices matching the deleted customer record is changed to match the one being retained. This way no purchase history is lost. Once this is done, recency, frequency, monetary value (RFM) must be recalculated to be accurate.

Old Data

If a database contains many years of customer history and older data is not desired, it can be purged. However, remember the following:

◆ Do not eliminate original source code information for any customer being retained.
◆ Eliminate only customers who have not bought for some time, not those who first bought several years ago. Some are likely to still be customers.
◆ Do not eliminate discontinued products if they are represented in any invoices that are being retained.

In general, it is best to stay on top of the health of the database and fix problems at the source. In the long run, this approach is far more practical.

Protecting Your Assets (Keeping Data Safe)

Any marketing database should be stored where it is safe from theft, fire, and vandalism. A backup copy should be made at least as often as the database is updated or any time a major change occurs. It is not a good idea to store backup tapes or disks in the same area as the computer, as something (fire, flood, etc.) could happen to both.

Seed names are phony names added to the database, names only the owner of the database is aware of. Seed names are particularly important to use when the list is rented, either directly or through a list manager. If a mailing comes using the seed name, and the owner did not create the mailing or rent the list, it is proof that the list has been stolen. Actually, seed names should be in the database whether the list is rented or not. If an employee leaves for a competitor and seed names start appearing on the competitor's mailings, the company can put a very quick stop to it!

Certain names should be suppressed and never mailed or called. People may specifically ask to be removed from the list, but if removed they could reappear and be mailed again. Better to keep the name and mark it "do not mail" to prevent this from happening. Other names are suppressed if they have bad credit or legal action pending (which does happen occasionally).

Database information should never be "shown off" to customers. Never write something like this to a customer: "Dear Mr. Jones, Now that you've had your third child, owe only $72,000 on your home, and earn $2,850 a month, we want to offer you a new banking plan." This sort of letter will succeed only in making Mr. Jones think you know too much about his business. Of course, all this information can be found on any bank loan application and any bank could send a letter like this, but fortunately most have the good sense not to.

In general, never use a database in such a way that customers feel "Big Brother" is watching them. It will make people uneasy about databases in general, and your database in particular.

CASE STUDY

DAY-TO-DAY DATABASE ISSUES AT ADOLPHSON'S (G)

Since Adolphson's has chosen to operate its catalog database separately from its store databases, the day-to-day work is much simpler than otherwise possible. The challenge for Adolphson's is to mine its store database(s) for catalog prospect names.

Store names, from either credit card customers or other sources, must be continuously entered correctly (in the right fields), standardized, and merge-purged. This will not be a small task! Then, when Adolphson's mails a catalog, the store list, which has had duplicates removed, must be merge-purged against the list of customers and catalog requesters from Adolphson's catalog software, Mail Order Wizard.

When these lists are merge-purged, Adolphson's will keep any catalog buyer names that match a store name and purge the store name from the list. This will provide a single, nonduplicated house list. With rented lists, if a name matches any name in the house file, the house file name is kept and the rented name is dropped.

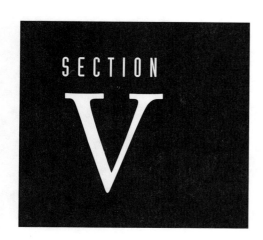

SECTION

V

Case Studies

Case Studies

Experience comprises illusions lost, rather than wisdom gained.

Joseph Roux (1834–86), French priest, writer. *Meditations of a Parish Priest* (1886).

DEALING WITH MULTIPLE CUSTOMER DATABASES: THE DATABASE NEEDS OF A CONGLOMERATE

A conglomerate that owns several companies is located in California. It does business primarily in one major metropolitan area. Over the course of several years, it purchased three smaller companies that sell baked goods through both stores and direct mail. The companies are similar in size and their offering of baked goods, but their customer bases, targeting of offers, and product selections are all quite different.

Since the three companies were originally independent, their databases were all quite different. However, under one owner, all the goods are now baked at and shipped from a central location. Phone orders are taken by an outside firm that specializes in inbound telemarketing. All orders are then sent electronically to the bakery to be fulfilled.

The database the telemarketers use is different from any of the three customer

databases, which are stored at the bakery and used for marketing purposes. Older customer data, therefore, could not be easily used in a single database with new customer data. What this conglomerate wanted to do was to standardize all three databases, be able to update with data generated by telemarketing, and streamline the process of using customer data for marketing.

Fortunately, someone on staff was working with all three databases and had helped set up the bakery and telemarketing arrangement. Rather than rely on a major computer system, the parent company chose to hire a consultant (J. Schmid & Associates Inc.) to set up a marketing database with its employee and to train the employee as the project went along.

The first step was to review the design of the telemarketing firm's database and compare it with the other databases. All the information that needed to be gathered from the customer (name, address, phone number, and so on) was being stored in the telemarketing database. It was not normalized in as ideal a manner as it perhaps should have been, but it was at least adequate as a basic structure.

The older information from the three databases (gathered before the telemarketing firm came on the scene) was "forced" into the same structure as the updates that telemarketing was providing. This made adding information easy, as the structure of incoming data did not have to be changed. It also prevented a major change in the inbound system, which would have been very costly.

The biggest challenge was getting the names into the same format (first, last, etc.) and the correct data in the company/secondary address/primary address fields. This had to be done to find duplicates and assign purchase histories accurately. It was possible for a customer to be in the old database with one customer number and some purchase history and to be in the newer database from telemarketing with another customer number and some purchase history. In addition to cleaning up the name and address fields, National Change of Address (NCOA) was run on all the names to improve matching accuracy.

Another challenge was that gift recipients were not given a unique ID number. Unfortunately, customers who had received a cake or box of cookies as a gift and later made a purchase were listed in two separate tables. Ideally, gift recipients should be given a customer number and be made part of the house file. Since this was not the case, the consultant had to match all the recipients by name and address to find duplicates and matches to the customer list.

Because all the corresponding fields in the tables of the three databases have the same field name, field length, and data types, programs that work for one work for all. This greatly sped up creating update programs for RFM, square-inch analysis, and revenue by source code reports. Also, because the databases have exactly the same structure, it is very easy to match customers across databases or to remove duplicates when cross-mailing between companies.

Another advantage to a common structure is that it makes learning to use the various databases easier. Unlike a single database, where something needs to be reported, printed, or analyzed once a month or once a week, having three databases requires three versions of each report. Forgetting how to operate the system is harder when there is more chance to practice!

Why didn't the conglomerate choose to have only one database with all three companies' customers? The answer is simple. Although the businesses are selling similar products (baked goods) in a similar manner (catalogs), they are quite separate in how they market and to whom they market. Keeping the databases apart makes it easier to focus on separate marketing for each company.

The resulting marketing database helps the whole group more easily determine who their customers are, which customers they want to mail, and what sort of sales they are getting from each catalog and each customer. In addition, the marketing database is far easier to use than the previous databases were. Even some of the non-marketing-related reports from an older system have been replaced by reports from the marketing database, which are more accurate, faster, and easier to obtain information from.

This project was completed over a four-month period, with the consultants working for two days every four weeks. The entire database was created on an existing PC, with the only additional expenses being a larger hard drive and a copy of FoxPro. A relatively low-budget project, given its scope, it is making a big difference in marketing for the conglomerate.

CASE STUDY 2

FIXING A "BROKEN" DATABASE

A catalog company sells upscale children's merchandise to new parents and grandparents. Items such as infant seats, toys, and unique bottle warmers fill its catalog, which features just about every baby accessory young parents might need.

The company, however, was having one simple problem that caused management to doubt the accuracy of its marketing database: sales figures obtained from the marketing database were consistently too high. When the company started to hear about customers not getting their catalogs, it decided to have J. Schmid & Assoc. Inc. review its database to see what was wrong.

In this case, there were really two databases—one at company offices, where the data was gathered (the cataloger did its own fulfillment), and the one at the list manager, which functioned as the marketing database. The company would send updated information, gathered through order fulfillment, to its list manager, and the list manager would create mailing lists.

To determine a customer's recency, frequency, monetary value (RFM), the M must be correct. If the two systems disagree on total sales, then individual customers will surely be different as well. The possibility existed that the wrong people were being mailed too often, and the right ones not often enough.

As it turned out, the data in the marketing database was incorrect. On a high percentage of the orders it was overstating the actual sales total. The reason was quite simple, and it is a very common mistake.

Looking at the two databases, the consultant compared invoice records of the two systems and found that the sale amount in the marketing database always equaled the sales total from the fulfillment system. However, it did not match the net sales amount. (Recall in Chapter 3 that the invoice header contains a gross sales field, as well as discounts, other charges, and the net sale amount.) The sale amount in the marketing database matched the gross sales from

the fulfillment system! Discounts and other charges (other charges were usually an additional discount) were not reflected. As a result, the net sales amount from the fulfillment system was usually less than the sales amount in the marketing database.

Another discovery bears a lesson for many direct marketers. This cataloger's customers are often young and recently married. As a result, many of its female customers have recently changed their last names. It was not taking this into account when removing duplicates that caused unneeded duplication in mailings. Because of its market, the company needed to adjust to make sure it handled changed last names properly.

These were just minor details to a programmer, but they were very big deals to marketers. They show clearly that it really pays to know what is going on with the database.

CASE STUDY 3

BUILDING A DATABASE THAT WORKS FOR EVERYBODY

The Kansas City Direct Marketing Association (KCDMA) is the third-largest local direct marketing association in the United States, just behind New York and Chicago. Until recently, it did not have a single database but rather had several versions of the membership list and nothing like an invoice table at all! It was not possible to tell who attended which meeting, and a member's name was likely to be spelled one way on the address label of the monthly newsletter and another way on a name tag.

The problem was not that the KCDMA didn't know who its members were or how to reach them. Several dedicated members spent a great deal of their own time maintaining a list of members, making corrections, and ensuring that the roster listings were correct. The problem was that the data had been dispersed to different places. Membership had a membership list, the roster committee worked on its own version of the membership list, and so on. If the people creating the roster found someone had moved, the information might not get back to the people sending out newsletters. This also frustrated the members, who could tell the association about a change, only to see the information reflected in one place and not another.

The KCDMA was also changing association management companies, and a new company would be handling its data day to day. Since the new company seemed very capable, the KCDMA decided to clean up and improve its database.

The first step was to gather all member and prospect names into one, and only one, database and use this one database as the master database. This was something of a culture change, as different groups were used to working on their own list. However, having one database that is kept updated and correct is much less work for everybody.

The next step was to look at transactions. KCDMA had never consistently tracked which members attended dinner meetings, for example; it simply tracked how many people came and what the total amount collected (charged) for the dinner was. By adding an invoice table to the database, KCDMA can now track who goes to which meetings and whether they are members or not.

The other benefit of using an invoice table is that the sum of the invoice totals for an event equals the total amount collected. This makes accounting much easier and far more accurate.

In the end, accuracy and credibility have been two of the biggest advantages in using a relational marketing database. Previously different people had different contact data for KCDMA members, depend-ing on which version of the membership file they had. Sales were just a total; there was no easy way to go back to where money came from. Now questions can be answered quickly and accurately.

The marketing advantages in targeting members for renewal and targeting prospects to become new members are substantial. However, the real benefit is the time the improved database saves the members of the KCDMA. Meeting time wasted trying to decide how many members the association had, how much it had taken in from last month's meeting, or how many attendees were nonmembers can now be used for better purposes.

Interestingly, the database design created at the KCDMA was adopted for the other associations the management company represents. It had never used an invoice table, nor had it kept all the members and prospects in one table. Similar to the bakery case study, once one database was set up, making others with structures just like it was easy.

CASE STUDY 4

USING THE DATABASE TO SELL SMARTER

A company owned and operated by veterinarians sells pet and veterinary supplies through direct marketing. It offers a wide variety of products to pet owners, kennels, breeders, and groomers.

With such a wide product offering, their catalog had over 3,000 SKUs in 144 pages. Yet the company had never done a square-inch analysis. It wanted to measure the sales per page and item and make sure each page was being used as efficiently as possible.

Even with hundreds of thousands of customers and a midrange computer running its fulfillment software, the cataloger was not too big to have a simple marketing database on a PC. Granted, it was a big PC (with an eight-gigabyte hard drive), but it was still a PC and quite capable of both square-inch and RFM analysis.

The biggest challenge to creating a square-inch analysis was the fact that each item on each page must be keyed into a file that includes the product ID (SKU), page number, and amount of selling space it covers in square inches.

The next challenge was to verify that the cost information in the product table was accurate. Commonly, data in a fulfillment system can be (or become) different from up-to-date accounting data; this case was no exception. With 50 or 100 products this is no big deal, but with 3,000+ it is a major task.

Once a file was created with page-by-page product and space data and the cost data was updated, the invoice header (which contained the key code that related to each catalog), the invoice detail table (which contained by-item sales and quantities), and the product table all had to be downloaded to the PC.

At this point, actually creating the square-inch analysis report was relatively simple. The hard part was that each page and each two-page spread had to be reviewed, which was a very large task. Reports were created by category as well, to aid in new product selection. Nevertheless, poring over 144 pages and 3,000 products, no matter how well the data is reported, still takes time and effort.

One company goal was to create a smaller, 60- to 90-page catalog for prospects, one that would cost less and use less paper than the 144-page book. Another square-inch analysis was created, using only sales from first-time buyers to see what appealed most to new customers.

Because of the number of items and pages involved, the project took several months. However, it had a big impact on catalog design—and on sales. The 144-page book was updated and improved, and a 72-page prospecting book was created. Although the goal had been 60 pages, it turned out that new customers were buying too broad a range of products to fit that. The 72-page book is the first smaller book that the cataloger used for prospecting that was more profitable with first-time buyers than a larger book.

CASE STUDY 5

CREATING A NONTRADITIONAL MARKETING DATABASE FOR AN ORCHESTRA

Most symphonies, like other performing arts organizations, use a computer ticketing system to process ticket transactions. Although these systems are good for processing tickets and maintaining ticket inventory records, they are usually quite difficult to use as marketing databases.

Also, direct marketing efforts (primarily mail and phone) by arts organizations generally are list driven rather than transaction driven. That is, someone is either a customer or a prospect, and the only distinction between customer groups is whether or not they are targeted as a renewal (last year's season ticket holders).

Often, for example, no distinction is made between someone who bought tickets the last two years in a row and someone who bought only last year. Also, little tracking is usually done by prospect segment or by which offer patrons responded to. This is because a very low percentage of key codes are entered correctly, or at all, when ticket sales are made. Some of this is due to high staff turnover in the ticket office, and some reflects the ticketing system's lack of sophistication in database-driven marketing.

As a result, targeting offers by most arts organizations typically amount to taking all the in-house names, merge-purging them with other arts organizations, and then calling or mailing them each season. Unfortunately, without accurate tracking, such organizations cannot tell how well any list segment is working.

In its database marketing efforts, a major urban orchestra used a four-step approach to attack these problems.

Step 1: Cleaning the List and Removing Duplicate Names

First, all customer and purchase information was taken out of the ticketing system and used to create a simple marketing database. Names and addresses were standardized and sent through National Change of Address (NCOA) and checks were made to be sure information was stored in the correct fields. This allowed the building of a nonduplicated customer list with each customer marked as to how many tickets bought, whether tickets were bought for classical music or pops events, and how much had been spent. Then the list of arts organization names was added, and the people who matched against the symphony's marketing database were marked.

The orchestra took two important extra steps at this point. Since it had changed ticketing systems two years before, the output from the old ticketing system was used in the marketing database. This way the group didn't lose any information needed for targeting offers to past ticket buyers. Then each and every name was "parsed," to make sure the first name was in the first-name field, the last name was in the last-name field, and the prefix, middle name, and suffix (Jr, Sr, III, etc.) were all in the correct fields. This made the merge-purge far more accurate.

Carefully building a marketing database with nonduplicated customers and their pur-

chase histories did two things. First, most of the work was required to build a clean mail file. Including purchase histories actually made it easier to decide how to rank the names when removing duplicates. Second, if this had not been done, any one customer would be judged the same as any other. To create a model that will help find prospects that resemble the best customers, it is essential to identify the best customers.

With a carefully assembled marketing database in place, tracking future ticket sales has become much easier. Just as finding duplicates is made more accurate, so is matching new ticket buyers with past customers and prospects, by segment, in the marketing database.

Step 2: Using a Statistical Model to Predict Ticket Sales

Ruf Strategic Solutions, a firm that specializes in predictive modeling, took the orchestra's initial database and used it to create a cluster-based model called Experian. The Experian model, based on household-level data, predicts how likely prospects are to buy tickets if they receive an offer. Household-level data was used to allow more precise modeling than could be done with only neighborhood-level data. The Experian model can be used either to select additional names and increase the number of prospects or to "score" each person in the prospect file on likelihood to purchase.

Using the Experian predictive model allows symphony managers to market smarter. The additional Experian names expanded prospecting efforts beyond the traditional lists, bringing in new people who would otherwise have been missed. Scoring arts trades makes it possible to do a better job of targeting prospect groups to mail or call as the season progresses. More likely ticket buyers are marketed to more frequently, and less likely ticket buyers are contacted less or not at all. This saves wasted marketing dollars while adding revenue from greater ticket sales.

STEP 3: COMMUNICATION PLANNING

Before mailing and calling were started, a communication plan was set up, detailing how many people would be mailed or called for each promotional effort during the season. It became possible to determine how many names were mailed from each segment, how many times, and so on.

Without the third step, setting up a communication plan, it would be very difficult to plan, track, or adjust as the season goes along. A simple plan-your-work and work-your-plan step makes tracking, segmenting, and learning go much better.

STEP 4: FOLLOW-UP AND TRACKING

As the season went on, comparisons were made between who was buying tickets and who was being targeted, and upcoming promotions were adjusted accordingly. At first, this was done by using key codes. However, very few key codes were being captured, which made for incorrect information on which to base decisions. For this situation, matching customers back to the mailing or calling list was found to be far more accurate. This "closed the loop" and provided accurate information for targeting future offers. Some specific examples show why this is the case.

Exhibit 21-1A shows a "season-to-date" communication plan update with the results based only on source codes. It accounts for only $48,800 in revenue, and nearly half of that is under "Mail unknown." Notice how poorly the KCPT (public television) list performed and that 233 buyers came from a total of over 200,000 contacts.

In contrast, Exhibit 21-1B is a sample communication plan based on actual name and address match results. Now $356,444 in

revenue is accounted for, a much more "reasonable" proportion of the ticket sales for this time period. The KCPT list, which appeared to be a poor performer, actually outperformed several other lists. "Mail unknown" is now eliminated, and 2,801 buyers match the original prospect file.

What does this mean from a marketer's point of view? First, good lists, such as the KCPT list, could end up being dropped due to poor tracking, and not-so-good lists could continue to be mailed. Second, each group was recontacted more than once. By using key codes, only 233 people were removed from the prospect file. That means 2,568 people were recontacted on multiple occasions about something they already bought.

In the address match example, each contact generated $1.53 in ticket sales. By failing to remove buyers from the prospect list and recontacting them, the orchestra lost money in two ways. First, on average, names were reached three to four times throughout the season, so the cost of mailing 7,500 to 10,000 pieces was probably wasted. Second, prospects who could have been contacted with those 7,500 to 10,000 pieces were not. Combined savings and incremental revenue totaled over $15,000.

The real trick to making the address matching work lies in cleaning both the customer and prospect list thoroughly, which is why the names were parsed so carefully. This requires some special software, as well as some handwork for the exceptions, to meet the standards required for truly accurate tracking.

Thorough cleaning and parsing allows for very good address matching. For example, Mr. John Doe, Mrs. Jane Doe, and Mr. and Mrs. John and Jane Doe, at 101 Main Street, are all Doe at 101 Main Street. This method also avoids overmatching, as a Smith and a Jones in the same office or condominium do not match. Particularly with arts organizations

Exhibit 21-1

COMPARISON OF TRACKING BASES FOR PROMOTIONS

A. Key Code Basis

Mail Date	List Type/Name	Source Code	Selection	Quantity Available	Quantity Mailed	Number of Orders	Percentage Response	Gross Sales	Dollars per Mailing	Average Order
All ex Sumr Fare	Current subscribers	MA			0					
	Former subscribers	MB	ZIP select 6	2,570	7,560	17	0.22%	$ 2,094.80	$0.28	$123.22
	Current singles	MC		2,316	7,623	27	0.35	5,330.20	0.70	197.41
	Former singles	MQ		5,818	19,421	12	0.06	2,954.00	0.15	246.17
	Big list/prospects	ME		8,231	26,921	13	0.05	2,534.45	0.09	194.96
	New prospects	NP		547	547					
	Nonrenewals	NR		139	139					
	KCPT	MK	Dropped	4,304	8,571	1	0.01	398.00	0.05	398.00
	Opera trade	ML	Dropped	17,854	42,030	15	0.04	3,805.20	0.09	253.68
	Missouri rep	MM	ZIP select 6	16,347	50,150	13	0.03	6,501.80	0.13	500.14
	Chamber orchestra	MO			0					
	TRW list	MR	Dropped	14,742	29,484	7	0.02	1,796.00	0.06	256.57
	State ballet	MS	Dropped	3,133	6,186	2	0.03	542.00	0.09	271.00
	Mail unknown	MU			0	125		22,150.70		177.21
	Camerata	MX	Dropped	1,156	2,920	1	0.03	696.00	0.24	696.00
			All Non SF	77,157	201,552	233		$48,803.15	$0.24	$209.46

Exhibit 21-1 (continued)

B. Address Match Basis

Mail Date	List Type/Name	Source Code	Selection	Quantity Available	Quantity Mailed	Number of Orders	Percentage Response	Gross Sales	Dollars per Mailing	Average Order
All ex Sumr Fare	Current subscribers	MA			0					
	Former subscribers	MB	ZIP select 6	2,570	7,560	191	2.53%	$24,459.55	$3.24	$128.06
	Current singles	MC		2,316	7,623	378	4.96	50,469.73	6.62	133.52
	Former singles	MQ		5,818	19,421	474	2.44	52,213.10	2.69	110.15
	Big list/prospects	ME		8,231	26,921	356	1.32	44,082.11	1.64	123.83
	New prospects	NP		547	547					
	Nonrenewals	NR		139	139					
	KCPT	MK	Dropped	4,304	8,571	109	1.27	12,752.10	1.49	116.99
	Opera trade	ML	Dropped	17,854	42,030	429	1.02	57,573.23	1.37	134.20
	Missouri rep	MM	ZIP select	16,347	50,150	567	1.13	75,992.82	1.52	134.03
	Chamber orchestra	MO			0					
	TRW list	MR	Dropped	14,742	29,484	154	0.52	22,813.04	0.77	148.14
	State ballet	MS	Dropped	3,133	6,186	142	2.30	16,088.80	2.60	113.30
	Mail unknown	MU		31,103		0				
	Camerata	MX	Dropped	1,156	2,920	1	0.00	0.00	0.00	0.00
			All Non SF	77,157	232,655	2,801		$356,444.48	$1.53	$127.26

and local nonprofits, this type of cleaning and matching is crucial (but not easy!).

The Ruf Experian model can be used either for finding new prospects to select or for scoring prospect files. In this example, any additional prospects selected with the Ruf model are not in any arts file or in the house file. As a result, they are known not to have attended the symphony or to hold tickets at the opera, ballet, and so on. Nevertheless, they did provide $1.53 in revenue per name.

When arts organization names were scored, each name and address was given a rank from 1 to 10, with 1 being the best. Some did not match the Experian database at all, so they were given no score. This was less than 10 percent of the arts names in this example. Exhibit 21-2 charts a breakdown of performance, measuring ticket sales per prospect by Experian score, for arts trade names.

Notice how well the first four groups performed, each returning $3.99 or more in sales per prospect. This score can be used to select names as the season goes along. For example, if a list such as the opera is a marginal performer, all the names from deciles 5 through 10 might be dropped in late-season efforts. For a list that performs very well, such as the ballet, all the names could continue to be contacted.

Recency, or how long ago someone last bought a ticket or requested information, is another important part in segmenting customers and prospects. Building the database to clearly mark and track who last bought one year, two years, and three years ago is an important part of managing the database marketing process. Otherwise, a customer who has not bought for three years will be contacted the same as someone who bought just last year.

This case study uniquely demonstrates how revenue can be generated and costs reduced by using a marketing database in an industry that up to now did not have cost-effective access to these tools.

Putting these tracking, planning, and targeting tools in place has a major effect on

Exhibit 21-2

SYMPHONY ARTS LIST PERFORMANCE BY DECILE

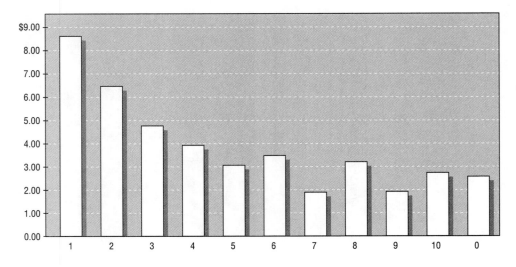

how marketing in general, not just database marketing, can be conducted. Demonstrating credibility through tracking and planning allows more time to focus on what is important and provides better tools to deal with what is urgent.

A Business-to-Business Case Study

OHIO PLUMBING SUPPLY

SITUATION

Ohio Plumbing Supply is a wholesale supply company located in central Ohio. In its 35 years it has built up a very nice regional business supplying product to a wide variety of small firms and plumbing contractors located within a 100-mile radius of its only facility. The business building combines a warehouse, wholesale supply store, and office facility that has been expanded a number of times as the business has grown.

Historically, Ohio Plumbing's business is 60 percent drive-up, where plumbers or other contractors either call or just stop and pick up the supplies they need for the job at hand. The other 40 percent of its business is phoned in, with delivery by one of four trucks or by UPS to the job sites of customers. Over the years, the owner, Tom Jones, has prided himself on his company's superb customer service and fair pricing. He has been very technology minded and invested in the latest telephone, inventory control, and computer systems to help him manage his business better. He has also selectively added key warehouse and telesales staff and two outside salespeople to help grow the business. His company's reputation as an innovator and strong customer service–

driven provider has helped the company grow and prosper economically.

One technical innovation that helped the business grow was the development before it was in vogue, of a simple customer database. Tom thought that the company could expand on the accounts receivable information used for billing to include such information as

◆ key company contacts: decision-makers and other purchase influencers (besides accounting or accounts payable)

◆ purchase history down to the items purchased, including

- date of last purchase
- total number of purchases
- total dollars spent with the company
- product categories purchased

◆ payment history

◆ key contact with the customer (direct sales or telesalesperson)

The database was rudimentary at first, almost more of a glorified accounting file. But as computer costs came down, Tom invested in continuously updating the hardware and making improvements in the software.

The second part of the database, which was almost as important, was the merchandise or product database. Every effort was made to keep a constantly updated inventory position. Every product was identified on the product database, with the following types of data:

◆ Item name

◆ Descriptive information and selling points, including colors, sizes, and so on

◆ Item number

◆ Vendor

◆ Inventory on hand and on order (and date anticipated)

- Vendor lead-time
- Minimum/maximum order points
- Cross-sell items (typically accessories that might be needed with the product for installation)

Communication with customers was done through simple flyers, billing inserts, and sales sheets. They were not elaborate— mainly product and price listings that most plumbers and other craftsmen could understand without a detailed explanation.

PLANNING TO GROW THE BUSINESS

Tom, an enterprising and entrepreneurial person, had a vision of growing the business beyond his limited geographical radius. Rather than adding more outside salespeople and more delivery trucks, he wondered if he could sell in a seven- or eight-state region. Tom felt that to make a success of this expansion he needed six things:

1. *Top-quality salespeople.* He wanted to expand his inside salespeople (technical sales reps, or TSRs) with top-notch communicators who knew and understood plumbing supplies and accessories. They needed to be almost technical consultants that could help customers solve their problems.
2. *A redefined product database* that could be maintained on-line with real-time inventory and with accurate forecasting capability.
3. *An expanded prospect and customer database* as the "driver" of all customer communication. A state-of-the-art house list database system with on-line access to every customer's detailed purchase history was deemed critical to the success of dealing with people who didn't buy across the counter at the store.
4. *An improved process of new customer acquisition* to let people know about this company with such good solid pricing and

the best customer service in the world. Tom was convinced that once he got buyers, they would be happy with the service and he could keep them long term. The challenge was to reach key industries and companies that purchased plumbing supplies. Tom felt they could be found in various types of companies:

- Plumbing contractors
- Mechanical contractors
- General commercial and residential contractors
- Home builders
- Water treatment and wastewater management companies
- Manufacturers
- Chemical companies
- Gas- and air-handling companies
- Other related Standard Industrial Classification (SIC) codes: almost anyone who works with piping, water handling, and drainage

5. *Shipping and delivery of product.* Tom noted that a good number of plumbing supplies and accessories are lightweight PVC and could be shipped via UPS or the U.S. Postal Service. Even larger, heavier, or bulkier items where a common carrier was needed could be delivered in two to three days to customers in the surrounding eight states.
6. *A strong visual presentation of the company's product line* to expand on Tom's proposition of top-quality service with knowledgeable salespeople. Tom proposed a detailed, visual catalog that he could mail to customers and prospects twice a year.

THE ACTION PLAN

The company did its long-term plan and agreed that this was a solid opportunity. Each of the key six critical needs was assigned to a team to accomplish.

Team 1: Sales Staff Headed by the sales manager, the team took the projected order volume from the financial plan and determined how many people would be needed to effectively staff an eight-state launch. Hiring and training were big requirements and were started immediately.

Team 2: Merchandise Database Headed by the warehouse manager and the comptroller of the company, this team analyzed how many SKUs the company had at present and how the product line would grow. An expansion of the database was necessary, and both hardware and software decisions were needed.

Team 3: Prospect and Customer Database This team was headed by Tom, the owner. As a technical innovator, he knew that expansion of the number of prospects and customers was critical to the company's success and that control and contact strategy were needed to implement the kind and level of communication he envisioned for customers.

Team 4: New Customer Acquisition The help of a marketing consultant was secured to help the team get started identifying compiled mailing lists, industry publications, and other potential contacts for companies and individuals in the eight-state area. Trade shows, card decks, space advertising, yellow page ads, and so on were investigated to reach potential new customers.

Team 5: Delivery The team studied alternative shipping options for getting the product to the customer in two, three, or four days. Overnight delivery was also explored for the customer who needed the product the next day.

Team 6: Catalog Also headed by Tom, the owner, this team explored how many pages would be needed to present the complete product line. Eventually a 120-page catalog

was envisioned, with a four-color cover and two-color inside pages.

RESULTS

Getting everything in order took about nine months, but it finally happened. A catalog was prepared, printed, and mailed to key prospects. Other prospecting—particularly soliciting of catalog requests—was run and advertising was initiated. The sales staff was expanded and trained. Finally, two new database elements were in place. The merchandise database was upgraded, using existing technology. The customer database and new fulfillment systems were purchased outside, and the old customer history was converted to the new system.

A major prospecting effort using a wide variety of outside lists was initiated. Since the existing customer list was small, it was included in the same catalog mailing as that to secure new customers. The type of lists that proved most responsive were subscriber lists such as those from

◆ *Industrial Equipment News*

◆ *Contractor Magazine*

◆ IMPO (Industrial Maintenance and Plant Operations)

◆ *Pollution Engineering*

From such lists, one could select readers by name and type of equipment they either ordered, specified, or influenced, or by specific title. All of these winning lists were controlled-circulation lists that update their information annually. Another positive aspect of controlled-circulation trade publications was that Ohio Plumbing Supply was able to either select or post-analyze buyers by SIC code and size of the company (by either number of employees or sales volume).

Compiled lists such as plumbing contractors, even though they had a name on each file, responded well down the list. The only exceptions were businesses in high-responding SIC codes, when they had 10 or more employees. Although it was originally planned that the TSRs would make outbound calls to compiled lists to get the correct contact person's name, this turned out to be a lower priority. The salespeople were so busy with responses from the higher-quality lists that little time was left over to cull through lower-performing lists.

The expectation of Tom Jones was correct. Once the buyer names were developed, they stayed with the company and became strong, regular buyers. The buyer file consistently outperformed the prospect lists by a factor of over five.

THE CUSTOMER COMMUNICATION PLAN

Based on the selling history of the original business, company management had a good idea of when to reach customers during the year and what the most effective customer contact strategy would be. The communication plan that was subsequently tested included the following:

- January, February, and March: 96-page catalog to buyers and prospects (catalog drops were spread during this time for maximum customer service)
- Three weeks after catalog drop to customers: a follow-up call made by TSRs (staggered drop was also helpful here in spreading outbound calls)
- April, May, and June: solo and self-mailers to buyers; testing to prospects
- July, August, and September: 96-page catalog to buyers and prospects (catalog drops were spread during this time for maximum customer service)
- Three weeks after catalog drop to customers: a follow-up call made by the TSRs

- October and November: solo and self-mailers to buyers; testing to prospects
- December: holiday greeting to all buyers

The business was a runaway success. Before half the initial catalog printing of 100,000 was distributed and mailed, the variable catalog costs (printing and postage) and the fixed creative costs were paid for.

CONCLUSION

The success of a marketing database will depend on many things. Is the product a good one? Is the offer enticing? Is the creative element effective? A marketing database won't turn dogs into winners, but it can help squeeze every profit dollar possible out of a desirable product.

What makes the type of database and type of database marketing featured in this chapter unique is that it is transaction driven. Rather than looking at the database as a list of names or thinking of a customer list simply as a mailing file, marketers always think of transactions and customers together. Is this person a first-time buyer or a repeat buyer? Has that company bought from us in the past? How much do they order at one time? Which offers did we send them? These are the kinds of questions database marketers are likely to ask. The focus is not just on their names and addresses. It is on who they are *and* what they do—especially what they do with "us."

By using the database to respond to people based on who they are, what they do with you, and what you do with them, you can carry on a true one-on-one, two-way relationship with them. That is what database marketing is all about!

Index

Access, to data warehouses, 39
Accounting software, 166
Active cluster analysis, 89
Advertising space, 213, 216
Advocates, 14
Alternative media, for prospecting,
    226–27
Append process, 75
Artificial intelligence, 89–90
Average order value (AOV), 14

Back-end marketing
    business-to-business sellers and,
        16–17
    catalog companies and, 16
    defined, 15–16
    retailers and, 16
Backups, 78
Basic research phase, of testing, 177–78
Beaver, D., 14
Bell-shaped curve, 86
Benchmarks, testing, 188
Bimodal graphs, 86–87
Bits, 77
Blank customer numbers, 69–70
Brand equity, 107

Brand loyalty, 107
Break-even analysis
    determining, 20–21
    for house circulation plans, 236–37
    for prospect circulation plans, 227–29
Brokers, list, 225–26
Browse windows, 96
Budgets, for testing, 188
Business lists, 201, 202
Businesses. *See* Large businesses;
        Medium businesses; Small
        businesses
Business-to-business clones, 201
Business-to-business data, 157
Business-to-business direct marketing,
        247
Business-to-business marketing
    customer communication and, 16–17
    database design considerations for,
        67–69
    media for, 217–19
Bytes, 77

Calculations, in reports, 100–101
Card decks, 217
Catalog marketers, 16, 246

Census data, 157–58

CHAID. *See* Chi-square automatic interaction detector (CHAID)

Chi-square automatic interaction detector (CHAID), 88–89

Circulation, defined, 206–7

Circulation lists, 207

Circulation planning, 206–7

Circulation plans
developing house, 219–20
developing prospect, 210, 214
long term use of space in, 217–19
prospect, 225–33

Clones
business-to-business, 201
consumer, 194–95

Cloning. *See* Customer cloning

Cluster analysis, 83–84, 89

Codd, E. F., 57

Codes, 183–84

Company as customer database design
problem, 67–69

Compiled files, 92

Compiled lists, 196–98, 199, 209

Computer systems
databases for, 36–37
decision support, 36
management information, 35–36
transaction processing, 35

Consumer clones, 194–95

Consumer data, 155–57

Consumer direct marketing, 246

Contact management software,
164, 166

Continuation lists, 195

Controls, 79

Co-op lists, 201

Cost replacement method, for customer
lists, 219

Credit card matching, 156–57

Customer circulation plans, 234. *See also*
House circulation plans

Customer cloning
defined, 190–91
statistical models for, 191–93

Customer communication
benefits of improved, 18
buyer hierarchy and, 16–17
customer hierarchy and, 13–14
strategy, 6–7
using database marketing for,
24–28

Customer data, 11–12

Customer files, flat, 56–57

Customer hierarchy, 13–14

Customer information, 44–48, 143–46

Customer lists
strategies, 222–24
valuation methods for, 219–20

Customer loyalty
defined, 107–8
tracking, 114–15

Customer numbers, blank, 69–70

Customer relationship marketing
pros and cons, 112–13
requirements for successful, 11

Customer value, 6

Customers
acquiring new, 207–209
as advocates, 14
deleting, with transactions, 70–71
determining profiles of, 193–94
as one-time buyers, 14
as prospects, 13–14
selection process of, 108
as suspects, 13
as two-time buyers, 14

Data. *See also* External data;
Information; Internal data
adding, 90–91
changing, 79
converting, for input, 149
enhancement, 90–92

external, 154–55
business-to-business, 157
census, 157–58
consumer, 155–57
mapping, 158–59
premodeled, 159
internal, 142, 152–53
limitations on using, 92–93
querying, 96
requirements, for database marketing, 11–12
updating, 150–51
Data cards
for business-to-business lists, 202
for compiled lists, 199
defined, 195
for response lists, 197
for subscription lists, 200
Data warehouses, 38, 80–81, 165
access to, 39
controlling, 39–40
security, 39
updating, 39
Data warehousing, defined, 34–35
Database fields, 42
Database files, 41–42, 43–44.
See also Tables
Database marketing
appropriateness, 8–9
capabilities, 7–8
data requirements for, 11–12
defined, 3
economics of, 24–28
lists and, 6
managing customer and prospect communication with, 24–28
procedures, 6–7
process, 208
Database records, 42
Database software. *See also* Statistical software
selecting, 81

storage, 73–74
weaknesses of, 80–81
Databases
customer relationship marketing and, 11
defined, 5
housekeeping functions, 79
quickchecks for, 151
robust, 73–74
Decision support computer systems, 36
Dedupe process, 213
Demographic information, 52–53, 193
Denormalization, 38, 67
Dependent variables, 82
Descriptive statistics, 85–86
Desktop database marketing
benefits, 4
defined, 3–4
future of, 9
Detail bands, 100–102
Direct marketing
business-to-business, 247
consumer, 246
Discounts, using marketing databases for, 115
Duplicates, 149–50

80/20 rule, 224
Enhancement data
types, 91
using, 91–92
Enhancement lists, 90–91
Enhancing, defined, 90
Exit strategies, 189
External data. *See also* Internal data
defined, 154–55
designing, into marketing databases, 160–61

Factor analysis, 83
Fields, database, defined, 42
Fifth normal form, 67

Files
   defined, 41–42
   flat, 54–57
Fingerhut Corporation, 179
First normal form, 59–61
Flat files
   customer, 56–57
   defined, 54
   transaction, 54–56
Footers, page, 100–102
Forecasting, mailing plans, 241
Fourth normal form, 64–66
FoxPro, 73, 96–98
Front-end marketing, 14–15
   business-to-business sellers and,
      16–17
   catalog companies, 16
   retailers and, 16
Future value method, for customer lists,
      219–20

Geographic segmentation, 210
Gift recipients, 71, 246
Group footers, 100–102

Hard drives, 77–78
Hardware, selecting, 81
Headers, page, 100–102
Hey data, 17
House circulation plans, 219–20, 234.
      See also Mailing plans; Prospect
      circulation plans
House list inventory
   defined, 220–21
   house circulation plans and, 234
Housekeeping functions, for
      databases, 79

Independent variables, 82–85
Indexes, 74–76, 95, 98, 165
Information. *See also* Data
   customer, 44–48, 143–46

demographic, 52–53, 193
   offer, 51, 148–49
   product, 49, 147–48
   salesperson, 49–50, 148
   survey, 52–53
   transaction, 48–49, 146–47
Inner joins, 80
Internal data. *See also* External data
   assembling, 152–53
   converting, for input, 149
   defined, 142

Key codes. *See* Source codes
Key fields, 43
   blank, 69–70

Large businesses, 170–71. *See also*
      Medium businesses; Small
      businesses
Lead generation, 248
Lifetime value (LTV), 6, 19, 21–24
   calculating, 137–40
   comparing, 140
   defined, 132–33
   establishing measurements of,
      136–37
   financial importance of, 135–36
   loyalty programs and, 115
   measuring success with, 140–41
   prerequisites for, 133–34
   strategy and budgeting and, 136
Linear regression, 86–87
List brokers, 225–26
List codes. *See* Source codes
Lists
   business, 201, 202
   circulation, 207
   compiled, 196–98, 199, 209
   continuation, 195
   co-op, 201
   customer, 219–20, 222–24
   database marketing and, 6

defined, 5
enhancement, 90–91
merge-purge of, 213
response, 193, 195–96, 197, 207
subscription, 198–99, 200
Log test histories, 187
Logit regression, 89–90
Loglinear regression, 87–88
Look-alikes, 194
Lookups, 77
Loyalty marketing, 108
Loyalty marketing programs, 11. *See also*
Customer relationship marketing
building successful, 109–12
catalog, 111
lifetime value (LTV) and, 115
need for, 108–9
range of, 110
using databases for, 113–15
LTV. *See* Lifetime value (LTV)

Magnetic tape, 77
Mail Order Wizard, 168–69
Mailing lists, 250–51
Mailing plans. *See also* Circulation plans;
House circulation plans; Prospect
circulation plans
developing seasonal strategies for,
222
forecasting, 241
organizing, 229–33, 237–41
tracking competitive, 188–89
Management information computer
systems, 35–36
Management Information Systems
(MIS), 39–40
Mapping data, 158–59
Maps, 191–93
Marketing briefs, 222
Marketing data
finding relevant, 37–38
summarizing, 38

Marketing databases
building blocks of, 41–44
building recency-frequency-monetary
(RFM) into, 122–23
business-to-business, 247
for business-to-business marketing,
67–69
company size and selection of,
164–71
consumer, 246
design considerations, 67–72
designing external data into,
160–61
determining users, 41
development costs, 171
discounts and, 115
duplicates and, 149–50
fixing broken, 251–52
goals for, 33–34
growing into new, 171–72
impractical situations for, 8–9
multi-source, 156
protecting, 252–53
relationship/loyalty programs and,
113–15
for retailers, 247
single-source, 156
supporting sales representatives and
dealers with, 250
updating, 150–51
Marketing plans, 222
Matching, 156–57
Mean, 86
Median, 86
Medium businesses, 168–69. *See also*
Large businesses; Small businesses
Merge-purge, 213, 250–51
Mode, 86
Modeling, postal code, 210
Models, 92, 93
Multibuyers, 213
Multi-source databases, 156

Name rental method, for customer lists, 219–20
National Change of Address (NCOA), 159, 251
NCOA. *See* National Change of Address
Net present value, 133
Neural networks, 89–90
New names, cost versus quality, 234
Nontraditional testing, 184–85
Normal forms, 58–67
Normalization
    defined, 38, 54
    principles, 58–67

Offer information, 51, 148–49
One-time buyers, 14
Oracle, 73, 171
Orphans, 70
Outer joins, 80
Output. *See* Reports

Page footers, 100–102
Page headers, 100–102
Passive cluster analysis, 89
Pelley, D., 92–93
Perk building, 224
Phone matching, 156–57
Postal code modeling, 210
Postal code segmentation, 210
Post-test analysis phase, of testing, 180
Post-test customer and noncustomer
    research phase, of testing, 180
Predictions, 82–83
Premodeled data, 159
Pretest phase, of testing, 178
Primary research, 154, 160
Product information, 49, 147–48
Profitability
    lifetime value (LTV) and, 115
    measuring, 113–15
Programs, 80
Prospect circulation, 207–9

Prospect circulation plans. *See also*
    House circulation plans; Mailing
    plans
    adding alternative media to, 213–16
    becoming financial plans, 225–33
    developing, 210, 214
Prospects
    data requirements for, 12
    hierarchy of, 13–14, 209–10
    using database marketing for com-
        munication with, 24–28

Quality checks, 149–50
Quantitative testing phase, of testing, 179
Queries, 80, 95, 96, 165
    optimizing, 98–99
    running, 96–98, 99
    versus spreadsheets, 102–3
Quick checks, for databases, 151

Random access memory (RAM), 77
Recency-frequency-monetary (RFM), 92
    building, into marketing databases, 122–23
    defined, 119–20
    marketing smarter with, 129
    PCs and, 121–22
    sample program for, 130–31
    strategy for use, 123
    using, 120–21
    value of, 67
    visual approach to, 123–29
Recency-frequency-monetary-
    profitability (RFM-P), 120
Record locking, 37
Records, defined, 42
Red Brick (software), 73, 171
Regression equations, 86–88
Relational databases, 54
    design rules, 58–67
    flexibility of, 57

Relational query by example (RQBE), 96–98
Relationship marketing, 108
Relationship programs. *See also* Customer relationship marketing
  building successful, 109–12
  need for, 108–9
  range of, 110
  using databases for, 113–15
Reliability, 181–83
Report writer software, 100
Reports, 95–96, 99–100
  calculations in, 100–101
  designing, 101–2
  parts, 100–102
  sections, 100
  versus spreadsheets, 102–3
Response files, 92
Response lists, 193, 195–96, 197, 207
Retail databases, 247–48
Retailers, customer communication and, 16
Retesting, 186
Reverse matching, 156–57
RFM-P. *See* Recency-frequency-monetary-profitability (RFM-P)
Robustness, 73–74
RQBE. *See* Relational query by example (RQBE)
Ruf, J., 57
Rule of 100, 182–83

Sales codes. *See* Source codes
Sales representatives
  contact strategies for, 217
  information, 49–50, 148
  supporting, with marketing database, 250
Sample sizes, 84
SAS, 73, 93–94, 171
Screens, 79
Scripts, 80

Searches. *See* Queries
Second normal form, 61–63
Secondary research, 154
Security, to data warehouses, 39
  See d names, 252
Single-source databases, 156
Skewness, 86
Small businesses, 165–68. *See also* Medium businesses; Large businesses
Soundalikes, 99
Source codes
  for testing and tracking, 183–84
  using, to expand business, 25–28
Source IDs, 71–72
Space advertising
  as alternative medium, 213, 216
  long-term planning for, 217
Spreadsheets
  versus databases, 102–3
  as statistical software, 93
SPSS, 93–94, 171
SQL. *See* Structured query language (SQL)
Standard deviation, 85, 86
Statistical controls, 181
Statistical models
  descriptive, 191–93
  predictive, 191
Statistical software
SAS, 93–94
  selecting, 93–94
SPSS, 93–94
Statistics
  techniques, 85–90
  uses, 82–85
String searches, 99
Structured query language (SQL), 78–79, 95
Subscription lists, 198–99
Summary bands, 100–102
Survey information, 52–53, 160

Suspects, 13
Sybase, 73, 171

Tables, defined, 38, 43–44
Telemarketers, 189
"Test back," 185–86
Test groups, 84
Testing, 84
    benchmarks, 188
    budgeting for, 188
    improving, 180–89
    log history, 187
    nontraditional, 184–85
    phases of basic research,
        177–78
    post-test analysis, 180
    post-test customer and noncustomer
        research, 180
    pretest, 178
    quantitative, 179
    regular, 188
    for reliability, 181–83
    tracking and, 183–84
    for validity, 181–83

Third normal form, 63–64
Time value of money, 133
Time value of money discount factor,
    138
Tracking
    for loyalty programs, 114–15
    testing and, 183–84
Trade publications, 201–2
Trade shows, 217
Transaction files, flat, 54–56
Transaction information
    common problems with, 146–47
    defined, 48–49
    lack of, for database design, 70
Transaction processing computer
    systems, 35
Tree analysis, 89–90
Two-time buyers, 14

Updating
    data, 150–51
    data warehouses, 39

Validity, 181–83